ZAGATSURVEY®
25TH ANNIVERSARY

2005

SAN FRANCISCO BAY AREA RESTAURANTS

Local Editor: Meesha Halm

Local Coordinator: Maura Sell

Editor: Troy Segal

Published and distributed by
ZAGAT SURVEY, LLC
4 Columbus Circle
New York, New York 10019
Tel: 212 977 6000
E-mail: sanfran@zagat.com
Web site: www.zagat.com

Acknowledgments

We thank Antonia Allegra, Alissa Bushnell, Erica Curtis, Heidi Cusick, Jon, Olive and Jude Fox, Vincent, Conor and Liam Logan, Leroy Meshel, Steven Shukow, Jeffrey Tappan and Willow Waldeck, as well as the following members of our staff: Reni Chin, Larry Cohn, Anuradha Duggal, Schuyler Frazier, Jeff Freier, Shelley Gallagher, Katherine Harris, Natalie Lebert, Mike Liao, Dave Makulec, Emily Parsons, Robert Poole, Robert Seixas, Kelly Sinanis, Yoji Yamaguchi and Sharon Yates.

Contents

About This Survey

Here are the results of our *2005 San Francisco Bay Area Restaurant Survey,* covering 953 restaurants as tested, and tasted, by 6,357 local restaurant-goers.

This marks the 25th year that Zagat Survey has reported on the shared experiences of diners like you. What started in 1979 in New York as a hobby involving 200 friends rating local restaurants has come a long way. Today we have over 250,000 surveyors and now cover entertaining, golf, hotels, resorts, spas, movies, music, nightlife, shopping, sites and attractions as well as theater. Our *Surveys* are also available on wireless devices and by subscription at zagat.com, where you can vote and shop as well.

By regularly surveying large numbers of avid customers, we hope to have achieved a uniquely current and reliable guide. This year's participants dined out an average of 3.2 times per week, meaning this *Survey* is based on roughly 1.1 million meals. Of these surveyors, 47% are women, 53% men; the breakdown by age is 15% in their 20s; 31%, 30s; 20%, 40s; 20%, 50s; and 14%, 60s or above. Our editors have synopsized our surveyors' opinions, with their comments shown in quotation marks. We sincerely thank each of these surveyors; this book is really "theirs."

Of course, we are especially grateful to our editor, Meesha Halm, Bay Area restaurant critic and cookbook author, and to our coordinator, Maura Sell, a specialty food industry consultant.

To help guide our readers to San Francisco's best meals and best buys, we have prepared a number of lists. See Most Popular (page 9), Top Ratings (pages 10–15) and Best Buys (page 16) for the Overall Bay Area. Top Ratings broken down by region can be found at the beginning of each section. In addition, we have provided 46 handy indexes and have tried to be concise.

To join any of our upcoming *Surveys*, just register at zagat.com. Each participant will receive a free copy of the resulting guide when published. Your comments and even criticisms of this guide are also solicited. There is always room for improvement with your help. You can contact us at sanfran@zagat.com. We look forward to hearing from you.

New York, NY
September 28, 2004

Nina and Tim

Nina and Tim Zagat

What's New

San Francisco's restaurant scene is experiencing a wave of irrational exuberance like we haven't seen since the dot-com days. None of the conventional indicators point to much change in the local economy; yet one-third of Zagat surveyors report they are eating out more often than they did two years ago – and 55% are spending more money in restaurants. Furthermore, there's been a burst of new branches from leading restaurateurs, as well as a spate of openings by some of the city's best-known chefs.

Neighborhood Noshing: Not surprisingly, many have chosen to debut Downtown, surveyors' No. 1 neighborhood for eateries. Among the top-shelf shops turning up are Daniel Patterson's (ex Elisabeth Daniel) late-night lounge Frisson, Michael Mina's (ex Aqua) eponymous establishment and George Morrone's (ex Fifth Floor) Tartare. However, the area to watch is SoMa, which is seeing a series of offshoots, including La Suite from Chez Papa's Jocelyn Bulow and Jack Falstaff from the PlumpJack people.

Global Gourmets: The Bay Area may have given birth to Californian cuisine, but its citizens think globally when it comes to their favorite foods. 81% of reviewers happily report that our fine-dining scene is becoming more diverse. Cases in point: paeans to the Pyrénées like Bocadillos and Iluna Basque, the Asian-Latin Circolo, Peruvian Fresca and the Burmese-inspired Roe.

It's a Small World After All: Some nights, it seems like San Francisco serves more tapas than San Sebastian. Small wonder, when 80% of surveyors approve of the proliferation of small-plates restaurants, putting such practitioners as À Côté, Isa and Tamarine on this *Survey*'s Most Popular list for the first time. Among newcomers, there are nearly 20 *petit plats* places of all types, from the Mediterranean Cortez to the Asian Lüx to the Indian-French Tallula.

We'll Never Quit Wine-ing: Given the proximity of the wine country, it's natural that Golden Gaters are fond of the grape. And such excellent new wine-by-the-glass venues as 1550 Hyde Café, Nectar Wine Lounge and Va de Vi indulge both those who order by the bottle (44% of surveyors) and those who prefer the pour (40%).

Popularity Contest Upset: The average cost of a meal, $33.75, dipped .9% from last year. But San Franciscans still love to splurge: this year, ritzy Gary Danko actually became the *Survey*'s Most Popular restaurant – ending Boulevard's seven-year hold on the title.

San Francisco, CA   Meesha Halm
September 28, 2004

Ratings & Symbols

Name, Address, Phone Number & Web Site

Zagat Ratings

Hours & Credit Cards

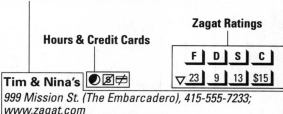

Tim & Nina's ● 🗷 ⊄

F	D	S	C
▽ 23	9	13	$15

*999 Mission St. (The Embarcadero), 415-555-7233;
www.zagat.com*

🗹 Open "more or less when they feel like it", this bit of
unembellished Embarcadero ectoplasm excels at seafood
with an Asian- Argentinean-Albanian twist; the staff seems
"fresh off the boat", and while the view of the garbage
barges is "a drag", no one balks at the bottom-feeder prices.

Review, with surveyors' comments in quotes

Restaurants with the highest overall ratings and greatest
popularity and importance are printed in CAPITAL LETTERS.

Before reviews a symbol indicates whether responses
were uniform ■ or mixed 🗹.

Hours: ● serves after 11 PM
🗷 closed on Sunday

Credit Cards: ⊄ no credit cards accepted

Ratings are on a scale of **0** to **30**. The Cost (C) column
reflects our surveyors' estimate of the price of dinner
including one drink and tip.

F Food	D Decor	S Service	C Cost
23	9	13	$15

0–9 poor to fair	**20–25** very good to excellent
10–15 fair to good	**26–30** extraordinary to perfection
16–19 good to very good	▽ low response/less reliable

For places listed without ratings, such as a newcomer or
survey write-in, the price range is indicated as follows:

I	$25 and below	**E**	$41 to $65
M	$26 to $40	**VE**	$66 or more

Most Popular

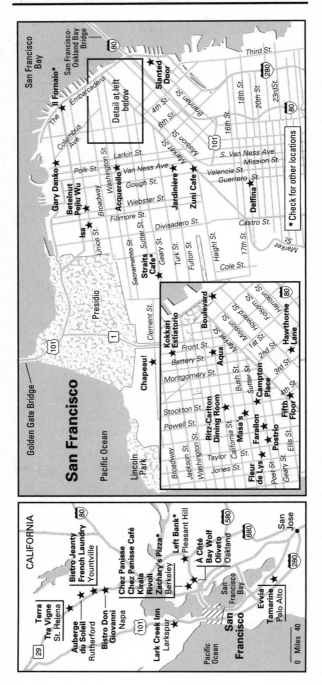

Most Popular

Places outside of San Francisco are marked as follows:
E=East of SF; N=North; and S=South.

The Bay Area's Most Popular

1. Gary Danko
2. Boulevard
3. French Laundry/N
4. Chez Panisse/E
5. Aqua
6. Slanted Door
7. Delfina
8. Chez Panisse Café/E
9. Bistro Jeanty/N
10. Zachary's Pizza/E
11. Farallon
12. Masa's
13. Evvia/S
14. Kokkari Estiatorio
15. Jardinière
16. Fleur de Lys
17. Rivoli/E
18. Tra Vigne/N
19. Chapeau!
20. Oliveto/E
21. Left Bank/E/N/S
22. Zuni Cafe
23. Bay Wolf/E
24. Postrio
25. À Côté/E
26. Auberge du Soleil/N
27. Hawthorne Lane
28. Terra/N*
29. Bistro Don Giov./N
30. Fifth Floor
31. Il Fornaio/E/N/S/SF*
32. Isa
33. Tamarine/S*
34. Betelnut
35. Ritz-Carlton D.R.*
36. Straits Cafe/S/SF
37. Campton Place
38. Kirala/E
39. Acquerello
40. Lark Creek Inn/N

It's obvious that many of the restaurants on the above list are among the San Francisco area's most expensive, but if popularity were calibrated to price, we suspect that a number of other restaurants would join the above ranks. Given the fact that both our surveyors and readers love to discover dining bargains, we have added a list of 80 Best Buys on page 16. These are restaurants that give real quality at extremely reasonable prices.

* Indicates a tie with the restaurant above

Top Ratings

Except where indicated by a ▽, top lists exclude places with low voting.

Top 40 Food

29 Gary Danko
28 French Laundry/N
    Masa's
    Fleur de Lys
27 Le Papillon/S
    Sushi Ran/N
    Charles Nob Hill
    Cafe La Haye/N
    La Toque/N
    Acquerello
    Chez Panisse/E
    Erna's Elderberry/E
    Ritz-Carlton D.R.
    Marché/S
    Fork/N
    Rivoli/E
    Boulevard
    Marinus/S
    La Folie
    Hog Island Oyster

    Aqua
    Chez Panisse Café/E
    Kabuto Sushi
26 John Bentley's/S
    Rest. at Stevenswood/N*
    Sierra Mar/S
    Chapeau!
    Isa
    Campton Place
    Bay Wolf/E
    Terra/N
    House
    Tartine Bakery
    Rosamunde Grill
    Bistro Jeanty/N
    Jardinière
    Kirala/E
    Auberge du Soleil/N
    Café Marcella/S
    Delfina

By Cuisine

American (New)
29 Gary Danko
28 French Laundry/N
27 Boulevard
26 John Bentley's/S
    Terra/N

American (Traditional)
26 Lark Creek Inn/N
24 Gordon's/N
23 Tarpy's Roadhse./S
    Hayes St. Grill
22 Blue Plate

Bakeries
26 Tartine Bakery
    Mama's on Wash. Sq.
24 Gayle's Bakery/S
    Downtown Bakery/N
23 Boulange de Cole/Polk

Barbecue
24 Foothill Cafe/N
    Brother's Korean
23 Buckeye Roadhse./N
22 Brother-in-Law
21 Bo's Barbecue/E

Cajun/Creole/Southern
23 Kate's Kitchen
21 Purple Plum/E
20 PJ's Oyster
    Everett & Jones/E
19 Kingfish/S

Californian
27 Charles Nob Hill
    Cafe La Haye/N
    Chez Panisse/E
    Fork/N
    Marinus/S

Chinese
26 Omei/S
25 Ton Kiang
    Koi Palace/S
    Mei Long/S
    Yank Sing

Continental
25 Fresh Cream/S
23 Anton & Michel/S
20 Dal Baffo/S
    Caprice, The/N
19 Shadowbrook/S

Dim Sum
25 Ton Kiang
Koi Palace/S
Yank Sing
24 Fook Yuen/S
22 Harbor Village

Eclectic
24 Willi's Wine Bar/N
23 Firefly
Willow Wood Mkt./N▽
Wappo Bar/N
22 Celadon/N

French
27 Le Papillon/S
26 Isa
25 Cafe Jacqueline
Chez Spencer
Seasons

French (Bistro)
26 Chapeau!
Bistro Jeanty/N
25 Clémentine
Fringale
24 Bistro Elan/S

French (New)
28 Masa's
Fleur de Lys
27 La Toque/N
Erna's Elderberry/E
Ritz-Carlton D.R.

Fusion
26 House
25 Flying Fish Grill/S
CAFÉ KATi
Eos Rest.
24 Roy's/Pebble Bch./S

Hamburgers
22 Taylor's Automatic/N/SF
21 Mo's
20 Burger Joint/S/SF
19 Barney Hamburger/E/SF
18 Balboa Cafe/E/SF

Indian/Pakistani
25 Amber India/S
24 Indian Oven
23 Ajanta/E
Shalimar/E/SF
Tallula

Italian
27 Acquerello
26 Delfina
Dopo/E
25 Quince
Oliveto/E

Japanese
27 Sushi Ran/N
Kabuto Sushi
26 Kirala/E
25 Hana Japanese/N
Kyo-Ya

Latin American
23 Limòn
Alma
Destino
Fonda Solana/E
Fresca

Mediterranean
27 Chez Panisse/E
Rivoli/E
Chez Panisse Café/E
26 Campton Place
Bay Wolf/E

Mexican
24 La Taqueria/S/SF
Doña Tomás/E
23 Pancho Villa/S/SF
Villa Corona/N
Maya

Middle Eastern
25 Cafe Gibraltar/S
24 Helmand, The
23 Truly Med./E/SF
Maykedah▽
20 Yumma's

Pizza
25 Zachary's Pizza/E
Pizzetta 211
24 Postrio
Tommaso's
Pauline's Pizza

Seafood
27 Hog Island Oyster
Aqua
25 Swan Oyster
Passionfish/S
Flying Fish Grill/S
Willi's Seafood/N*

Top Food

Spanish/Basque
25 Piperade
   Fringale
23 César/E
   Zarzuela
   Destino

Steakhouses
25 Cole's Chop Hse./N
   House of Prime Rib
24 Harris'
   Ruth's Chris
23 Morton's

Tapas (Latin)
23 César/E
   Zarzuela
   Destino
   Zuzu/N
22 Charanga

Thai
25 Thep Phanom
24 Marnee Thai
   Soi 4/E
   Royal Thai/N
22 Basil Thai

Vegetarian
28 French Laundry/N
   Fleur de Lys
24 Greens
23 Millennium
16 Herbivore

Vietnamese
26 Slanted Door
25 Tamarine/S
   Thanh Long
23 Crustacean
   Tu Lan

By Special Feature

Breakfast
26 Tartine Bakery
   Mama's on Wash. Sq.
   Dottie's True Blue
25 Oliveto/E
24 Gayle's Bakery/S

Brunch
27 Erna's Elderberry/E
26 Campton Place
   Lark Creek Inn/N
25 Pacific's Edge/S
   La Forêt/S

Child-Friendly
25 Yank Sing
22 Taylor's Automatic/N/SF
19 Barney Hamburger/E/SF
16 Max's/E/N/S/SF
15 Pasta Pomodoro/E/N/S/SF

Hotel Dining
28 Masa's
     Hotel Vintage Ct.
27 Ritz-Carlton D.R.
     Ritz-Carlton Hotel
   Marinus/S
     Bernardus Lodge
26 Rest. at Stevenswood/N
     Stevenswood Lodge
   Sierra Mar/S
     Post Ranch Inn

Late Night
24 Zuni Cafe
   Bouchon/N
   Brother's Korean
23 Pancho Villa
   Shalimar

Newcomers (Rated)
26 Dopo/E
25 Quince
   Willi's Seafood/N
   Cortez
23 1550 Hyde Café

Newcomers (Unrated)
   Eccolo/E
   Frisson
   Michael Mina
   Pilar/N
   Tartare

People-Watching
27 Boulevard
26 Jardinière
24 Zuni Cafe
23 Town Hall
22 Spago Palo Alto/S

Small Plates
27 Fork/N
26 Isa
   Slanted Door
25 Tamarine/S
   Willi's Seafood/N

Tasting Menus

29 Gary Danko
28 French Laundry/N
  Masa's
27 Le Papillon/S
  Charles Nob Hill

Trendy

26 Manresa/S
25 Tamarine/S
  Willi's Seafood/N
  Cortez
  Piperade

Wine Bars

25 Eos Rest.
23 César/E
  1550 Hyde Café
22 bacar
18 Hayes & Vine

Winning Wine Lists

29 Gary Danko
28 French Laundry/N
  Masa's
  Fleur de Lys
23 Rubicon

Worth a Trip

28 French Laundry/N
  Yountville
27 Sushi Ran/N
  Sausalito
  Cafe La Haye/N
  Sonoma
  La Toque/N
  Rutherford
  Chez Panisse/E
  Berkeley

Top 40 Decor

28 Sierra Mar/S
Garden Court
Ahwahnee/E
Pacific's Edge/S
Navio/S
27 Farallon
Ana Mandara
Auberge du Soleil/N
Ritz-Carlton D.R.
Fleur de Lys
Madrona Manor/N
El Paseo/N
26 Jardinière
Erna's Elderberry/E
Shadowbrook/S
Gary Danko
French Laundry/N
Martini Hse./N
Marinus/S
Alexander Valley/N

Cetrella Bistro/S
Grand Cafe
25 Fifth Floor
BIX
Wente Vineyards/E
Le Colonial
Kokkari Estiatorio
Campton Place
Nepenthe/S
Boulevard
Roy's/Pebble Bch./S
Tonga Room
Seasons
Tra Vigne/N
Aqua
Lark Creek Inn/N*
Masa's
Domaine Chandon/N
Ozumo
Carnelian Room

Outdoors

Alexander Valley/N
Angèle/N
Auberge du Soleil/N
Bay Wolf/E
B44
Bistro Aix
Brix/N
Casanova/S
Chez Spencer
Domaine Chandon/N
Doña Tomás/E
Enrico's Sidewalk
Ferry Plaza Seafood

Foreign Cinema
General's Daughter/N
Hurley's Rest./N
Isa
Lark Creek Inn/N
Martini Hse./N
Pinot Blanc/N
Plouf
Ritz-Carlton Terr.
Tra Vigne/N
Wente Vineyards/E
Willi's Seafood/N
Zinsvalley/N

Romance

Acquerello
Applewood Inn/N
Auberge du Soleil/N
Aziza
Cafe Jacqueline
Casanova/S
Chez Panisse/E
Chez Spencer
Citron/E
El Paseo/N
Erna's Elderberry/E
Fleur de Lys
Jardinière

Julius' Castle
Khan Toke
La Forêt/S
Le Papillon/S
Madrona Manor/N
Manka's Inverness/N
Marinus/S
Martini Hse./N
Ritz-Carlton D.R.
Sierra Mar/S
Tallula
Venticello
Zaré

Rooms

Ahwahnee/E
Ana Mandara
Applewood Inn/N
A.P. Stump's/S
Aqua
Asia de Cuba
Azie
BIX
Boulevard
Cetrella Bistro/S
Emporio Rulli/N/SF
Evvia/S
Farallon
Garden Court
Grand Cafe
Jardinière
Jeanty at Jack's
Kokkari Estiatorio
Le Colonial
Martini Hse./N
Masa's
Pinot Blanc/N
Poggio Rist./N
Ritz-Carlton D.R.
St. Orres/N
Tallula

Views

Ahwahnee/E
Albion River Inn/N
Angèle/N
Auberge du Soleil/N
Beach Chalet
Bella Vista/S
Brix/N
Carnelian Room
Cityscape
Greens
Guaymas/N
Hog Island Oyster
Jordon's/E
Julius' Castle
Ledford Hse./N
Napa Valley Train/N
Navio/S
Nepenthe/S
Pacific's Edge/S
Poggio Rist./N
Roy's/Pebble Bch./S
Scoma's/N/SF
Sierra Mar/S
Slanted Door
Waterfront Rest.
Wente Vineyards/E

Top 40 Service

28 Ritz-Carlton D.R.
Gary Danko
27 French Laundry/N
Masa's
La Toque/N
Erna's Elderberry/E
Le Papillon/S
26 Acquerello
Rest. at Stevenswood/N
Albona Rist.
Campton Place
Fleur de Lys
Seasons
Charles Nob Hill
Chapeau!
25 Ritz-Carlton Terr.
Chez Panisse/E
Terra/N
Chez TJ/S
John Bentley's/S
La Folie
Cafe La Haye/N
Silks
Emile's/S
Fifth Floor
Sierra Mar/S
Quince
Marinus/S
Marché/S
Pacific's Edge/S
Auberge du Soleil/N
Boulevard
24 Madrona Manor/N
Little River Inn/N
Lalime's/E
Fresh Cream/S
Jardinière*
Bay Wolf/E
Aqua
Manresa/S

Best Buys

Top 40 Bangs for the Buck

1. Rosamunde Grill
2. Caspers Hot Dogs/E
3. Taq. Can-Cun
4. Yumma's
5. Pancho Villa/S/SF
6. Cactus Taqueria/E
7. Downtown Bakery/N
8. El Balazo
9. La Taqueria/S/SF
10. Jay's Cheese Steak
11. La Cumbre Taq./S/SF
12. Truly Med./E/SF
13. Burger Joint/S/SF
14. Boulange de Cole/Polk
15. Tartine Bakery
16. Caffe 817/E
17. Vik's Chaat/E
18. Jimtown Store/N
19. Mama's Royal/E
20. Fenton's Creamery/E
21. Dottie's True Blue
22. Emporio Rulli/N/SF
23. It's Tops Coffee
24. Pork Store Café
25. Chloe's Cafe
26. Villa Corona/N
27. Taylor's Automatic/N/SF
28. Kate's Kitchen
29. Picante Cocina/E
30. Citrus Club
31. Lovejoy's Tea Rm.
32. Café Fanny/E
33. Frjtz Fries
34. Asqew Grill/E/SF
35. Bette's Oceanview/E
36. Mama's on Wash. Sq.
37. Mario's Bohemian
38. Joe's Taco/N
39. King of Thai
40. Barney Hamburger/E/SF

Other Good Values

Alamo Sq.
A La Turca
Amici East Coast/N/S/SF
Angkor Borei
A 16
Axum Cafe
Baker St. Bistro
César/E
Chapeau!
Charanga
Chow/Park Chow/E/SF
Christophe/N
Dipsea Cafe/N
Dopo/E
Firefly
Gayle's Bakery/S
Happy Cafe/S
Helmand, The
Home
Hotei
Hyde St. Bistro
JoAnn's Café/S
jZCool/S
La Table O&CO
Le Charm
L'Osteria del Forno
Luna Park
Osha Thai
Pacific Catch
Pakwan/E/SF
Pizzetta 211
Shalimar/E/SF
Ti Couz
Tommaso's
Udupi Palace/E/S
Vicolo
Vi's/E
Watercress
Watergate
Zachary's Pizza/E

Bargain Prix Fixes
($30 & Under)

Ajanta/E	15.00
Baker St. Bistro	14.50
Bistro Liaison/E	26.00
Bizou	29.95
Caffe Delle Stelle	21.95
Cetrella Bistro/S	24.95
Chapeau!	25.00
Chez Panisse Café/E	28.00
Christophe/N	22.00
Cozmo's Corner	28.00
Fook Yuen/S	20.00
Gayle's Bakery/S	10.50
girl & the fig/N	20.00
Jordan's/E	29.95
La Luna	19.95
La Scene Café	29.95
La Table O&CO	18.00
Le Charm	25.00
L'Olivier	29.50
Mandarin, The	28.00
Marica/E	24.00
Market/N	24.95
Maya	29.95
Mecca	29.95
Moose's	29.95
Palomino	29.00
Passage to India/S	18.95
Pinot Blanc/N	28.00
Rist. Bacco	25.00
RNM	25.00
Robert's Whitehse./S	27.00
Roy's	30.00
Sanraku	30.00
South Park	29.95
Stinking Rose	24.95
Town's End	13.50
Watercress	19.95
Zazie	17.50

City of San Francisco

Top Ratings

Top lists exclude places with low voting.

Top Food

29 Gary Danko	Kabuto Sushi
28 Masa's	**26** Chapeau!
Fleur de Lys	Isa
27 Charles Nob Hill	Campton Place
Acquerello	House
Ritz-Carlton D.R.	Tartine Bakery
Boulevard	Rosamunde Grill
La Folie	Jardinière
Hog Island Oyster	Delfina
Aqua	Mama's on Wash. Sq.

By Cuisine

American (New)
- **29** Gary Danko
- **27** Boulevard
- **24** Postrio
  - Woodward Garden
- **23** Chenery Park

American (Traditional)
- **26** Mama's on Wash. Sq.
- **23** Hayes St. Grill
- **22** Blue Plate
  - Taylor's Automatic
  - Liberty Cafe

Bakeries
- **26** Tartine Bakery
- **23** Boulange de Cole/Polk
- **22** Liberty Cafe
  - Town's End
- **20** Citizen Cake

Californian
- **27** Charles Nob Hill
  - Aqua
- **26** Jardinière
- **24** Hawthorne Lane
  - PlumpJack

Chinese
- **25** Ton Kiang
  - Yank Sing
- **23** Tommy Toy's
  - Eliza's
  - R & G Lounge

French
- **26** Isa
  - Jardinière
- **25** Cafe Jacqueline
  - Chez Spencer
  - Seasons

French (Bistro)
- **26** Chapeau!
- **25** Clémentine
  - Fringale
- **24** Chez Papa Bistrot
- **23** South Park

French (New)
- **28** Masa's
  - Fleur de Lys
- **27** Ritz-Carlton D.R.
  - La Folie
- **26** Fifth Floor

Fusion
- **26** House
- **25** CAFÉ KATi
  - Eos Rest.
- **24** Ma Tante Sumi
  - Silks

Hamburgers
- **22** Taylor's Automatic
- **21** Mo's
- **20** Burger Joint
- **19** Barney Hamburger
- **18** Balboa Cafe

Indian/Pakistani

24 Indian Oven
23 Shalimar
    Tallula
21 Pakwan
20 Zante's Pizza

Italian

27 Acquerello
26 Delfina
25 Quince
    Albona Rist.
24 Rist. Milano
    Venticello*

Japanese

27 Kabuto Sushi
25 Kyo-Ya
24 Ebisu
    Maki
23 Sushi Groove

Latin American

23 Limòn
    Alma
    Destino
    Fresca
22 Charanga

Mediterranean

26 Campton Place
25 Kokkari Estiatorio
    Cortez
    Frascati
24 Ritz-Carlton Terr.

Mexican

24 La Taqueria
23 Pancho Villa
    Maya
    Taq. Can-Cun
21 La Cumbre Taq.

Middle Eastern

24 Helmand, The
23 Truly Med.
20 Yumma's
    La Méditerranée
17 Kan Zaman

Pizza

25 Pizzetta 211
24 Postrio
    Tommaso's
    Pauline's Pizza
    Pazzia

Seafood

27 Hog Island Oyster
    Aqua
25 Swan Oyster
24 Farallon
    Pesce

Spanish/Basque

25 Piperade
    Fringale
23 Zarzuela
    Destino
21 B44

Steakhouses

25 House of Prime Rib
24 Harris'
    Ruth's Chris
23 Morton's
22 Anzu

Tapas (Latin)

23 Zarzuela
20 Alegrias
    Esperpento
18 Ramblas
17 Picaro

Thai

25 Thep Phanom
24 Marnee Thai
22 Basil Thai
    Khan Toke
21 Thai Hse.

Vietnamese

26 Slanted Door
25 Thanh Long
23 Crustacean
    Tu Lan
22 Three Seasons

---

* Indicates a tie with restaurant above

Top Food

By Special Feature

Breakfast
26 Tartine Bakery
　　Mama's on Wash. Sq.
　　Dottie's True Blue
23 Boulange de Cole/Polk
　　Kate's Kitchen

Brunch
26 Campton Place
25 Ton Kiang
　　Yank Sing
24 Ritz-Carlton Terr.
　　Zuni Cafe

Child-Friendly
25 Yank Sing
22 Taylor's Automatic
21 Mo's
19 Barney Hamburger
13 Mel's Drive-In

Late Night
24 Zuni Cafe
　　Brother's Korean
23 Pancho Villa
　　Shalimar
　　Taq. Can-Cun

Newcomers (Rated)
25 Quince
　　Cortez
23 1550 Hyde Café
　　Tallula
　　Town Hall

Newcomers (Unrated)
　　Bocadillos
　　El Raigon
　　Frisson
　　Michael Mina
　　Tartare

Outdoor Seating
26 Isa
25 Chez Spencer
24 Ritz-Carlton Terr.
23 Sociale
22 Foreign Cinema

People-Watching
27 Boulevard
26 Jardinière
24 Postrio
　　Zuni Cafe
23 Sushi Groove

Power Scenes
27 Boulevard
　　Aqua
23 Rubicon
　　Town Hall
22 One Market

Romance
29 Gary Danko
28 Masa's
　　Fleur de Lys
27 Charles Nob Hill
　　Acquerello

Small Plates
26 Isa
　　Slanted Door
25 Eos Rest.
24 Baraka
　　Pesce

Tasting Menus
29 Gary Danko
28 Masa's
27 Charles Nob Hill
　　Acquerello
　　Ritz-Carlton D.R.

Trendy
25 Cortez
　　Piperade
23 Limòn
　　Talulla
　　Town Hall

Winning Wine Lists
29 Gary Danko
27 Acquerello
26 Fifth Floor
24 PlumpJack
23 Rubicon

By Location

Castro/Noe Valley
- *24* Incanto
- Ma Tante Sumi
- *23* Firefly
- Rist. Bacco
- Destino

Chinatown
- *23* R & G Lounge
- Great Eastern
- *21* Hunan Home's Rest.
- Brandy Ho's
- *20* Yuet Lee

Civic Center/Hayes Valley
- *26* Jardinière
- *24* Zuni Cafe
- *23* Hayes St. Grill
- *22* Axum Cafe
- *21* Absinthe

Cow Hollow/Marina
- *26* Isa
- *24* PlumpJack
- Greens
- *23* Emporio Rulli
- Pane e Vino

Downtown
- *28* Masa's
- *27* Aqua
- *26* Campton Place
- *25* Kokkari Estiatorio
- Cortez

Embarcadero
- *27* Boulevard
- Hog Island Oyster
- *26* Slanted Door
- *23* Ozumo
- *22* Taylor's Automatic

Fisherman's Wharf
- *29* Gary Danko
- *22* Ana Mandara
- Grandeho's
- *21* Mandarin, The
- Scoma's

Haight-Ashbury/Cole Valley
- *25* Eos Rest.
- *23* Boulange de Cole/Polk
- *22* Grandeho's
- *21* Zazie
- *20* Citrus Club

Mission
- *26* Tartine Bakery
- Delfina
- *25* Chez Spencer
- *24* Woodward Garden
- La Taqueria

Nob Hill/Russian Hill
- *28* Fleur de Lys
- *27* Charles Nob Hill
- Ritz-Carlton D.R.
- *25* Frascati
- *24* Ritz-Carlton Terr.

North Beach
- *26* House
- Mama's on Wash. Sq.
- *25* Cafe Jacqueline
- Albona Rist.
- *24* Helmand, The

Pacific Heights/Japantown
- *25* Quince
- CAFÉ KATi
- *24* Maki
- *23* Chez Nous
- Eliza's

Richmond
- *27* Kabuto Sushi
- *26* Chapeau!
- *25* Ton Kiang
- Clémentine
- Pizzetta 211

SoMa
- *26* Fifth Floor
- *25* Fringale
- *24* Hawthorne Lane
- Pazzia
- *23* Maya

Sunset
- *25* Thanh Long
- *24* Ebisu
- Marnee Thai
- *21* Pomelo
- *20* Yumma's

Van Ness/Polk
- *27* Acquerello
- La Folie
- *25* Swan Oyster
- House of Prime Rib
- *24* Harris'

Top Decor

28	Garden Court	Le Colonial
27	Farallon	Kokkari Estiatorio
	Ana Mandara	Campton Place
	Ritz-Carlton D.R.	Boulevard
	Fleur de Lys	Tonga Room
26	Jardinière	Seasons
	Gary Danko	Aqua
	Grand Cafe	Masa's
25	Fifth Floor	Ozumo
	BIX	Carnelian Room

Top Service

28	Ritz-Carlton D.R.	**25** Ritz-Carlton Terr.
	Gary Danko	La Folie
27	Masa's	Silks
26	Acquerello	Fifth Floor
	Albona Rist.	Quince
	Campton Place	Boulevard
	Fleur de Lys	**24** Jardinière
	Seasons	Aqua
	Charles Nob Hill	Clémentine
	Chapeau!	Frascati

Top Bangs for the Buck

1. Rosamunde Grill
2. Taq. Can-Cun
3. Yumma's
4. Pancho Villa
5. El Balazo
6. La Taqueria
7. Jay's Cheese Steak
8. La Cumbre Taq.
9. Truly Med.
10. Burger Joint
11. Boulange de Cole/Polk
12. Tartine Bakery
13. Dottie's True Blue
14. Emporio Rulli
15. It's Tops Coffee
16. Pork Store Café
17. Chloe's Cafe
18. Taylor's Automatic
19. Kate's Kitchen
20. Citrus Club

City of San Francisco

Absinthe ❶
21 | 22 | 19 | $40

398 Hayes St. (Gough St.), 415-551-1590; www.absinthe.com
◪ Hayes Valley's "hip" "imitation of 1920s Paris" is "everything a brasserie should be" – "jolly", with a "dark, lush" "bohemian atmosphere" ("I was half expecting can-can girls to appear"), "great people-watching" and "*très délicieuse*" "French-Med fare"; while addicts' "hearts grow fonder after one of the super-strong", "snazzy" cocktails, the "busy, noisy" room and "snobbish staff can dull" the "buzz", particularly "during the rush hours before or after performances" at the theaters nearby.

Ace Wasabi's
21 | 15 | 16 | $31

3339 Steiner St. (bet. Chestnut & Lombard Sts.), 415-567-4903; www.acewasabis.com
◪ This "wild and noisy" "Marina sushi joint" feels like a "fraternity party", with "lots of twentysomethings" "packed like sardines" into the "dinerlike" room "dropping sake shots in their beers" and "finding someone to hook up with"; but "if you can stand" the "blaring rock music" and "long waits", the "creative rolls" "are well worth" it say those "embarrassed to admit how much they like this place"; P.S. "you get a nice $20 break off your bill if you win" at weekday bingo.

Acme Chophouse
19 | 18 | 17 | $44

24 Willie Mays Plaza (bet. King & 3rd Sts.), 415-644-0240; www.acmechophouse.com
◪ "Who wouldathunk" sustainably farmed vegetables and meat "could be found underneath home plate", but that's the lineup at this "booming" sports bar/"steakhouse that cares" located "next to the ballpark"; while the "Giants portions" hit "a home run" with fans, foes call foul over the "mediocre-for-the-price" meals, "uneven service" and the "cavernous" room, which is "total mayhem before a game", "deserted" "when there isn't one."

ACQUERELLO ⌧
27 | 23 | 26 | $60

1722 Sacramento St. (bet. Polk St. & Van Ness Ave.), 415-567-5432; www.acquerello.com
■ It's closed Sunday, but other days are fine times "to worship" at this Italian "in a refurbished chapel" near Polk Street, considered a "mercifully quiet", "Venetian-themed" "jewel" of "linen tablecloths" and "hand-carved decanters" by an "older" "blue-blooded crowd"; simply "put your faith in Giancarlo Paterlini" who "waits on you

hand and foot" and creates some "killer wine pairings" off his "incomparable list", while co-owner/chef Suzette Gresham's "rich" *cucina* "brings you to your knees."

Alamo Square   ▽ 20 | 19 | 19 | $25 |
803 Fillmore St. (bet. Fulton & Grove Sts.), 415-440-2828
◪ "All neighborhood restaurants should be as good" as this "lovely little French fish place" in the Western Addition offering a "unique" "mix-n-match menu (you pick the preparation and the sauces)" "at a decent price"; while locals are less forgiving about the "Gallic service", a Decor score solid suggests they consider the tight quarters "cozy but quaint."

A La Turca   ▽ 22 | 7 | 13 | $14 |
869 Geary St. (Larkin St.), 415-345-1011
◪ There's "no need to regret not making that trip" to Turkey when you can "just eat" "amazingly authentic" "tasty" "Turkish treats" at this hole-in-the-wall offering a bit of "Istanbul in the Tenderloin"; the "outstanding kebobs", "tomato and feta pide (pies)" and other items listed on a dry-erase board are "cheap" and "good enough to go back for more" "despite a complete lack of atmosphere" (it's "an oasis for the stomach, not the eyes").

Albona Ristorante Istriano ⊠   25 | 15 | 26 | $38 |
545 Francisco St. (bet. Mason & Taylor Sts.), 415-441-1040
■ This "offbeat" "little find" in North Beach is something out of a *Saturday Night Live* skit, where "comical" owner Bruno Viscovi "greets every customer like a long-lost friend", then "sits down" with them to patter on "about the days of yore" and his "marvelous", "unusual Istrian fare" that's "unlike any Italian you've ever had"; the valet parking is nothing to laugh at, however.

Alegrias, Food From Spain   20 | 16 | 18 | $29 |
2018 Lombard St. (Webster St.), 415-929-8888
◪ "Anyone nostalgic for Spain" would enjoy this "low-key" tapas bar cranking out "reasonably priced" "down-home style" "*comida*" that's "the real thing"; trendsters irritated by "slow service" (which dipped in ratings) and the "kitschy" "outdated decor" cry it just doesn't cut it in the "hip" Marina, but the forgiving say "drink enough of the sangria and you won't notice the flaws."

Alfred's Steak House ⊠   22 | 19 | 21 | $46 |
659 Merchant St. (bet. Kearny & Montgomery Sts.), 415-781-7058; www.alfredssteakhouse.com
◪ "Atkins dieters will love" this "old-boys'-network type" of steakhouse, "hidden in a back alley in Downtown", that's been "perfectly preparing" and "professionally serving" the same "refreshingly old-fashioned menu" since 1928; modernists moan it's time to "update this dinosaur", but nostalgists appreciate the "clubby", "dark interior" that,

along with the comparatively "reasonable prices", sets it apart from the chains.

Alice's
19 | 15 | 17 | $19

1599 Sanchez St. (29th St.), 415-282-8999

☑ Purists may pout "give me a hole-in-the wall Chinese anytime", but it's the "healthy-tasting", artfully presented twists on Sino standards that "lure diners" to this "family-friendly" Noe Valley neighborhood spot; with its "simple" yet "eye-catching decor" ("beautiful orchids and glass vases"), it's "a good alternative" to the "remarkably similar" Eric's and Eliza's, even though the "parking's still bad."

Alioto's
17 | 16 | 17 | $37

8 Fisherman's Wharf (bet. Jefferson & Taylor Sts.), 415-673-0183; www.aliotos.com

☑ "Owned by a family with long political ties", this "Fisherman's Wharf institution" (circa 1925) is "exactly what it's supposed to be" – a "friendly" "must-visit" for the "the Midwest fanny-pack crowd" with "old-style" Sicilian seafood and "sunsets over the Golden Gate Bridge"; advocates argue "the view's so beautiful you won't mind" that the eats are "well prepared but not special"; but locals lament "oh, dear – it's still here", this "tourist trap"?

Alma ☒
23 | 19 | 19 | $34

1101 Valencia St. (22nd St.), 415-401-8959; www.almacomida.com

☑ "Go, Johnny, go!" sing supporters of chef-owner Johnny Alamilla, whose "chic" venture "distinguishes itself from the rest" of the Mission's "trendy" "Nuevo Latino bunch" thanks to "ferociously delicious" *comida* ("one hell of a pork chop"), "unique South American wines" and "upscale" hacienda decor; however, the "crowds make for a stressed-out staff" and unless you go for the "great midweek prix fixe", it's "slightly overpriced", as "those seviches he's famous for feed only a goldfish."

Amici's East Coast Pizzeria
21 | 12 | 16 | $18

2033 Union St. (Buchanan St.), 415-885-4500; www.amicis.com

☑ Literally and figuratively, this Cow Hollow chain link delivers "the best brick-oven", "NY-style" "crispy, thin-crust pizza" "this side of the West Side Highway", with "friendly" "drivers who are like Manhattan cabbies, getting you hot 'za in under 15 minutes" (the preferred option, since the site's "nothing special"); still, some old boys from the boroughs decry the "expensive" prices for pie ("they must be paying for shipping from NY as well"); N.B. there are branches throughout the Bay Area.

ANA MANDARA
22 | 27 | 21 | $44

Ghirardelli Sq., 891 Beach St. (Polk St.), 415-771-6800; www.anamandara.com

■ This "stunningly beautiful" celebrity-backed hot spot boasts a "swank colonial decor" that "transports you to the Pacific" (or at the very least "the movie set of *The Quiet American*"); you'll pay for the "creative Vietnamese fare with New French influences" complemented by a "superior wine list", but "it's a great alternative to all the bad food along the Wharf" and "worth a visit", even if you just "enjoy the ambiance with a unique cocktail" in the jazz-serenaded lounge upstairs.

Andalu   21 19 18 $33

3198 16th St. (bet. Guerrero & Valencia Sts.), 415-621-2211; www.andalusf.com

☑ "Mission hipsters mingle" with "the bridge and tunnel crowd" at this "boisterously noisy" "velvet-draped" hot spot serving a "stellar variety" of Eclectic "multinational small plates" (from Coke-braised ribs to "amazing doughnut holes") "with a kickin' wine bar"; just "be prepared to spend a lot" 'cuz the portions, while "big in flavor", are "laughably" "Lilliputian"; P.S. "take public transit", as the only thing harder to find than an often-"slow" server is a parking spot.

Angkor Borei   ▽ 22 13 23 $19

3471 Mission St. (Cortland Ave.), 415-550-8417; www.angkorboreisf.com

■ For "a little bit of Cambodia right here" in Bernal Heights, head to this often "overlooked" "little place" serving up "consistently" "delicious" dishes (including "amazing" "fake-meat vegetarian choices") that haven't been "too *farang*-ized" (they're "authentic", that is); true, there's "little atmosphere, but the family that owns the place is attentive and charming" and "they deliver" citywide, too.

Angkor Wat   21 18 19 $23

4217 Geary Blvd. (bet. 6th & 7th Aves.), 415-221-7887

■ "Lit candles on the tables", a choice of dining on "standard seats or lower to the floor in a cushioned booth" and "dancing on weekend nights" "add to the pleasing" ambiance (reflected by a ratings rise) of this "special-occasion" Inner Richmond Cambodian, whose fare is "authentic and delicious"; "the ebullient staff" "makes sure everyone's having a good time" and "customers celebrating birthdays, etc. receive a silk scarf."

Anjou ⌧   23 18 22 $39

44 Campton Pl. (bet. Post & Sutter Sts.), 415-392-5373; www.anjou-sf.com

☑ "Owners Gail and Pierre" Morin make you believe "it's Paree just one block from Union Square" at their "homey" "jewel box" that, like any "authentic bistro", gets "cramped" and "loud", but is "worth dealing with" for the "excellent" "traditional French fare" that's its "raison d'être"; it doesn't hurt that the "well-informed" waiters are "not stuck-up" and the prices offer the area's "best bang for the buck" making it popular "pre-show" or for a "shopping break."

Antica Trattoria
23 | 18 | 21 | $35

2400 Polk St. (Union St.), 415-928-5797

☑ "North Beach can't hold a candle to" this "boisterous, fun" Russian Hill trattoria where "chef-owner Ruggero Gadaldi puts his personal touch" on the "authentic, soulful, hearty" Tuscan fare, "made that much better by the charming staff" and "wonderful selection of lesser-known Italian wines"; however, "be prepared to shout" over the din of "yuppie types" who crowd this "dark, wooded" "neighborhood joint."

Anzu
22 | 20 | 21 | $48

Hotel Nikko, 222 Mason St. (O'Farrell St.), 415-394-1100; www.restaurantanzu.com

☑ "Outstanding beef", "stellar sushi" and a "tasty Sunday buffet brunch" await at this "Japanese take" on a surf 'n' turf house; while the "secluded" "location at the back of the Hotel Nikko" "isn't ideal" and prices are hefty for "small portions", "sturdy pours at the bar", "attentive service" and "free" "validated parking" make it a "good pre-theater place."

Aperto
21 | 15 | 20 | $29

1434 18th St. (Connecticut St.), 415-252-1625

☑ A "down-to-earth" staff doles out "inventive homemade pasta" and "wonderful nightly specials" at this "relatively unknown" trattoria on Potrero Hill; it's "one fantastic outlet for meals with friends", but you better count on some "long waits" in the small, "plain dining room" as "reservations aren't accepted."

AQUA
27 | 25 | 24 | $65

252 California St. (bet. Battery & Front Sts.), 415-956-9662; www.aqua-sf.com

☑ Take the plunge and "treat yourself" to SF's "best damn seafood" site, which stays "in the swim" under new chef Laurent Manrique; "high ceilings" and "stunning floral displays provide the perfect backdrop" for his "piled-up" French-Cal "feats of fresh fish" and foie gras, offered by "service so polished it shines"; while it's "cacophonous", "crowded and pricey" ("the food's rich, but we weren't after paying the bill"), Downtown power-lunchers and the "breathlessly chic" fall for it hook, line and sinker.

A. Sabella's
18 | 17 | 19 | $38

2766 Taylor St. (Jefferson St.), 415-771-6775; www.asabellas.com

☑ "If you have out-of-towners who insist on going to the Wharf for dinner", take 'em to this fourth-generation "family-owned" waterfront "standby"; sure, the "prices are high", but the "incredible views" of the Bay, seafood "right from the tank", an "amazingly reasonable wine list" and "professional servers" "make up for it", most say; still, sophisticates sniff it's "a tour-bus stop, stuck in time" (must be that "*Jetsons* decor").

Asia de Cuba　　　　20 | 25 | 18 | $50
Clift Hotel, 495 Geary St. (Taylor St.), 415-929-2300;
www.ianschragerhotels.com
☑ "Edgy, loud and as NY as you can get in Downtown SF", this "Ian Schrager–owned" "scene" is "frequented by celebrities" who slip past "the velvet rope" to share "giant portions" of "tasty" Asian–Nuevo Latino combinations "served to thumping techno music" in the "darker-than-a-bat-cave" dining room that's "as pretty as the staff is snooty"; it's "outrageously expensive", "but that's the price you pay for posing" with "the S&M (stand and model) crowd that gathers in the adjoining Redwood Room."

AsiaSF　　　　16 | 18 | 19 | $37
201 Ninth St. (Howard St.), 415-255-2742;
www.asiasf.com
☑ The "crazy" floor show of "gender illusionists" is the "claim to fame" (and what you pay for) at this "festive" SoMa supper club overrun with "bachelorette parties" and locals "freaking out" their out-of-town guests; the "creative" cocktails and Asian small plates are "better than expected", but "don't expect great service" since hourly your "cross-dressing waiter takes to the bar to lip sync" and "shake 'her' coconuts to a Josephine Baker number."

A 16　　　　21 | 20 | 19 | $31
2355 Chestnut St. (bet. Divisadero & Scott Sts.), 415-771-2216;
www.a16sf.com
☑ You'll "feel like you are in Naples", not the Marina, at this "slick" new wine bar/restaurant (named for the Campania-traversing motorway), thanks to its "incredibly authentic Neapolitan pizza", "adventurous Southern Italian boutique wines" "by the glass, carafe and bottle" and even a "classic foosball table"; although the "rocky service" pales in comparison to the "great ambiance", "with a little time everything should be *perfecto.*"

Asqew Grill　　　　18 | 12 | 14 | $13
1607 Haight St. (Clayton St.), 415-701-9301
3348 Steiner St. (Chestnut St.), 415-931-9201
www.asqewgrill.com
☑ "They do one thing and they do it well" at these "mix-n-match" Cal "kebab houses" in Haight-Ashbury and the Marina that offer "any kind of" skewered meat, sauce and side "you can think of"; while the counter staff and decor "leave something to be desired", "considering the price", "huge portions" and "quick service", it can't be beat for "grab-n-go meals" "before a movie"; P.S. a suburban Emeryville branch is ideal pre- or post-"marathon shopping trips to IKEA."

Axum Cafe
22 | 8 | 14 | $16

698 Haight St. (Pierce St.), 415-252-7912
1233 Polk St. (Bush St.), 415-474-7743 🏠
www.axumcafe.com

◪ "Get ready to eat with your fingers and lick them clean"
at this pair proffering "hands down" the "best Ethiopian
food in the city" – "spicy, satisfying" and "amazingly
cheap"; "abundant" portions "make up for the rather sad
atmosphere" and "slow service" (whose score has sunk)
at the Haight Street "hole-in-the-wall", while "posh booths"
and "smoking hot jazz" at "the more upscale sister" in Civic
Center "make it a one-stop evening."

Azie
22 | 22 | 19 | $42

826 Folsom St. (bet. 4th & 5th Sts.), 415-538-0918
◪ Fans find SoMa's "onetime dot-com hangout" has
gotten "less expensive" yet "even better with the addition
of the new chef", whose "Asian-inspired New French" menu
consists of "creative fare, offered up family-style" and
complemented by "hip cocktails", served in a setting that's
"good for romance" ("especially in the private booths");
but the less enamored opine it's still "overpriced", noting
"as more and more fusion restaurants open", this one's
"just not worth wading through all the attitude to get to."

Aziza
24 | 23 | 21 | $43

5800 Geary Blvd. (22nd Ave.), 415-752-2222; www.aziza-sf.com
■ "Amazing nouvelle Moroccan cuisine" along with "nice
touches" like plush cushioned seats and ritual rosewater
hand washing "contribute to the experience of being
carted off to a faraway land" at this Casbah-inspired
Outer Richmonder; while the "exotic cocktails" can be
"exorbitantly priced", the "tasting menu is a steal and gets
you a little of everything"; most enjoy the "entertaining
belly dancers", but you "can avoid them on weekdays" if
they're not your cup of mint tea.

bacar
22 | 23 | 21 | $48

448 Brannan St. (bet. 3rd & 4th Sts.), 415-904-4100;
www.bacarsf.com
■ A "wall of wine", "cool jazz licks" and "late-night
dining" on weekends are "the makings of a great night
out" at this "industrial" "NYC-style" SoMa lounge that's
"still holding on after the dot-bomb"; while the "mix of
business and trendy types, with a little goth thrown in",
mainly "go for the vino" (on "the most extensive list in
town"), the "pricey" Med–New American "vittles are
"surprisingly good" as is the "informed service."

Baker Street Bistro
20 | 15 | 19 | $28

2953 Baker St. (bet. Greenwich & Lombard Sts.), 415-931-1475
■ "Well loved by locals", this "quaint" Marina "sidewalk-
style bistro" offers frugal Francophiles "well-prepared"

"standard" classics "at substandard prices" (particularly the $14.50 nightly prix fixe); like its Parisian counterparts, it's "crowded, noisy" and "slow" (despite the "considerate" "French-speaking staff's" efforts); but at these prices, "you can order 'another bottle of wine, *s'il vous plâit.'"*

Balboa Cafe   18 | 17 | 17 | $31 |
3199 Fillmore St. (Greenwich St.), 415-921-3944;
www.plumpjack.com
🅭 Although "our esteemed mayor" no longer "owns the joint", this "mainstay of the trendy Triangle" in Cow Hollow is still "dominated by" politicos and "highbrows" supping on "dependable" American lunches and brunches paired with "unique wines" "without the markup"; however, "after hours" "it's hard to get any attention from the staff" when the "dark-paneled bar" turns into a "pickup scene" for the "lonely mid-30s crowd"; P.S. there's a branch "at the bottom of the slopes" at Squaw Valley.

Baldoria   ▽ 19 | 18 | 20 | $33 |
2162 Larkin St. (Green St.), 415-447-0441;
www.baldoriarestaurant.com
🅭 This "affordable, hidden" hole off Van Ness is "all a neighborhood restaurant should be – inviting, cozy and consistently good" (if "nothing special"), with its "solid Italian" standards; however, while the waiters are "cute enough to make you blush", "horrendous parking" means it's better suited for "those who can walk to it."

Bambuddha Lounge ⓩ   18 | 24 | 15 | $38 |
Phoenix Hotel, 601 Eddy St. (bet. Larkin & Polk Sts.),
415-885-5088; www.bambuddhalounge.com
🅭 An "awesome" Bali-meets-*Wallpaper** atmosphere beckons "hipsters" to this new "lounge/lively club" in "the 'loin's" funky Phoenix Hotel; and while most prefer to "chill" by the "poolside patio", "smoking and drinking" "tropical cocktails" or to "dance the night away" after 10 PM, the French–Southeast Asian small plates are "surprisingly delicious and well priced"; however, the bam-boozled bark "it's neither as quiet as Buddha would like, nor does the service leave you feeling particularly Zen."

Baraka   24 | 22 | 19 | $38 |
288 Connecticut St. (18th St.), 415-255-0370; www.barakasf.net
🅭 "Refreshingly different" and "hip for the Hill", Potrero's packed, "high-energy" hideaway has supporters swooning "take me to the Casbah" for "simply amazing" Moroccan-Med tapas with "tastes out of this world – or at least this country"; the "exotic" decor "lets you pretend you're in Marrakesh", but unfortunately the "real French" staff serves up "an unusual helping of attitude" and "reservations mean nothing"; N.B. a new chef has expanded the menu post-*Survey.*

Barney's Gourmet Hamburger   19 | 12 | 14 | $14 |
3344 Steiner St. (bet. Chestnut & Lombard Sts.), 415-563-0307
4138 24th St. (Castro St.), 415-282-7770
www.barneyshamburgers.com
See review in East of San Francisco Directory.

Basil Thai Restaurant & Bar   22 | 16 | 19 | $23 |
1175 Folsom St. (bet. 7th & 8th Sts.), 415-552-8999;
www.basilthai.com
■ "In a city full of Thai" eateries, this "upscale, modern" one, though set in a "so-so" section of SoMa, "stands out" as it is a "bit hipper" and even makes a mean mojito; while it's packed with "lots of byte heads" and conventioneers at lunch and neighborhood noshers at night who appreciate the "quick, solid" fare and "friendly service", it's also "fantastic for delivery" or "takeout" "for the money."

Beach Chalet Brewery   11 | 19 | 12 | $27 |
1000 Great Hwy. (bet. Fulton St. & Lincoln Way), 415-386-8439;
www.beachchalet.com
◪ Surveyors admit they "frequently take out-of-towners" to this "casual brewery" for the "swoon-worthy views" of the ocean and "interesting WPA murals"; sure, the "simple" New American food is "nothing to write home about" and "service is slow at best", but "live band jam sessions" on some days and "homemade brews" "redeem it."

Bella Trattoria   21 | 17 | 20 | $30 |
3854 Geary Blvd. (3rd Ave.), 415-221-0305; www.bellatrattoria.com
■ This "sweet little" "neighborhood trattoria" in the Richmond doesn't get "a lot of fanfare" but with its "top-notch homemade pastas", "cozy" atmosphere and "couldn't-be-friendlier" staff (who come complete with "hot Italian accents"), it "could easily become the place you go back to again and again."

BETELNUT PEJIU WU   23 | 22 | 17 | $33 |
2030 Union St. (Buchanan St.), 415-929-8855;
www.betelnutrestaurant.com
◪ "Good luck getting into" Cow Hollow's "original" Pan-Asian "small-plates paradise" that's "still jumping" "after all these years"; the "frightfully" loud bar area is "jammed to the max" with "young Marina hipsters and the bartenders they stalk", while in the "dramatically lit and furnished" dining room, "grown-ups fight over the green beans" and other examples of "wok magic"; now if only the "snotty staff" "cared half as much as the kitchen", it would "make many a naysayer a faithful follower."

B44   21 | 17 | 18 | $35 |
44 Belden Pl. (bet. Bush & Pine Sts.), 415-986-6287
◪ Tucked away "in a closed-off alley", this "fine, festive" Downtown boîte is "like being transported to Madrid",

where an "international crowd" tucks into "fabulous paella" ("heaven in cast-iron and rice") and "authentic" Catalan dishes while "catching airborne Spanish sherry poured from a carafe"; however, most opt for "lunch in the sun" or dinner "under the heat lamps" as the "industrial" interior gets "cramped" and "ear-splittingly loud."

Big 4   21 | 24 | 23 | $52 |

Huntington Hotel, 1075 California St. (Taylor St.), 415-771-1140; www.big4restaurant.com

■ You "almost expect to see the Big Four" railroad barons "of San Francisco long gone" at this "very old-school" hotel dining room whose "dark" "polished wood paneling", "extraordinary" "formal service" and "scrumptious", surprisingly Contemporary American food make it *the* "place to rub elbows with the old Nob Hill elite" (so "this is what it feels to be rich"); while "suits set up shop on weeknights", others enjoy the "clubby" bar.

Bistro Aix   23 | 18 | 21 | $34 |

3340 Steiner St. (bet. Chestnut & Lombard Sts.), 415-202-0100; www.bistroaix.com

◪ For "a romantic dinner" "without spending an arm and a leg", head to this "wonderful oasis" in the "hectic" Marina; fans find the Cal–French bistro menu is "better than the food in Aix" and "among the best" on Restaurant Row, yet "lacking the pretension associated" with either, thanks to a "congenial staff" that also proffers "a wine list you can afford"; however, dining on the "heated, covered patio" "is the way to go" as the inside can be "cramped and noisy."

Bistro Clovis   19 | 16 | 18 | $36 |

1596 Market St. (Franklin St.), 415-864-0231

■ This "oh-so-French", yet oh-so-affordable "stalwart" may "look like it's straight out of Paris" with its "art deco–style" decor, "classic service" and "authentic bistro" fixings, but the pre-show throngs are thrilled to have it so "close to Civic Center concert venues"; accompanying the "nothing fancy, but mm-mm-good" fare, "the wine palettes are a great way to learn about" varietals from Beaujolais and beyond.

Bistro La Mooné   21 | 17 | 18 | $31 |

4072 18th St. (bet. Castro & Hartford Sts.), 415-355-1999; www.bistrolamoone.com

◪ Supporters swoon that this "surprising little gem in the Castro", "with a name like a louche drag queen's", "is not to be missed", citing the "innovative Fusion small plates, a good selection of sake cocktails" and an interior that is "as cool as the blue lava in the middle of the tables"; however, many are "not completely over la moone about it", citing "slooow service" and food that "tries too hard to impress."

BIX   22   25   22 $49
56 Gold St. (bet. Montgomery & Sansome Sts.), 415-433-6300;
www.bixrestaurant.com
■ "Only Bogart is missing" from this "knockout" Downtown
"back alley" supper club featuring "swank art deco decor",
"bartenders in starched jackets" and a piano bar that
"evokes memories" of the Jazz Age; though it's "better
known as a gin joint" with "perfect martinis" for "the coat-
and-tie after-work crowd", if you can "get a table on the
balcony", the "high-back chairs", "impeccable service" and
"delicious" French-American fare make for pleasurable
"power lunches" or "sexy" dinners.

Bizou ☒   22   19   20 $41
598 Fourth St. (Brannan St.), 415-543-2222;
www.bizourestaurant.com
■ Chef-owner Loretta Keller's "unsung" "French-Med in
gritty SoMa" "continues to make magic" thanks to her
"short" but "distinctive", "hearty" menu ("beef cheeks all
the way!") delivered by "spot-on" servers in an "airy",
"mustard-colored" dining room that, though "noisy", is
equally "comforting"; and while prices are considered
"major" league for a neighborhood joint, the "prix fixe
lunches and dinners", particularly before a baseball game,
are a real steal.

Blowfish, Sushi to Die For   22   21   17 $37
2170 Bryant St. (20th St.), 415-285-3848; www.blowfishsushi.com
☑ "Japanese MTV" meets *Iron Chef* at this "surreal" sushi
joint in the Mission, packed with "party kids" who pay
"fancy prices" for "stunning sculptures" of raw fish,
"nouveau" rolls and "deadly" cocktails served in a "Sino-
tech" nightclub setting; but skeptics snap it's "not worth
dying for" the "surly service" and "sensory overload" from
the "deafening house music" and "semi-pornographic
anime" flashing "everywhere you look"; P.S. there's an
equally "über-hip" sibling in San Jose.

Blue Plate, The ☒   22   18   20 $32
3218 Mission St. (29th St.), 415-282-6777; www.blueplatesf.com
■ "Tucked among the taqueria joints" at the base of
Bernal, this "hidden treasure" ("with a secret garden to
boot") buzzes with a "blue-collar-meets-trendy vibe", as
"homestyle hipsters" huddle over the "innovative takes on
American classics" (e.g. macaroni and drunken Spanish
goat cheese); "the waiters flirt just the right amount", and
while the tabs "aren't particularly cheap", they "won't leave
you blue", either.

Bocadillos ☒   –   –   –   I
710 Montgomery St. (Washington St.), 415-982-2622
Bargain Basque bites are the buzz at this Downtown wine
bar and cafe, a casual outpost of Piperade owners Gerald

and Cameron Hirigoyen, specializing in small, Spanish-style sandwiches (hence the name), salads and soups by day and tapas and vino well into the night (don't miss the 'innard circle' – tripe, trotters and foie gras); the bright modern interior features two long counters with bar stools plus a long communal table.

Boulange de Cole/de Polk ⊟　　23 | 16 | 15 | $13
1000 Cole St. (Parnassus St.), 415-242-2442
2310 Polk St. (Green St.), 415-345-1107
☑ "The smell of fresh bread" and "transcendent" pastries "wafts over" Pascal Rigo's "Parisian boulangeries/cafes" in Cole Valley and Russian Hill that fill up with Francophiles fantasizing they "just stopped off in Saint-Germain for a café au lait" and an open-faced tartine; "harried", "surly service" and a "cramped interior" notwithstanding, the "long lines", particularly "on weekend mornings", "speak for themselves."

BOULEVARD　　27 | 25 | 25 | $55
1 Mission St. (Steuart St.), 415-543-6084;
www.boulevardrestaurant.com
■ There's no better place to "show off our fair city" than at this Embarcadero "icon" that, while "anything but cheap", remains the "sine qua non of SF dining"; in Pat Kuleto's "over-the-top" belle époque setting, the "brisk" but "professional" "waiters whiz by", serving Nancy Oakes' "extraordinary" French–New American creations ("you feel guilty eating 'cuz they look like works of art"), along with wines that "would turn anyone into a wanna-be sommelier"; P.S. go for "the back with the killer Bay Bridge view."

Brandy Ho's　　21 | 12 | 16 | $21
217 Columbus Ave. (bet. Broadway St. & Pacific Ave.),
415-788-7527; www.brandyhos.com
☑ "Eater beware": "get out the fire hoses" or "have a bottle of Tsing Tao on hand" at this cheap Chinatown "hole-in-the-wall" where the "super-spicy" "smokin'" Hunan eats may be a "bit more than you bargained for" ("medium is hot, and hot borders on inedible"); "sitting at the counter" and watching the "woks blazing away" distracts from the "no-decor" look.

Brazen Head ◗⊟　　20 | 20 | 20 | $32
3166 Buchanan St. (Greenwich St.), 415-921-7600;
www.brazenheadsf.com
■ "This longtime local favorite doesn't even need a sign to attract a loyal crowd" that flocks to the Cow Hollow "secret hideaway" to "indulge a red-meat craving" (the best choice on the American menu) and have "quiet conversation" in the "dark, boozy" "publike atmosphere" – "especially late at night, when most places are closed"; P.S. being "cash only makes it seem all the more exclusive."

Brindisi Cucina di Mare ⑤   ▽ 22 | 18 | 18 | $28
88 Belden Pl. (Pine St.), 415-593-8000; www.brindisicucina.com
■ "A nice addition to Belden" Place's predominantly
French Restaurant Row, this "small" Italian cafe "looks
promising", with its "well-prepared" Adriatic seafood tapas
served in a rustic, terra-cotta and tile-floored dining
room; as with most newcomers, the "service has kinks",
but they still "go out of their way to please."

Brother-in-Law's Bar-B-Que   22 | 4 | 12 | $15
705 Divisadero St. (Grove St.), 415-931-7427
▣ Looking for the "best 'cue in the city"? – "just follow that
cloud of smoke" over the Western Addition to this "run-
down storefront" cranking out slabs of "fall-of-the-bone",
"finger-licking good" "classic Southern BBQ meats"; since
the service is "slow", the decor "decrepit" and seating
limited, "get it to go" or visit "when you have no one to
impress but your stomach."

Brother's Korean Restaurant   24 | 6 | 15 | $23
4014 Geary Blvd. (bet. 4th & 5th Aves.), 415-668-2028
4128 Geary Blvd. (bet. 5th & 6th Aves.), 415-387-7991 ◗
▣ Seoul searchers for the "absolute best Korean BBQ"
find it at these "cook-it-yourself" Inner Richmonders
featuring a "great assortment" of "complementary side
dishes", a gregarious owner who "gives you free stuff"
(spurring a rise in the Service score, despite "horrendous
waits") and "zero ambiance" – "unless barbecue smoke
counts as decor"; "just don't wear your finest threads"
since you end up "smelling like the bulgoki you just ate."

Buca di Beppo   14 | 16 | 16 | $24
855 Howard St. (bet. 4th & 5th Sts.), 415-543-7673;
www.bucadibeppo.com
See review in South of San Francisco Directory.

Burger Joint   20 | 12 | 15 | $11
700 Haight St. (Pierce St.), 415-864-3833
807 Valencia St. (19th St.), 415-824-3494
www.burgerjointsf.com
▣ "Damn fine" "responsibly" raised meat and veggie
burgers make these Lower Haight and Mission "retro
dineresque shops" the "rich man's In-N-Out"; some find
the "*Jetsons* decor" "univiting" and the "service distracted
at times", but there's nothing like eating "beef from happy
cows" to "assuage the guilt" of fast-food indulgences;
N.B. there's a SFO branch as well.

Butler & The Chef Cafe, The ⑤   ▽ 17 | 20 | 19 | $21
155A South Park St. (bet. 2nd & 3rd Sts.), 415-896-2075;
www.oralpleasureinc.com
■ It's as if this "charming" daytime Lilliputian cafe, filled
with "French antiques" and sidewalk seating overlooking

"quaint South Park", was "cut out of a Parisian scene"; the "simple", "*authentique*" crêpes and croque monsieurs are "nothing special", but make a fine "escape" for a "workday lunch" or "on a sunny weekend"; N.B. no longer related to the similarly named furniture store.

butterfly embarcadero   18 | 20 | 17 | $37 |
(fka butterfly)
Pier 33 (Bay St.), 415-864-8999; www.butterflysf.com
☑ With a "marvelous location" "right on the pier", this ex-Mission restaurant/club with "hip decor" is an "exciting" "addition to the Embarcadero" proclaim the "flocks of beautiful people" who flutter over the "surprisingly good" Cal-Asian fare; but killjoys counter this high-flier "doesn't have as much panache since it moved", while the "loud" noise level prompts pessimists to proclaim "disco and dining are not a good combination."

Cafe Bastille ⌧   18 | 16 | 16 | $28 |
22 Belden Pl. (bet. Bush & Pine Sts.), 415-986-5673;
www.cafebastille.com
■ On days when "patio seating is a must", surveyors storm this "sweet and romantic" Belden Alley mainstay, "a small slice of Paris" where "everything is authentic, including the accents" and the "*toujours bon*" "basic French bistro food"; think of it as "a cheap trip to the continent."

Café Claude ⌧   19 | 17 | 15 | $29 |
7 Claude Ln. (bet. Grant Ave. & Kearny St.), 415-392-3515;
www.cafeclaude.com
☑ Downtowners say "*oui, oui, oui*" to "this grande dame of the French ghetto" serving "authentic" bistro fare, like a "very good croque monsieur", in a "cute but tight" room and alley-side patio that's "great for playing hooky on a Friday afternoon"; while "brusque" service has marred past visits, some assert it's getting "better" and praise the "live jazz" on weekends.

Cafe For All Seasons   18 | 14 | 19 | $25 |
150 W. Portal Ave. (bet. 14th Ave. & Vicente St.), 415-665-0900
☑ This "modest" West Portal "stalwart" isn't a place where you should expect "gourmet cuisine or a fancy setting", but rather is "a comfortable place to go" for "good basic American food", "warm" service and weekend brunch that "satisfies everyone" from the "older folks" to "your most picky friends"; just anticipate "long waits during prime hours" and a "high noise level."

Cafe Jacqueline   25 | 17 | 17 | $42 |
1454 Grant Ave. (bet. Green & Union Sts.), 415-981-5565
☑ Madame Jacqueline oversees "everyone's Valentine's Day dream" at this longtime country French set in a "romantic", if "small", North Beach storefront whose sole raison d'être is "heavenly soufflés" (from lobster to

"scarily rich but oh-so-good" chocolate); and if the wait is "long" and the staff "uppity at times, don't worry": after "one bite, all is forgiven."

CAFÉ KATi   25   17   22 $43
1963 Sutter St. (bet. Fillmore & Webster Sts.), 415-775-7313; www.cafekati.com
☑ "It's always a treat to go" to this Japantown "pioneer" of Cal-Asian "fusion food before it was trendy", as chef-owner Kirk Webber's "joie de vivre" shines through his "superb", "eye-popping" creations; but some confess to a "love-hate relationship" with the place because those "wonderful treats on the menu" and "delightful" service have to contend with "crammed-together" tables and noise.

Cafe Marimba   18   17   14 $25
2317 Chestnut St. (bet. Divisadero & Scott Sts.), 415-776-1506
☑ Purveying "earthy, rustic" moles and other Oaxacan-style dishes, this Marina Mexican offers an appreciated "break from the Mission"; it's also known as a "loud, lively" drinking spot complete with "great margaritas" and "crazy", "colorful" decor; but "disaffected" service and "lapses in quality control" provoke many to think it's "coasting on its reputation."

Cafe Maritime ◉   –   –   –   M
2417 Lombard St. (Scott St.), 415-885-2530
Hoping to fill the void of middle-ground seafood restaurants (not too pricey, not too cheesy), this casual Marina newcomer is reeling in diners with the promise of reasonably priced, simply prepared fin fare and a well-stocked raw bar; and while the cocktails flow until closing, so does the food (1 AM), a rarity in this early-to-bed town.

Café Niebaum-Coppola   16   20   15 $31
916 Kearny St. (Columbus Ave.), 415-291-1700; www.cafeniebaum-coppola.com
☑ A hit with "out-of-towners who want a taste of Italy and Hollywood" (at least Francis Ford Coppola's version of them), this North Beach cafe/wine bar is best for "thin, crispy" pizzas and "simple dishes" along with "glasses of vino", including those from the master's own vineyard; if critics claim they're "overhyped" and suffer from "snooty" staff, fans remind that you can "purchase the *Rumble Fish* soundtrack or *Dracula* posters" here; N.B. there is another branch South of SF.

Cafe Riggio   19   16   18 $28
4112 Geary Blvd. (bet. 5th & 6th Aves.), 415-221-2114; www.caferiggio.com
☑ Owner "John Riggio makes sure you're happy" at this Inner Richmonder that "hasn't been around for so long without a good reason", namely "cheap and good" Italian staples served in a "friendly", no-frills atmosphere; but not

everyone can "figure out why it's so popular", saying that it "gives a decent try but doesn't cut the mustard."

Café Tiramisu ⊠　　20　15　18　$35
28 Belden Pl. (Bush St.), 415-421-7044;
www.cafetiramisu.com

■ "Who needs North Beach when you can get quality food" "cooked by real Italians" plus "fine wine" "right in the Financial District"?; "flirty waiters" "do a great job of keeping everyone happy in the cramped", frescoed dining room and in the "wine cellar downstairs", but "when the weather is pleasant, enjoy it outside under an umbrella."

Caffe Centro ⊠　　▽ 18　12　14　$14
102 South Park St. (bet. 2nd & 3rd Sts.), 415-882-1500;
www.caffecentro.com

■ Having survived the "dot-com bust", this former "focal point" for the "legions of multimedia artists and engineers" that once plied South Park "still delivers" "good coffee", sandwiches, salads and cookies "quickly" and at "affordable" prices; so "don your hipster glasses", "tap on your handheld" and grab a seat in the "cramped quarters" or outside on the green.

Caffe Delle Stelle　　16　13　16　$27
395 Hayes St. (Gough St.), 415-252-1110

◪ A "good bet" when you have "ballet, opera or symphony tickets and forgot to make a reservation", this Hayes Valley trattoria serves "generous portions" of "classic" Tuscan fare "with no surprises"; to cynics, this signals a lack of "verve", but the atmosphere's "friendly", prices are "moderate" and they "get you to your show on time."

Caffè Greco ●⇎　　▽ 18　14　15　$13
423 Columbus Ave. (bet. Green & Vallejo Sts.),
415-397-6261

◪ "Super-strong coffee", "homemade tiramisu" and great sidewalk seating are the hallmarks of this North Beach cafe frequented by a mix of "local writers", "older gentlemen chatting with their *amici*" and tourists; they stop in to "read a novel" or "Italian newspapers" on "weekday afternoons" when it's more tranquil or "after dinner" for an affogato and gelato.

Caffe Macaroni ⊠⇎　　19　15　18　$27
59 Columbus Ave. (Jackson St.), 415-956-9737;
www.caffemacaroni.com

◪ This "pleasantly wacky" North Beach Italian is just like what you'd "find in Rome, including crying babies and family arguments" – which you can't help but overhear given the "tiny" proportions – and flirty waiters who "will do wonders for your self-esteem"; as for the food, it's "authentic", "really good" and includes "more than its name" indicates.

Caffè Museo
18　15　12　$17

San Francisco Museum of Modern Art, 151 Third St.
(bet. Howard & Mission Sts.), 415-357-4500;
www.caffemuseo.com

☑ Attached to SFMOMA, this "bustling", "self-service" cafeteria is "better than a museum concession needs to be", offering "well-made, varied" "nouvelle" Italian-Med salads, sandwiches and desserts at somewhat "inflated" prices; "delightful" for "resting your weary legs" after "viewing modern art" or for "people-watching with a glass of wine" from sidewalk tables, it's also handy for a day at Yerba Buena Gardens with the kids.

Caffe Sport ⊠⊄
18　16　14　$30

574 Green St. (bet. Columbus & Grant Aves.), 415-981-1251

☑ When "your visiting friends demand to eat at a North Beach Italian", take them to this "loud", "festive" Sicilian that plays the part, complete with "family-style" dishes laden with "lots of garlic" and "hilariously" "surly waiters" who are just "part of the show"; unabashedly "touristy and tacky", it's "packed with all kinds of odds-and-ends" to gaze on while waiting to be seated.

CAMPTON PLACE
26　25　26　$67

Campton Place Hotel, 340 Stockton St. (bet. Post & Sutter Sts.),
415-955-5555; www.camptonplace.com

■ "Chef Daniel Humm might be young, but he's a genius" gush those who've sampled his "exquisite" Provençal-Med creations (he "should be awarded Best Use of Foam") at this hotel restaurant off Union Square; "ultrasmooth" service, a "classy", "whisper-quiet" room, "wonderful wine list" and "staggering prices" make it "perfect for a special occasion" underwritten by your "rich maiden aunt" or a meal "on the company"; N.B. jackets suggested.

Capp's Corner
16　15　18　$24

1600 Powell St. (Green St.), 415-989-2589; www.cappscorner.com

☑ "Little has changed over the years" at this North Beach Italian "institution" that's "been there forever" (since 1960); while "not for gourmets", it's "fun for families" and "out-of-towners faced with SF sticker shock" or en route to *Beach Blanket Babylon*; the "photos of famous faces who've dined here will be lost on the kids", but they'll appreciate the "friendly" service and slightly "zany" atmosphere.

CARNELIAN ROOM
17　25　20　$57

Bank of America Ctr., 555 California St., 52nd fl. (bet. Kearny &
Montgomery Sts.), 415-433-7500; www.carnelianroom.com

☑ "You can't beat the exterior decoration", i.e. "astonishing" sight lines of SF and beyond, at this American located at the "top of the world" (aka the Bank of America building) Downtown; but "the best views do not mean the best food", which is both "uninspired and pricey", so "skip dinner and opt for drinks in the lounge", and whatever you do, avoid it on foggy nights.

Catch   18 21 19 $32
2362 Market St. (Castro St.), 415-431-5000; www.catchsf.com
◪ A "sleeker version of the standard seafood house", this Castro entry has generated "high buzz" with its "contemporary" decor, nightly piano music, "fun" staff and potential for "catching a cutie after oysters on the half shell"; indeed, the "chief attraction" is the "heated" patio where lots of "preening and cruising goes on", as the "food quality's uneven" and the interior "loud."

Cha Am Thai   19 13 16 $18
Museum Parc, 701 Folsom St. (3rd St.), 415-546-9711
◪ In SoMa, there's no slack in demand for this longtime Thai's "consistently well-prepared", "reasonably priced" dishes, even if those with "asbestos mouths" say the stuff's "too sweet to be authentic"; the "decor leaves a lot to be desired" and service wavers between "spotty" and "friendly", making it more of a "takeout–worthy" option; P.S. the Berkeley branch is also "perennially busy."

Cha Cha Cha   19 17 15 $24
1801 Haight St. (Shrader St.), 415-386-5758
2327 Mission St. (bet. 19th & 20th Sts.), 415-648-0504
◪ "Always fun with a rowdy group", these "huge scenes" in the Upper Haight and Mission blur the dining and "nightlife" boundary, purveying tapas-style "small plates" of "jammin'" Pan-Caribbean food and "lethal sangria" from their "well-stocked bars"; service can be "surly" and the waits for a table are "harsh" and "hectic", so "get there early" or "don't bother on a Friday or Saturday night."

CHAPEAU!   26 18 26 $43
1408 Clement St. (15th Ave.), 415-750-9787
■ "Get kissed by a Frenchman" – or at least receive a "handshake" – at the door to this Inner Richmond "boutique" bistro where owner Philippe Gardelle and his "gracious" wife, Ellen, "will charm you with their hospitality" and "perfectly presented", "authentic *classiques françaises*; their "contagious energy" infects the "superb" staff and keeps the "awfully cramped" room "lively with conversation", while "affordable wines" ensure it's among "the best values in the Bay Area."

Charanga   22 16 19 $24
2351 Mission St. (bet. 19th & 20th Sts.), 415-282-1813; www.charangasf.com
■ "Everything is prepared with care and creative flair" at this "hip", "intimate" Mission address that serves small plates of Latin-Caribbean fare, including "memorable" seviche and some of "the best fried yucca this side of the equator", until 11PM; sangria that will "knock your socks

off", an "unpretentious attitude" and "affordable" tabs are "just what the doctor ordered after a busy day in the city."

CHARLES NOB HILL 27 | 23 | 26 | $77
Clay-Jones, 1250 Jones St. (Clay St.), 415-771-5400;
www.charlesnh.com
■ "An aura of luxury" wafts over this "jewel box" atop Nob Hill, where "waiters perform like a synchronized swim team" in the "hushed", low-lit rooms, "bringing little gifts from the chef"; "if you've got a Benjamin burning a hole in your pocket", "spring for" the "spectacular" Cal–New French tasting menu "enhanced by perfect wine pairings"; sure, it's "old-school and stuffy" ("who else sends you a thank-you letter?"), but there's no better place for "closing a big deal" or "pitching the woo."

Chaya Brasserie 22 | 22 | 20 | $45
132 The Embarcadero (bet. Howard & Mission Sts.),
415-777-8688; www.thechaya.com
☑ Boasting a "fantastic view from the foot of the Bay Bridge" at the Embarcadero, this "swank" Asian–New French draws a corporate crowd with its "adventuresome" culinary stance that sees "sushi and venison on the same menu" and "fun bento boxes" at lunch; if critics call it a "hit-or-miss" "holdover from the fusion era" and jab at "variable" service, they nonetheless praise the "cool bar scene."

Chaz Restaurant ▽ 24 | 17 | 21 | $42
3347 Fillmore St. (bet. Chestnut & Lombard Sts.), 415-928-1211
■ "One-man-wonder Charles Solomon" "does it all and really well" at his "hidden Marina gem" whose "dark", plain-Jane room "gives no hint how sophisticated" the New American–French cuisine is; if it's too "relaxed" to be "a see-and-be-seen scene", it's appreciated for "prices that are reasonable for the quality."

Cheesecake Factory, The 16 | 16 | 15 | $25
Macy's, 251 Geary St., 8th fl. (bet. Powell & Stockton Sts.),
415-391-4444; www.thecheesecakefactory.com
☑ "Convenient for dessert cravings" or dining with a group, this Union Square outpost of the national chain is laudably "consistent", offering an "astounding variety" of American eats from a "book-sized" menu; there's "always a long wait" for a table and you'll risk being "attacked by shopping bag"–wielding tourists, but since portions are scaled for "sumo wrestlers", be sure to pace yourself or you might "never get to try the famed cheesecake"; N.B. there's a sister in San Jose.

Chenery Park 23 | 19 | 23 | $35
683 Chenery St. (Diamond St.), 415-337-8537;
www.chenerypark.com
■ Imagine a "neighborhood restaurant with big-city atmosphere" and you've got a reason (some say "the only

reason") "to venture out to Glen Park", where this New American's "terrific" comfort food, Cal-conscious wine list and an "informed staff" rival the big boys Downtown, but the prices don't; from the "full bar that knows how to make the perfect Manhattan" to the "children's menu on Tuesdays", they keep everyone happy, "cleaning their plates (I made the dishwashers' job very easy)."

Chez Maman   23 | 13 | 20 | $26 |
1453 18th St. (bet. Connecticut & Missouri Sts.),
415-824-7166
☑ "If you can snag a seat" – there are only 14 – Potrero Hill's "low-key French" bistro/crêperie (the "country cousin to Chez Papa") "is hard to beat" for "great Gallic standards" – whipped up "right in front of you" – that "we wish *maman* herself would have prepared"; only downside is there's "usually a wait – with no place to wait."

Chez Nous   23 | 15 | 19 | $32 |
1911 Fillmore St. (bet. Bush & Pine Sts.), 415-441-8044
☑ In 2000, this "darling" *petit* Pacific Heights hangout "helped make SF the leader in the small plates" phenomenon and today it still "stuffs the place like sardines" with "close friends (you have to be because it's so cramped)" sharing "an amazing array" of nicely priced Med tapas that "whiz out of the kitchen" and are delivered by a "hip" yet "remarkably accommodating staff"; now that "it takes reservations", those "bummer" "hour-long waits" may become passé (yeah, right).

Chez Papa Bistrot   24 | 17 | 20 | $39 |
1401 18th St. (Missouri St.), 415-255-0387;
www.chezpapasf.com
☑ "The Left Bank has nothing on" this "buzzing" "Potrero Hill bistro" that exudes "that wonderful feel of Paris" "down to the cramped" "shoebox dining room", "flirty" waiters ("if you can manage to hear them") who "seem French even if they're not" and "delicious" Provençal classics, many served in *nouveau* small plates style; it even offers "great views of the city while you're waiting for a table."

Chez Spencer ⊠   25 | 23 | 22 | $51 |
82 14th St. (Folsom St.), 415-864-2191;
www.chezspencer.com
■ "A diamond in the rough" stretch of the Mission, this "incredibly cool" bistro serves "impeccable French" "foie gras, oysters and truffle oil"–infused cuisine ("better than an orgasm, maybe") in a "candlelit", "loftlike" interior or on the "lovely" garden patio; service is "attentive" "without all the formality", but a preponderance of "unusual selections" ("amazing antelope") prompts some to ask, where's the beef and "other ordinary meats"?

Chloe's Cafe ⌿   23 | 13 | 19 | $15 |
1399 Church St. (26th St.), 415-648-4116
■ A contender for "the best breakfast" in the city – "with
the long lines to prove it" on weekends – this Noe Valley
"sunny" snug storefront has seen its Food ratings climb for
its "big" helpings of "pancakes that rock" and "excellent
scrambles", "served indoors or out", that "make the calories
worthwhile"; "they'll even give you coffee" while you
wait, which might explain the Service score surge.

Chou Chou Patisserie   ▽ 21 | 20 | 21 | $36 |
Artisinal & French Bistro
400 Dewey St. (Woodside Ave.), 415-242-0960;
www.chouchousf.com
■ Tucked away in "sleepy" Forrest Hills, this "wildly busy"
new patisserie/bistro has the "authentic" ambiance, eats
and "French staff" to "transport one straight to Paris"
("you'll want to put the charming maître d' in a doggy bag
to take home"); don't miss the "incredible" signature
"pastry-shell covered stews", but leave room for dessert,
as the owner, a Montmartre chef, bakes up fruit and
chocolate tarts that are "out of this world."

Chow/Park Chow   19 | 15 | 18 | $21 |
215 Church St. (bet. 15th & Market Sts.), 415-552-2469
1240 Ninth Ave. (bet. Irving & Lincoln Sts.), 415-665-9912
◩ Consumers love to chow down at this "casual", convivial
duo in the Castro and Inner Sunset that takes a self-styled
'Sanfransiscan' approach (e.g. organic produce and free-
range meats) to its "eclectic", "flavorful" array of New
American "comfort food at comfortable prices" ("more
yum for the buck!"); they're "almost always crowded", a
fact the "friendly" "staff isn't well-trained to handle"; but
a "call-ahead waiting list works" to beat the "annoying"
lines; N.B. there's a third East of SF.

Circolo ◖🖻   – | – | – | M |
500 Florida St. (Mariposa St.), 415-553-8560; www.circolosf.com
Arguably one of the most ambitious venues since the dot-
com era, this multilevel Potrero Hill restaurant/lounge,
created by club impresario Jon Mayeda, includes a
cascading waterfall in the entryway and a metallic mesh
curtain; chef Martin Castillo of Limón has designed a
Nuevo Latino–meets-Asia menu, to be paired with inventive
cocktails, sake and an extensive fusion-friendly wine list; the
45-seat Fiat Room has dancing on weekends till 2:30 AM.

Citizen Cake/Cupcake   20 | 16 | 17 | $33 |
399 Grove St. (Gough St.), 415-861-2228
Virgin Megastore, 2 Stockton St., 3rd fl. (Market St.), 415-399-1565
www.citizencake.com
◩ "Eat dessert first" at this "high-tech" Hayes Valley
bakery/eatery, since "the pastries and desserts are what

this place is all about"; citizens are conflicted over the Cal "spa-like" savory dishes ("sumptuous" vs. "overpriced") and chilled by the often-"icy service"; still, it's a "hip" "stop on the way to and from the opera or symphony"; N.B. the Citizen Cupcake spin-off in the Union Square is unrated.

Citrus Club
20 | 14 | 17 | $15

1790 Haight St. (Shrader St.), 415-387-6366

☑ "For what it is" – a source of saketinis and "bland" but "good, quick" "Pan-Asian eats" that's "cheaper than going to the grocery store" – this "hot and steamy" Haight Street noodle shop is "tough to top"; during peak hours, "expect a wait but the line goes quickly" and the "energetic" "hepcat clientele" "makes for good people-watching."

Cityscape
▽ 19 | 25 | 20 | $43

Hilton San Francisco, 333 O'Farrell St., 46th fl. (bet. Mason & Taylor Sts.), 415-923-5002; www.cityscaperestaurant.com

■ Like the name says, an "incomparable city view from the 46th floor" is the main draw of this "top-of-the-Hilton" aerie; however, "after settling down from the oohs and ahs", folks find the "Traditional American cuisine" is "surprisingly good" and service "attentive", making it an ideal place to "do holidays" or an "amazing Sunday brunch" whose "soft live jazz, free flowing champagne and a huge variety of food" is the stuff of dreams (albeit at sky-high prices).

Clémentine
25 | 21 | 24 | $41

126 Clement St. (bet. 2nd & 3rd Aves.), 415-387-0408

■ "You don't need to be a miner 49er to fall for this darlin'" bistro; an unusual find in the Inner Richmond, it "never misses" with its "flawless French classics"; locals line up early for "bargain" prix fixe and "Gallic waiters who are actually nice" as they operate in close but comfortable digs "accented by wood tones and soft lighting."

Cortez
25 | 24 | 21 | $46

Adagio Hotel, 550 Geary St. (Taylor St.), 415-292-6360; www.cortezrestaurant.com

☑ "Small plates strike again" at this "sceney" Downtown newcomer from "the Bay Bread folks", which "merits a trip" as much for the "memorable" mix of Mediterranean "masterpieces", "heavenly desserts" and "affable staff" as for the "flatteringly" lit, "numbingly loud" "*Sex and the City*" atmosphere and "glamorous bar"; however, "prices can sneak up on you", since you "have to order a lot" of the *petit* portions (e.g. "soups that come in shot glasses").

Cosmopolitan ⌀
20 | 22 | 19 | $41

Rincon Ctr., 121 Spear St. (bet. Howard & Mission Sts.), 415-543-4001; www.thecosmopolitancafe.com

☑ The namesake cocktail could well be the "the best in town" at this "sultry, Gotham City"–like SoMa site, a "stylish hangout" "for happy hour and dinner afterwards", thanks to the "homey yet swank" New American eats and "slow-but-friendly service"; overall, it's "good enough to impress business or romantic contacts", provided you "sit away from the noisy bar."

Cote Sud ☒   21 17 18 $36
4238 18th St. (Diamond St.), 415-255-6565;
www.cotesudsf.com
☑ Bringing "a touch of Provence to the Castro", this "little bistro" attracts "even those skeptical of venturing" to 18th Street for its "authentic" "simple country" fare that matches the somewhat "cramped" but "charming cottagelike feel", replete with a "nice covered patio"; some say the "service should be more attentive", but all are "pleasantly surprised" by the "decently priced" prix fixe.

Cozmo's Corner Grill   15 16 15 $30
2001 Chestnut St. (Fillmore St.), 415-351-0175;
www.cozmoscorner.com
■ It's "more about the crowd than the food", but this "cool and casual" "Marina singles hangout" does dish out "solid, if undistinguished" Cal cuisine; "J.Crew-clad twenty- and thirtysomethings" gather for dinner, then move to the "crazed bar" for "a different kind of meat than what's on the menu."

Crustacean   23 17 18 $45
1475 Polk St. (California St.), 415-776-2722; www.anfamily.com
■ "Crack, crack, crack go the diners" at this "upscale Vietnamese" on Polk Street (with a celebrated sibling in LA) where locals "ignore virtually everything" except "the specialties of the house"– "amazing roasted Dungeness crab" and "ultra-famous garlic noodles" (warning: you'll "smell for days after"); yes, the *Finding Nemo* decor "is just silly" and "yes, you'll spend a fortune" but "no, you shouldn't miss it."

Deep Sushi   22 18 17 $34
1740 Church St. (bet. 29th & 30th Sts.), 415-970-3337;
www.deepsushi-sf.com
☑ Despite a lack of signage, this "über-cool sushi spot" in Noe Valley "has been discovered" by a "terribly hip" clientele that packs into the "edgy" space for "fish so fresh it jumps into your mouth"; but as a Decor score dip attests, it's "so tiny" ("more people can fit into my living room") and "noisy" (due to the DJ's "bass beats that bump throughout your meal" most days), you can "forget it" for "quiet conversation."

Delancey Street   16 14 19 $26
600 The Embarcadero (Brannan St.), 415-512-5179
☑ "If niceness were part of the rating system", this Eclectic on The Embarcadero "would be No. 1", as its proceeds go

to "people trying to get their lives back in order"; alas, it's "average in all regards", from the "menu with ethnic items from around the U.S." to the staff, individuals whom its parent non-profit assists (their serving style can be "a touch unique"); still, it's "priced right" and sweethearted surveyors swear the "worthy" "cause makes the food taste better."

DELFINA   26 | 19 | 23 | $41
3621 18th St. (bet. Dolores & Guerrero Sts.), 415-552-4055; www.delfinasf.com

☑ What secret makes this small storefront "jam-packed" nightly? – it's chef-owner Craig Stoll's "exquisite", "simple" Northern Italian preparations "notched up" with "impeccable, seasonal ingredients", "hot" waitresses who are "always jazzed to serve" and a "Mission-hip-minus-the-attitude" vibe; yes, it's "loud tight quarters" but that's a "small price to pay" for what's "arguably the best of its kind in San Francisco"; P.S. they now do validated parking, alleviating that "nightmare."

Desiree Café ☒   ▽ 23 | 14 | 19 | $17
San Francisco Film Ctr., 39 Mesa St. (Lincoln Blvd.), 415-561-2336; www.desireecafe.com

■ Chef-owner Anne Gingrass (ex Hawthorne Lane) shines her "bright light" in this "simple but inviting" Cal cafe tucked away in The Presidio; weekday worker bees from the SF Film Center line up at the counter for "desirable" "made-to-order" breakfast, sandwiches and "pastries to die for", but savvy slackers "pick up a box lunch" and head elsewhere for a "SF-at-its-best picnic."

Destino ☒   23 | 20 | 20 | $32
1815 Market St. (bet. Guerrero & Valencia Sts.), 415-552-4451; www.destinosf.com

☑ "Part of the Nuevo Latino invasion" of SF, this Castrolite fulfills its destiny by delivering "fantastic", "inventive" tapas plus "well-chosen" South American wines and potent "pisco sours, the national drink of Peru"; the occasional flamenco dancers, "flirting waiters" and "fiery red walls make for a lively atmosphere" in the "narrow" room, but the "deafening noise" leads to pleas of "please hang some serapes up."

Dottie's True Blue Cafe   26 | 13 | 17 | $15
522 Jones St. (bet. Geary & O'Farrell Sts.), 415-885-2767

■ For over a decade, surveyors have stayed "true blue" to this daytime diner in the "raffishly charming Tenderloin", which serves "surprisingly sophisticated" "breakfasts that will keep you full until dinnertime" (if not, lunch is "impossibly good", too); "the service is quick, because it has to be"; even so, there's "always a line . . . but it's always worth it."

Dragon Well | 22 | 16 | 19 | $20 |
2142 Chestnut St. (bet. Pierce & Steiner Sts.), 415-474-6888;
www.dragonwell.com

☑ It doesn't deliver, so Marina mavens drag-on in to this
"favorite", one of the few Asians in the area; though some
wail it's "white-bread Chinese", scores support those who
praise the "simple pleasures" of "food your body can feel
good about" ("all the taste but a fraction of the oil");
however, it may be "better to take it out", because the
"sparse decor" "lacks ambiance."

E&O Trading Company | 19 | 20 | 17 | $33 |
314 Sutter St. (bet. Grant Ave. & Stockton St.), 415-693-0303;
www.eotrading.com

☑ "Rotating bamboo fans" are just part of the "kitschy,
Indiana Jones–themed" decor that dominates this "crazy,
busy" trading post "close to Union Square"; it "attracts the
after-work crowd" and those "contemplating the $400 they
just spent on shoes" with a "trendy formula" of "sweet"
cocktails – perhaps a pomegranate margarita? – and
Southeast Asian "appetizers that can make a meal"; all is
"easily consumed, and easily forgotten"; P.S. its southern
sibling is "one of the hipper places in San Jose."

E'Angelo ⊄ | 21 | 11 | 20 | $22 |
2234 Chestnut St. (bet. Pierce & Scott Sts.), 415-567-6164

■ It's the "ultimate crowded mob scene" at this "Marina
classic", "more pasta shack than trattoria", "where you sit
more or less on your neighbor's lap" consuming Northern
Italian eats that are "nothing fancy, just stuff grandma
from the old country used to make"; it's "one of the best
values" for the tony neighborhood, which might explain
the jump in Food and Service scores.

Eastside West | 18 | 17 | 17 | $29 |
3154 Fillmore St. (Greenwich St.), 415-885-4000

■ Perhaps the American cuisine "is an afterthought"
("food? do they do food?") at this Cow Hollow/"Marina
meet market" "known more for its bar scene"; but actually,
the seafood specialties are "solid" and certainly "better
than your normal pub grub" opines the "under-30, upwardly
mobile, well-tanned" set dancing to DJ-spun or live
tunes Wednesdays–Saturdays.

Ebisu | 24 | 13 | 18 | $33 |
1283 Ninth Ave. (Irving St.), 415-566-1770;
www.ebisusushi.com

☑ Prepare to be "packed like canned tuna" awaiting entry
to this Inner Sunset Japanese; but once in, "sit at the bar"
where "charismatic" chefs and fellow "sushi jocks" "party
with you" as you eat "transcendent" "fish so fresh you
know it was flopping on the deck that morning"; naturally,
naysayers wonder if it is really worth "the insane lines", but

for most, it still has an iron-chef "grip on its title" as one of the town's tops.

El Balazo   19 | 12 | 14 | $10 |
1654 Haight St. (Clayton St.), 415-864-2140
■ "Hippie meets Hispanic in the Haight" at this "alternative to the standard Mexican places", which cranks out "gigantic" portions of "yuppie" burritos and tacos (some named for the Grateful Dead), in both "classic" and "good vegetarian" versions; with its "funky" kaleidoscope-colored set and cafeteria-style service, it's a fine, fast stop for refueling "as you stroll around, and over, the denizens" of the block.

Elite Cafe   17 | 18 | 16 | $35 |
2049 Fillmore St. (bet. California & Pine Sts.), 415-346-8668
◪ This Upper Fillmore "mainstay" is "as New Orleans as SF gets", sporting an "amazing" oyster bar, "decadent Cajun cuisine" and "heavy" brunches; while the jaded joke the food and service are "as tired as a Bourbon Street whore", the "cute" booths remain "the place to be" with a "secret date", the "bar in full swing" when you're looking for one.

Eliza's   23 | 18 | 16 | $22 |
2877 California St. (bet. Broderick & Divisadero Sts.), 415-621-4819
1457 18th St. (bet. Connecticut & Missouri Sts.), 415-648-9999
◪ An "alternative to formula Asians", this Pac Heights and Potrero Hill pair offers "nontraditional", "vibrantly" "fresh" fare ("Chinese gone yuppie") in a "bright, airy" atmosphere; while there's "instant food arrival", you literally have to "hold on to the dishes and silverware" else the "brisk servers" will turn your table "like another widget on the assembly line"; P.S. lunch is an especially good "bang for the buck."

Ella's   21 | 15 | 17 | $21 |
500 Presidio Ave. (California St.), 415-441-5669; www.ellassanfrancisco.com
◪ "Dot-com refugees" brave "a huge drag of a wait" to scale Presidio Heights' "upscale greasy spoon"; admirers argue "you couldn't ask for a finer breakfast" of "homey" but "creative" American grub ("don't miss the blood orange juice"); but baffled bashers bark "one of the great mysteries" is why people "starve in line", given the "indifferent service" and "underwhelming decor"; P.S. "a better bet is breakfast during the week", and they do dinner too.

El Raigon 🅢   – | – | – | M |
510 Union St. (Grant Ave.), 415-291-0927; www.elraigon.com
South Beach Diet disciples will delight in this North Beach *estancia* (ranch-style) steakhouse – the city's first – specializing in meats grilled over wood and charcoal; chef Eric Hollis (ex La Folie) puts out an array of carnivore-friendly items from rib-eye and lamb loin to sweetbreads

and blood sausage, all served with traditional chimichurri sauce; a cowhide-wrapped bar, vintage ranching photos and other rustic bric-a-brac complete the home-on-the-pampas look.

Emmy's Spaghetti Shack ⊄   17 | 17 | 15 | $21 |
18 Virginia Ave. (Mission St.), 415-206-2086
◪ "Bring a flashlight to read the menu, bring earplugs on the weekends" (when the "DJ spins"), but be sure to "bring an appetite" to this Bernal Heights Italian, a "hipster magnet" where "sexy staffers "with a wee bit of attitude" serve up spaghetti with "monster meatballs" and 40-oz. beers at "bang-for-the-buck" prices; however, some huff "you go for the vibe, not the food"; P.S. the "bar next door provides a good waiting spot (you'll need it)."

Emporio Rulli   23 | 23 | 16 | $16 |
2300 Chestnut St. (Scott St.), 415-923-6464
333 Post St. (bet. Powell & Stockton Sts.), 415-433-1122
www.rulli.com
See review in North of San Francisco Directory.

Enrico's Sidewalk Cafe   17 | 19 | 16 | $32 |
504 Broadway St. (Kearny St.), 415-982-6223;
www.enricossidewalkcafe.com
◪ A "humming jazz vibe, busy sidewalk and neighborhood feel" – not to mention "muddled drinks that are the best in town" – brings in both guidebook-toting tourists and locals to this legendary Beat Generation destination; and if the "decent but unmemorable" Cal-Med cuisine seems a "sidebar to the scene", the patio is "the perfect place to waste away a sunny afternoon" or enjoy jazz into the night.

Eos Restaurant & Wine Bar   25 | 20 | 21 | $41 |
901 Cole St. (Carl St.), 415-566-3063; www.eossf.com
■ "The move to tapaslike dishes fixes the primary problem" of this fusion favorite with adjacent wine salon – namely, that "there was no way to sample all the fabulous" Cal-Asian creations before; they're "great for sharing, thus bringing the costs down", but happily, the "lower prices haven't decreased the service" nor the "industrial" space's "hip" vibe; but better cab it to Cole Valley because "parking is horrible" – and you'll want to partake of the "awesome, affordable wine list" anyway.

Eric's   22 | 15 | 17 | $19 |
1500 Church St. (27th St.), 415-282-0919
◪ Noe Valley-ites have this "Californian-cuisine" Chinese's number "pre-programmed into the phone", knowing it's a source for "solid eats" that, while not the most "authentic", are "delicious" nonetheless; the airy "Indochine colonial setting is a perfect" backdrop, but "don't expect to linger" as the extremely "efficient" servers have you "in and out in 45 minutes, no matter how you try otherwise."

Esperpento　　20　14　15　$23
3295 22nd St. (Valencia St.), 415-282-8867
◪ The young bar set shakes its maracas at this Mission
tapas place for the "tasty" if "standard" small plates
and paella, at "lower-than-expected prices"; "hot" and
"crowded", the "relaxed atmosphere" gets downright
"raucous with roaming mariachis" on weekend afternoons,
so that "it seems like everyone is shouting in this
place" – but the fare's good enough so "you don't want to
talk anymore" anyway.

Espetus Churrascaria ⊠　　▽ 22　16　21　$42
1686 Market St. (Gough St.), 415-552-8792
■ "Atkins dieters will go berserk" at this Hayes Valley
all-you-can-eat Brazilian steakhouse where *espetus*
(skewers) of fire-roasted meats are paraded through the
dark, nondescript dining room and sliced tableside by
"friendly" gauchos; the fixed-priced menus include a
bottomless salad bar ("the best buffet idea to hit SF")
overflowing with "delicious sides", the one bone they
throw to any vegetarian friends in tow.

FARALLON　　24　27　23　$57
450 Post St. (bet. Mason & Powell Sts.), 415-956-6969;
www.farallonrestaurant.com
■ "When you need to dazzle guests", this "splashy"
Downtown fish house "will do the trick"; after they "drink
in" Pat Kuleto's "whimsical" "nautical fantasyland" decor,
they can gobble up chef Mark Franz's "luscious", "creative"
seafood ("with a great wine list to go with it") brought by
well-schooled servers who know "when to attend and
when to blend into the background"; and while it'll cost
you an arm and a gill, the ambiance is refreshingly "less
stuffy than at other high-end" piscatorial places.

Faz ⊠　　17　18　17　$33
Crocker Galleria, 161 Sutter St. (bet. Kearny & Montgomery Sts.),
415-362-0404; www.fazrestaurants.com
◪ Located in the Crocker Galleria, this Italian-Med is
handy for a "business lunch" or an alfresco meal "when
the patio's open"; but convenience aside, most concede
that the food, while "generously portioned", is "rather
pedestrian" and service is "under par"; N.B. locations
East and South of SF too.

Ferry Plaza Seafoods　　▽ 22　18　18　$24
Ferry Bldg., 1 Ferry Plaza (Market St.), 415-274-2561;
www.ferryplazaseafood.com
■ Oyster lovers "step up to the bar and slide 'em down" at
this seafooder/fish market in the "bustling" Ferry Building,
which is "less touristy" than Fisherman's Wharf and has
views of "boats and the Bay Bridge that can't be beat"; all
wines and produce on the "simple" menu come from

neighboring merchants, making it an enticing stop for a "casual lunch" or early supper.

1550 Hyde Café & Wine Bar 23 18 21 $41

1550 Hyde St. (Pacific St.), 415-775-1550; www.1550hyde.com
☑ "Only in SF" can you find a "tiny", "reasonably priced" neighborhood "gem" offering "fantastic" Med fare of "all-organic, sustainable ingredients" and a "stunning wine bar" located right "on the cable car line" (lucky, since "parking's scarce" on Russian Hill); locals "try to keep it a secret" but they can't hyde the fact this newcomer is "worthy of discriminating out-of-towners", despite its "stark" industrial digs and "nice but uneven service."

FIFTH FLOOR ⌦ 26 25 25 $78

Hotel Palomar, 12 Fourth St. (Market St.), 415-348-1555
■ "The elevator stops at the fifth floor, but it's more like heaven" gush those besotted by this "ultramod" yet "clubby" SoMa hotel dining room where chef Laurent Gras' "cerebral" New French menu pairs with an "exceptional" wine list ("did they leave any Burgundies in France?") and served with fitting "pomp and circumstance"; although "priced as if the city remained full of dot-com zillionaires", it's still one "tough table to get."

Fillmore Grill 17 20 18 $35

2298 Fillmore St. (Clay St.), 415-776-7600; www.fillmoregrill.com
☑ Some Upper Fillmore locals laud this yearling for its "basic" New American bistro menu, "efficient service" and "middle-of-the-road prices", calling it "one of the least-pretentious tablecloth restaurants" in the 'hood; thrill-seekers contend the food's "dull" but admit "they've done a great job with the space" and recommend sitting in the "booths for privacy."

Firecracker ⌦ 20 17 17 $26

1007½ Valencia St. (21st St.), 415-642-3470
☑ Missionites hankering for a taste of the "exotic" head to this "thoroughly modern" Chinese whose dishes have "a real edge" "without being too fusion-y"; purists call the stuff "gringo" fare and some suspect it's "not as good as it used to be", but "long waits" on the weekends illustrate that even if it's "not dynamite, it's still a sparkler."

Firefly 23 20 22 $36

4288 24th St. (Douglass St.), 415-821-7652; www.fireflyrestaurant.com
■ "A little glow in the cold night", this "arty", "homey" Noe Valley "gem" "gracefully spans the neighborhood restaurant/destination-spot divide"; you can "dress up or down" and either way, you'll be rewarded with Eclectic and "ever-changing" takes on "comfort food" served by a staff "with no pretense"; P.S. the weekday "prix fixe makes it even better", so "make sure you reserve."

First Crush ◗ | 17 | 15 | 17 | $37 |

101 Cyril Magnin St. (Ellis St.), 415-982-7874; www.firstcrush.com
☑ With a location convenient "for those who've decided that dinner is just the beginning of the night", this Downtown French serves food that's regarded as "ambitious but flawed" in a setting now looking a bit "tired"; but consumers aren't crushed, 'cuz most come for the "well-balanced California"-only wine list, which is popularly "ordered flight-style"; N.B. there's a new branch North of SF.

500 Jackson | 17 | 21 | 18 | $40 |

500 Jackson St. (bet. Columbus Ave. & Montgomery St.), 415-772-1940; www.500jackson.com
☑ "Who would expect a clam bake" in such "elegant, classy" digs replete with "big booths" fawn fans of chef-owner Todd Kniess' (of Bistro Liaison fame) "newcomer" in historic Jackson Square; while the "safe", "reasonably priced" regional fare reels in diners yearning for a "quick trip to the shore", crabby critics carp the "chaotic service" and "unoriginal recipes" "make it as fun as a cold fish."

FLEUR DE LYS ⌘ | 28 | 27 | 26 | $87 |

777 Sutter St. (bet. Jones & Taylor Sts.), 415-673-7779; www.fleurdelyssf.com
■ Be "treated like *un roi*" at Hubert Keller's long-running "flirtation with excess" on Nob Hill that "still amazes after all these years"; the "flawless" staff guides you through an "unparalleled gourmet experience" via the "heart-stopping" New French prix fixes (including a "veritable vegetarian feast") "while you float away" "under the big top" in one of the "prettiest rooms in town" and depart feeling those "big dollars were well spent."

Florio | 21 | 20 | 20 | $39 |

1915 Fillmore St. (bet. Bush & Pine Sts.), 415-775-4300; www.floriosf.com
☑ "A slice of Paris" in Pacific Heights, this "neighborhood haunt" for the adult set is the "definition of a bistro" with its "cramped, noisy" room, "great bar" and French-Italian "hearty basics", like "addictive" steakfrites and "divine" roasted chicken; service is "hit-or-miss" and tabs can get a "little pricey" (a "good-value" prix fixe aside), but plenty feel "the whole is greater than the sum of its parts" here.

Fly Trap | 18 | 18 | 18 | $35 |

606 Folsom St. (2nd St.), 415-243-0580; www.flytraprestaurant.com
☑ Buzz into SoMa and get trapped in time at this "funky", historic spot where ghosts of "old SF places that have disappeared" are reflected in the Traditional American menu; service ranges from "personable" to "absent", and if fly-swatters fuss the "active" "atmosphere is better than the food", they concede it's always "good for drinks."

Fog City Diner
19 | 18 | 18 | $31

1300 Battery St. (The Embarcadero), 415-982-2000;
www.fogcitydiner.com

☒ Located on the Embarcadero, this "SF classic" is a "diner only in name and cool chrome-trimmed decor", for the American menu showcases "high-class comfort food" and "enough fusion fare to keep the food snobs interested" at "thoroughly modern prices"; and though "tourists love it", locals also confess a "soft spot for this old favorite", despite the "disinterested" service.

Foreign Cinema
22 | 24 | 19 | $40

2534 Mission St. (bet. 21st & 22nd Sts.), 415-648-7600;
www.foreigncinema.com

☒ "Redefining dinner and a movie" is this multitasking Mission Cal-Med that "projects old flicks on the back wall" of its "wonderful" patio, which is more in-demand than its "stylish, loft"-like interior, especially for the "busy brunch"; the kitchen delivers an uneven performance ("uninspired" vs. "underrated") and service can be "indifferent", but even if you "can't hear" what's on the screen, it's worth "going for the people-watching."

Fountain Court
19 | 12 | 16 | $21

354 Clement St. (bet. 4th & 5th Aves.), 415-668-1100

☒ Courtiers confess "everyone should have the menu" to this Inner Richmond Chinese, either in anticipation of dining in or taking out the "exceptional dim sum and Shanghai dishes"; but some report that "poor" service detracts from the experience and add "it would be nice if they dressed up" the place a bit.

Fournou's Ovens
22 | 21 | 23 | $60

Renaissance Stanford Ct. Hotel, 905 California St. (Powell St.),
415-989-1910; www.renaissancehotel.com

☒ Abiding fans of this "SF warhorse" in Nob Hill note that it has "endured while others have faltered", delivering "good" "roasted meats" and other Cal-Med–style dishes; and if modernists mutter it's "a little pretentious" and the "ovens are cooling off", others find it "charming" and appreciate its "quiet", "pleasant" confines.

Frascati
25 | 21 | 24 | $40

1901 Hyde St. (Green St.), 415-928-1406;
www.frascatisf.com

■ Those looking for a "non-formula" dinner spot and a base for "showing off the charm of Russian Hill" hop on the cable car or "burn calf muscle" to reach this "adorably charming", "always buzzing" address that also happens to serve "first-rate", "well-priced" Cal-Med fare matched with a "terrific wine list"; the owners "make everyone feel at home whether you live around the corner or in Ohio", but some suggest they install a fan in the "warm upstairs."

Fresca   23 | 17 | 18 | $30

2114 Fillmore St. (California St.), 415-447-2668
24 W. Portal Ave. (Ulloa St.), 415-759-8087

☑ "Peruvian appears to be the latest thing", and this
"busting-at-the-seams" Upper Fillmore spot (with a West
Portal offshoot) "lives up to its name" by serving "generous
portions" of *nuevo* "Inca delights", like "innovative
seviches", made from "the freshest ingredients around";
while the room might leave you "smelling like a short-order
cook", it's fun to "sit at the bar and watch the chefs in
action" while you wait for a table; N.B. at press time, a sib
was slated to open at 3946 24th St.

FRINGALE 🏷   25 | 18 | 22 | $45

570 Fourth St. (bet. Brannan & Bryant Sts.), 415-543-0573

☑ In SoMa, this "small", "noisy" yet "beloved neighborhood
bistro" continues to regale those with "Montparnasse"
on the mind via its "wonderful" French-Basque fare; if
skeptiques sniff "the pizzazz is gone" with the exit of its
founding chef, many say it remains a "charming place for a
cozy evening", thanks to its "lively" air and "attentive" staff.

Frisson ◗   – | – | – | E

244 Jackson St. (bet. Battery & Front Sts.), 415-956-3004;
www.frissonsf.com

This snazzy new French-Cal hopes to create a little frisson
Downtown, thanks to a circular, mod two-tiered sunken
dining room demarcated by honeycombed-shaped Lucite
panels and set under a backlit dome; adding to its appeal
is a bar (with live DJ booth), an urban garden patio and
chef Daniel Patterson's (of Elisabeth Daniel fame) small-
plates menu served until 10 PM, with more casual nibbles
available until 1 AM.

Frjtz Fries   19 | 14 | 14 | $14

579 Hayes St. (Laguna St.), 415-864-7654
Woolin Mill Bldg., 900 North Point St. (bet. Larkin & Polk Sts.),
415-928-1475
www.frjtzfries.com

☑ "As the name suggests", you'll be having "delectable"
fries along with a "seemingly endless" choice of dipping
sauces and crêpes at these "Generation Y" hangouts in
Hayes Valley and the Wharf that also boast "Belgian beers
on tap", outdoor seating and DJs spinning "hypnotic
beats"; unfortunately, "the staff seems more focused on
having fun than anything else", causing "eternal waits" for
your "Flemish fix."

Galette   18 | 13 | 14 | $20

2043 Fillmore St. (bet. California & Pine Sts.), 415-928-1300

☑ Francophiles and frugal gourmets beat a path to this
Pacific Heights perch specializing in sweet and savory
"Brittany-style" buckwheat *galettes* (crêpes), "melt-in-

your-mouth" brioche French toast and other "light" Gallic treats; "outdoor tables are best" because "you can watch the world go by" and be entertained while waiting on the "sunny" but somewhat "lacking" service.

GARDEN COURT
19 | 28 | 22 | $48 |

Palace Hotel, 2 New Montgomery St. (Market St.), 415-546-5010; www.gardencourt-restaurant.com

☑ A "spectacular" site for "ladies' high tea", "ostentatious" brunches and "awe-inspiring" holiday "cornucopias", this "historic" dining room Downtown is "a lovely place to take out-of-towners" or yourself when "you're all dressed up"; "say what you like" about the "good if not exceptional" Californian cuisine – "when the crystal chandeliers light up" the glass conservatory ceiling, "you could feast on the decor" alone.

Garibaldis
22 | 22 | 20 | $40 |

347 Presidio Ave. (bet. Clay & Sacramento Sts.), 415-563-8841

☑ Be it for a date, a "moms' lunch" or "work parties", this "sophisticated", "high energy" Presidio Heights address is "always a great choice" as "everyone will find something for his palate" on the "slick but reliable" Cal-Med menu; evenings, the "bar is where it's really happening", but "don't plan on intimate conversation" as "the noise level's deafening"; N.B. there's also a branch East of SF.

GARY DANKO
29 | 26 | 28 | $88 |

800 North Point St. (Hyde St.), 415-749-2060; www.garydanko.com

■ "Danko's is to dining as *The Producers* is to Broadway" – a three-hour "extravaganza" that's "worth every $100 bill" and phone call to get in; "applause goes to Gary" for his "dazzling" New American prix fixes ("if you skip the cheese course, go to foodie jail"), the "beautifully choreographed service" and the "Armani suit"–like ("subdued, elegant") digs; yes, it gets "cramped and loud", but "there's a reason" this Wharf wonder "ends up on so many No. 1 lists" – including this *Survey*'s for Food and Most Popular.

Gaylord India
19 | 16 | 18 | $31 |

1 Embarcadero Ctr. (bet. Battery & Sacramento Sts.), 415-397-7775; www.gaylordsrestaurant.com
Ghirardelli Sq., 900 North Point St. (bet. Larkin & Polk Sts.), 415-771-8822; www.gaylords.com

☑ This veteran "upper-end" Indian pair is "consistently pleasant", turning out "good", if "pricey", subcontinental specialties that work for a "quiet lunch" or "pre-movie dinner" on the Embarcadero or at the Ghirardelli branch "overlooking the Bay"; but critics take this "legacy" to task for "living off its 1970s reputation" and say "there are too many alternatives around" these days; N.B. there's a sibling South of SF also.

Geranium   – | – | – | M
615 Cortland Ave. (Anderson St.), 415-647-0118;
www.geraniumrestaurant.com
Brightly colored potted geraniums signal a homey welcome
at this attractive, family-friendly Bernal Heights vegetarian,
which skips the agitprop and simply cooks straightforward
meatless and vegan versions of international comfort food;
there's even a kid's menu for budding believers.

Giorgio's Pizzeria   21 | 11 | 18 | $17
151 Clement St. (3rd Ave.), 415-668-1266; www.giorgiospizza.com
■ "An oasis of thin crust in the thick-crust desert", this
"warm, bustling and good-smelling" "old-fashioned pizza
experience" in Richmond "packs" legions of pie-eyed fans
into "plastic red booths" in a space recalling a "1970s
basement"; given the number of youthful consumers
("didn't know so many kids lived in SF"), amorists warn "if
you're trying for romance", "it's better to do takeout."

Gira Polli   20 | 13 | 17 | $22
659 Union St. (bet. Columbus Ave. & Powell St.), 415-434-4472
☑ "Succulent" "rotisserie chicken and down-home
fixings" are the draws at this Southern Italian–style North
Beach rotticceria; if bird-watchers enjoy seeing them
"roasted over an open fire", fowl-weather friends suggest
it's "better for takeout than eating in" the "glorified-
cafeteria" setting; N.B. there's a branch North of SF.

Globe ◐   21 | 16 | 18 | $40
290 Pacific Ave. (bet. Battery & Front Sts.), 415-391-4132
☑ In a town that retires early, this Downtown American-
Italian "burns the midnight olive oil" to the great pleasure
of nightcrawlers who arrive "in jeans or a tux" and
"restaurant workers after their shifts"; the "cramped"
dining room has an "understated cool", but service can
turn chilly "if you're not in the chef/hipster crowd" and
some hint "the pizzazz has been missing" since the
globe-trotting owners flew south to open an LA branch.

Godzila Sushi   19 | 8 | 14 | $23
1800 Divisadero St. (Bush St.), 415-931-1773
☑ Watched over by a painted likeness of its namesake
lizard, this "no-frills" Pac Heights veteran is "always
packed" thanks to its reputation for "fun" times and
"creative rolls" "made sweeter" by "low prices"; but some
"question the hype around this place", saying "it's fairly
typical of the high caliber of sushi omnipresent in SF."

Golden Turtle   ▽ 19 | 16 | 17 | $28
2211 Van Ness Ave. (bet. Broadway & Vallejo Sts.),
415-441-4419; www.goldenturtle.net
■ Specializing in "real, not designer Vietnamese", including
some "sizzling" crab dishes, this sleeper on Van Ness is

"as good" as its swankier brethren but "without the pretension or the price"; as a bonus, "you can actually hold a conversation" in the "beautiful carved-wood interior."

Gordon Biersch   14 | 15 | 15 | $24 |
2 Harrison St. (The Embarcadero), 415-243-8246;
www.gordonbiersch.com
See review in South of San Francisco Directory.

Grand Cafe   21 | 26 | 20 | $44 |
Hotel Monaco, 501 Geary St. (Taylor St.), 415-292-0101;
www.monaco-sf.com
■ You'll "feel swank just walking into" the "larger-than-life art deco"–style digs of this restaurant located "just a hop from the theaters" in the Hotel Monaco Downtown; plenty praise the French-inflected New American food, but others sigh the kitchen "doesn't rise to the level of the beautiful room" (my, those are "soaring ceilings") and service seems "stretched"; still, there's always the bar, a "classy" place "to catch a drink."

Grandeho's Kamekyo   22 | 15 | 20 | $29 |
943 Cole St. (bet. Carl St. & Parnassus Ave.), 415-759-8428
2721 Hyde St. (bet. Beach & North Point Sts.),
415-673-6828
◪ There's something fishy going on at this Cole Valley and Wharf sushi duo; loyalists still line up for the "deliciously fresh fish with creative" rolls and "warm neighborhood feel"; but a Food score slide sides with those who "think it's just alright" at best, and "overrated, overbooked" and "overpriced" at worst.

Great Eastern ◑   23 | 13 | 16 | $27 |
649 Jackson St. (bet. Grant Ave. & Kearny St.),
415-986-2500
◪ "If you want Chinatown", this spacious – albeit "dull"-looking – seafooder is "one of the best in the area" (though cynics snap "that says very, very little"); however, locals say "you must order the exotic stuff" found swimming in the "tanks along the back wall" and "don't let the waiters talk you into ordering *gwailo* food", or this "affordable" site becomes "just like any other" "tourist destination."

Greens   24 | 23 | 21 | $37 |
Fort Mason Ctr., Bldg. A (Buchanan St.), 415-771-6222;
www.greensrestaurant.com
■ It's probably SF's most "famous veggie heaven", but even conservative carnivores "don't get hung up on the vegetarian" label, because the "delicacies are fit for even a burger king", with "flavors as stunning as the Golden Gate Bridge view from a window table" in the "earthy", "open" room; dead-headers may dislike paying "serious greens for eating greens", but can't deny that dining at this Marina mainstay is a "calming experience."

Habana
18 | 23 | 18 | $35

2080 Van Ness Ave. (Pacific Ave.), 415-567-7606;
www.habana1948.com
☑ "Everyone seems to be having a good time" at this Van Ness "Cuban high-end" hideaway; while the dining room's "sultry" "dramatic decor" "transports you to old Havana", the "thirtysomething" set prefers "sitting at the bar where friendly baristas serve fabulous seviche" and "killer" mojitos with "little sugar-cane stir sticks"; the kitchen gives it "a good shot", but some embargo it arguing, "do you really have to pay so much for rice and beans?"

Hamano Sushi
22 | 11 | 15 | $30

1332 Castro St. (24th St.), 415-826-0825; www.hamanosushi.com
☑ Longtimers lament it's "not the same as it used to be", but most say the situation's "still stellar" at this "old steady" that has served sushi in "fresh", "huge pieces" in Noe Valley for nigh on 15 years; despite "long waits" for seats, you're "best off sitting at the bar", thus avoiding the back room's "cheap shopping-center decor" and "surly" staff.

Harbor Village
22 | 17 | 15 | $32

4 Embarcadero Ctr. (bet. Clay & Sacramento Sts.),
415-781-8833; www.harborvillage.net
☑ "There's something delicious on every cart that passes" in this "large" locale that daily dishes up an "awesome" array of "arguably the best dim sum in SF", along with a "fabulous view" of the Embarcadero; on the down side, service can be "inattentive", there are "crazy long waits" on weekends and "it's more expensive than Chinatown" eateries – though not to worry: one surveyor "got a raise after taking my boss."

Hard Rock Cafe
12 | 18 | 14 | $22

Pier 39, Bldg. Q1 (Beach St.), 415-956-2013;
www.hardrock.com
☑ "For a touristy Wharf spot, it's actually not bad" confess fans of this (in)famous site, whose "solid burgers and sandwiches" and rock 'n' roll mementos (the "memorabilia alone makes a visit worthwhile") will "satisfy in a pinch" "that 13-year-old who needs that T-shirt"; all others are tired of "the textbook service" and "very average" American eats, wondering "why won't this chain go away?"

Harris'
24 | 20 | 23 | $53

2100 Van Ness Ave. (Pacific Ave.), 415-673-1888;
www.harrisrestaurant.com
■ Clusters of carnivores call this venerable Van Ness "temple to beef" among "the best in town", citing its "dark, clubby atmosphere", "memorable martinis", servers that make you "feel pampered" and, above all, "perfect steaks"; of course, "perfection can be expensive", but no matter to the "blue-haired blue bloods from Pacific Heights"

that patronize the place; besides, what's a few bucks to enjoy "a throwback to the gracious days of SF dining"?

HAWTHORNE LANE   24 24 22 $53

22 Hawthorne St. (bet. Folsom & Howard Sts.), 415-777-9779; www.hawthornelane.com

☑ Maybe it's not as jazzy as it was "before the dot-com boom", but this "tucked-away haven in SoMa" is "still going strong", plying "posh" patrons with "ornate dishes" of "rich and rewarding" "Asian-influenced Cal cuisine" in an "elegant dining room and classy bar" that's "conducive to whatever you want it to be" – from the site of a "romantic evening to a business meeting"; some of the "young, hip crowd" call the service "rather stuffy", but overall this is a "consistent" address "for a civilized meal."

Hayes & Vine Wine Bar ◗   18 20 19 $28

377 Hayes St. (bet. Franklin & Gough Sts.), 415-626-5301; www.hayesandvine.com

☑ "It's all about the wine (ok, and maybe the cheese and olive oil)" at this Hayes Valley vino bar/lounge with a "bible" of 1,200 labels and "extremely knowledgeable" (if a bit "hipper-than-thou") staff; it's "not exactly a place to have a meal" – just a site to "sip, nibble and dish" the Eclectic eats "before you get the party started" or "post-symphony."

Hayes Street Grill   23 17 20 $41

320 Hayes St. (bet. Franklin & Gough Sts.), 415-863-5545

☑ While "well away from the Wharf", the "always-fresh", "simply" and "superbly prepared" seafood shines at this "bustling" bistro in Hayes Valley, where you "pick a fish, any fish" and pair it with a traditional sauce and "fabulous french fries"; symphony subscribers shout "bravo" for waiters who "have pre-performance service down to a science", and if scolds say this "standard" seems "kinda tired", most praise this ship for being "steady as she goes."

Helmand, The   24 17 20 $29

430 Broadway St. (bet. Kearny & Montgomery Sts.), 415-362-0641; www.helmandsf.com

☑ Burkas off to this "excellent Afghan" that's "like a gem amid the rough" "seediness" of North Beach's "strip club central"; the cooks are "wizards with pumpkins" and other "flavorful foods" that will "expand your horizons" and "the staff couldn't be more polite"; pity the so-called "exotic decor" is "getting a little shabby"; P.S. the "resurrected lunch buffets" constitute one of "the best values" around.

Herbivore   16 14 14 $18

531 Divisadero St. (bet. Fell & Hayes Sts.), 415-885-7133
983 Valencia St. (21st St.), 415-826-5657
www.herbivore-restaurant.com

☑ "You don't notice the lack of dairy" or meat at these "hip" "noncarnivorous nuggets" in the Western Addition and Mission that "pleasantly surprise" "vegan virgins" with the "variety of options" at "decent prices"; however, even herbivores huff "the food always sounds better on the menu than it tastes" – and "you have to practically light a signal flare to get the staff's attention."

HOG ISLAND OYSTER COMPANY & BAR
27 18 19 $28

Ferry Bldg., 1 Ferry Plaza (Market St.), 415-391-7117; www.hogislandoysters.com
■ Mollusk mavens are in "hog heaven" at this boisterous new oyster bar/shop located in the Ferry Building; "sit, slurp and relax" at the U-shaped bar or "snag a seat outside" and waterside while watching the "spunky staff" shuck the "freshest" Tomales Bay beauties; some "wonder at the wisdom" of the prices, but conclude it's "well worth it" for these "tastes of the sea."

Home
– – – E

2100 Market St. (Church St.), 415-503-0333; www.home-sf.com
A new owner and chef have taken over this celebrated Castro citizen at press time; well aware there's no place like home, they intend to keep the focus on "well-crafted" "comfort food at comfort prices", while expanding the hours and the take-out business; the "romantic Backyard" bar should remain home base for the local "beautiful people."

Hotei
18 15 17 $18

1290 Ninth Ave. (Irving St.), 415-753-6045; www.hoteisf.com
☑ "Noodles that will remind you of home – if home is Tokyo" – are the draw at this "cute mom-and-pop" Inner Sunset Japanese decorated with "kitschy Christmas lights"; along with the "hot soups" at "rock-bottom prices", you can "get your sushi rolls here, avoiding the line at Ebisu", its sister across the street; but several snipe that "quality seems to be sliding" – certainly the Food score has.

HOUSE
26 16 21 $36

1230 Grant Ave. (bet. Columbus Ave. & Vallejo St.), 415-986-8612; www.thehse.com
☑ At this Asian-European in "Italian-centric North Beach", "every dish sparkles", from the "off-the-hook" "orgasmic sea bass" to the really decadent desserts"; in addition, "exceptional service" makes it seem an "excellent value"; and even naysayers who note "they pack you in pretty tightly" succumb to the "consistently creative" kitchen ("I can't hear you, but the food is great").

House of Nanking
20 4 10 $17

919 Kearny St. (bet. Columbus Ave. & Jackson St.), 415-421-1429
☑ "Famously snarling, surly" staffers and a "grungy, cramped" location can't deter fans of this Chinatown dive, who take it all in stride – "curt service is part of the charm" – in exchange for "oh-so-cheap" Chinese food

that's "unbeatable", especially if you "let the waiter order for you"; foes, however, wonder "why would anyone wait in line to get abused and end up eating what the kitchen made too much of?"

House of Prime Rib   25 | 18 | 22 | $40 |

1906 Van Ness Ave. (Washington St.), 415-885-4605

■ "With a name like this, the prime rib better be good" – and indeed, this "dark-paneled" Van Ness "institution" "doesn't disappoint"; the "theatrical presentation" could be considered "a little corny" – they wheel a "*Jetsons*-like" cart to your table and carve a "hearty portion" "right before your eyes" (and later, "if you're still hungry, they'll cut you some more") – but the "nostalgic" deem it a "great old-school experience", like taking "a trip back to the '50s."

Hunan   20 | 7 | 15 | $19 |

(aka Henry's Hunan)
1016 Bryant St. (8th St.), 415-861-5808 ☒
110 Natoma St. (2nd St.), 415-546-4999 ☒
674 Sacramento St. (bet. Kearny & Montgomery Sts.), 415-788-2234 ☒
924 Sansome St. (Broadway St.), 415-956-7727

☑ Fans admit they gladly wait "in the cold and fog just to have our insides burned out" by the "slightly greasy" "freakin' hot food" found at this chain of "cheap" Chinese; "you might get burned by the service as well" – "dishes arrive almost immediately after you order" – but who wants to linger in the "no-decor" rooms anyway?

Hunan Home's Restaurant   21 | 10 | 17 | $20 |

622 Jackson St. (bet. Grant Ave. & Kearny St.), 415-982-2844

☑ "Down-home" Hunan fare – spicy, "reasonably priced and authentic" – is on hand at this "Chinatown haunt"; expect "quick, utilitarian service" and "your standard, fluorescent-lit no-fuss, no-muss decor" – but homebodies holler "who cares, let's eat"; N.B. the digs at the younger Los Altos branch are a cut above the city counterpart's.

Hyde Street Bistro   22 | 18 | 21 | $36 |

1521 Hyde St. (bet. Jackson & Pacific Sts.), 415-292-4415

■ "Ooh-la-la! a little bit of France in Russian Hill" exclaim enthusiasts who "hop off the cable car" and into this "quintessential bistro" for "no-fuss comfort food"; tote up the *très* "reasonable" prix fixe, "romantic and relaxing" digs, and service "as warm as the fish en papillote" and it's clear why locals want to hyde this "jewel" for themselves.

IL FORNAIO   19 | 20 | 18 | $34 |

Levi's Plaza, 1265 Battery St. (bet. Greenwich & Union Sts.), 415-986-0100; www.ilfornaio.com

☑ "Wonderful aromas in the air" – from fresh-baked bread baskets that are arguably "the best part of the meal" – arise from this Embarcadero "old standby" and "flagship" of a growing Bay Area fleet; "snobs run away when they hear the word 'chain'", but actually the "familiar" Italian eats, if "never fabulous, are always good", with "monthly regional menus to keep things interesting"; the "Tuscan-trattoria ambiance" is "inviting", as are the "friendly" waiters – though they "could be better" "when it's busy."

Iluna Basque ●🅩   ▽ 22 | 20 | 21 | $32

701 Union St. (Powell St.), 415-402-0011;
www.ilunabasque.com
■ Basking in the popularity of his native Basque cuisine, ex-pat chef Mattin Noblia has opened this North Beach late-nighter; but unlike the all-you-can-eat family-style eateries of yore, he specializes in "stunning", "unusual tapas", served in the modern, red room that features communal dining both at the 150-year-old farm table and at the large stainless bar; early reports are it's *un poco* "pricey", "but a pleasant experience"; N.B. a daytime coffee shop, Eguna Basque, has opened nearby.

Incanto   24 | 23 | 23 | $40

1550 Church St. (Duncan St.), 415-641-4500;
www.incanto.biz
■ "Escape to Tuscany" without leaving Noe Valley at this "sublime, seductive and sensual" spot that enchants with Cal–Northern Italian food "prepared with love"; the wine list and "educated, helpful sommelier" get constant kudos, and although critics chant the "cavernous" room is "lovely" but "noisy, noisy, noisy", most call it a "keeper."

Indian Oven   24 | 17 | 18 | $27

233 Fillmore St. (bet. Haight & Waller Sts.), 415-626-1628;
www.indianovensf.com
☑ In an area overrun with Indian eateries, this upscale option in the Lower Haight is "one of the best in show" with "lines out to the sidewalk all the time"; "if you can find a parking space and don't mind the cramped quarters", you'll be "lovin' what's comin' outta that oven" – "fabulous curries", nonpareil naan and korma that's like "velvet on the tongue"; in addition, "you can't beat the sweet waiters in their hip native outfits."

Indigo   20 | 20 | 20 | $39

687 McAllister St. (Gough St.), 415-673-9353;
www.indigorestaurant.com
■ "A sleeper that wakes you up" with "lickalicious" New American food, "phenomenal" vino ("by the glass or half bottles") and a "cool blue" vibe (literally, as the name suggests); it's "ideal" for a "pre-show" meal in the Civic Center area as ticket-holders are "never rushed but out in time"; but for the ultimate bargain, "go for the Ultimate Wine Dinner after 8 PM", "which includes all-you-can-drink bubbly" and other pours.

ISA ⌧ | 26 | 20 | 21 | $40 |

3324 Steiner St. (bet. Chestnut & Lombard Sts.), 415-567-9588

☑ On "Restaurant Row in the Marina", co-owners "Luke and Kitty Sung go out of their way" at this leader in the "shared plates" dining trend – though Luke's French *petits plats* are so "superb", and surprisingly filling, that "you won't want to share anything"; the mod interior is "far more appealing post-expansion", but the "place to be is the [covered, heated] back patio"; however, those who "haven't bought into the concept of serially served" dishes lament the food's "slow", "chaotic" arrival.

It's Tops Coffee Shop ◗ | 15 | 17 | 17 | $14 |

1801 Market St. (bet. Guerrero & Valencia Sts.), 415-431-6395

☑ Breakfast "in the wee hours" is the come-on at this "campy" Upper Market, where "the tired 'old '30s diner' theme is not a theme – it just *is* an old '30s diner"; hipsters queue up for "heavenly" hot cakes in the morning and return 'round midnight with "after-party munchies", but nary in between, because a) they're closed mid-afternoon and b) in the glare of daylight the "scattered service" and "greasy" digs cause critics to call it "It's Bottoms."

Izzy's Steak & Chop House | 19 | 16 | 18 | $36 |

3345 Steiner St. (bet. Chestnut & Lombard Sts.), 415-563-0487

☑ "Indulge your inner carnivore" at this "time-warp" chophouse, with a "rowdy", boozy atmosphere that's more "frat house" than men's club and "old-school service" (or lack thereof) that's "a welcome refuge from all the Marina trendiness"; the steaks "are a cut below" the "pricier places'", but so is the tab, since the sides (the "scalloped potatoes and creamed spinach are the way to go") are "not à la carte"; N.B. it also has branches North and South of SF.

Jackson Fillmore | 22 | 13 | 17 | $33 |

2506 Fillmore St. (Jackson St.), 415-346-5288

☑ They still "pack 'em in" at "Jackmo" (as "neighborhood regulars" call this Upper Fillmore "institution") for traditional trattoria standards laced with "lots of garlic and love in the recipe"; no reservations for small parties means waiting "at the counter", munching the "free bruschetta" and "guzzling the house wine"; but even "snarky service" and "rock-concert loud" digs "don't stop the lines"; P.S. "its San Anselmo location is now called Cucina."

Jai Yun ⊟ | ▽ 23 | 6 | 16 | $42 |

923 Pacific Ave. (Mason St.), 415-981-7438; jaiyun.menuscan.com

☑ The prix fixe series of "small dishes, some of them sublime, all of them interesting", prepared and served by "wizard Shanghai chef" Nei Chia Ji causes converts to call this Chinatown "hole-in-the-wall" "The Chinese Laundry"; you can "phone ahead, give the chef a budget and he'll craft you a customized menu" "depending on the day's ingredients"; however, the jai-ded say it's "a novelty to go once", but the "pricey" routine becomes "repetitive" and "Christmas lights" alone do not a decor make.

JARDINIÈRE   26 | 26 | 24 | $61 |
300 Grove St. (Franklin St.), 415-861-5555; www.jardiniere.com
■ "For a special night out", few can match the savoir faire (or the "green business" practices) of this "seriously stylish" Hayes Valley haunt; "try for an upstairs table near the jazz duo for a bird's-eye view" of the "champagne-themed bar" buzzing with "ballet/symphony-goers" who drink in Pat Kuleto's "celebratory mood"-inducing decor while savoring the "sumptuous", "fantastic" "French fare with a California flip" and "staffers who treat you like royalty, no matter how fancy the rest of the crowd" is.

Jay's Cheese Steak   17 | 9 | 15 | $10 |
553 Divisadero St. (bet. Fell & Hayes Sts.), 415-771-5104
3285 21st St. (Valencia St.), 415-285-5200 ∅
◪ A "choice for dining on the fast and cheap", this duo is "where kids who live in the Western Addition and the Mission eat" when they "want to sink teeth into" a "Philly-style sub" and – "Dracula beware! – some of the best garlic fries around"; the veggie versions are "bold and much appreciated" ("hail, seitan cheese") – even if they make purists pout "have any of the cooks been east of Tahoe?"

Jeanty at Jack's   22 | 22 | 21 | $49 |
615 Sacramento St. (Montgomery St.), 415-693-0941;
www.jeantyatjacks.com
◪ "Don't lament the passing of Jack's, but hail Jeanty" exhort enthusiasts of the go-getting Gallic chef-owner, who's "lovingly restored" this "turn-of-the-century" site, combining its "old-timey SF" atmosphere with "old-fashioned" "French classics" ("even if you ate too much, don't miss the crêpes suzette") and "solicitous service"; while wine-country whiners wail the "noisy" brasserie "lacks the magic of the Yountville original", cosmopolites crow about having a Bistro Jeanty "offshoot" Downtown.

Jitney's Bar & Grill ⧄   ▽ 16 | 19 | 18 | $30 |
501 Broadway St. (Kearny St.), 415-982-5299; www.sfjitneys.com
◪ From a prime base in North Beach, this newcomer's "attentive" staff services tourists and locals with "generally good, if not memorable" American "homestyle cuisine" in a handsome, vaguely "art deco–style" interior; but the main draw, besides the "freshly made potato chips served in lieu of bread", seems to be that "diners can go downstairs and listen to live music without paying a cover charge."

Juban   20 | 18 | 17 | $32 |
Japan Ctr., 1581 Webster St. (bet. Geary Blvd. & Post St.),
415-776-5822; www.jubanrestaurant.com
See review in South of San Francisco Directory.

Julius' Castle
17 | 25 | 20 | $50

1541 Montgomery St. (Union St.), 415-392-2222;
www.juliuscastle.com

☑ "The view's the thing" at this historical landmark "perched on Telegraph Hill", "but the old-school atmosphere and service also make it a reliable romantic destination" or "place to wow tourists"; of course it's "way expensive", especially given that the New French–Italian cuisine is "in serious need of updating"; but keepers of the castle quip the sight of Alcatraz and the Bay Bridge "is incredible, so the food doesn't have to be."

KABUTO SUSHI A & S
27 | 14 | 19 | $35

5121 Geary Blvd. (15th Ave.), 415-752-5652;
www.kabutosushi.com

☑ Thriving in his "more cheerful" new locale across the street (as the Decor score jump attests), venerable "master chef Sachio Kojima" "reinvents sushi" in the Outer Richmond, with "adventurous" specials "not found anywhere else", plus "incredibly fresh" fish that's almost "too good to put into a roll"; unfortunately the "smaller location means longer waits", especially given the "slow service" at table.

Kan Zaman
17 | 19 | 13 | $21

1790 Haight St. (Shrader St.), 415-751-9656

■ "Smack in the middle of Haight-Ashbury", decadent diners "lounge on a cushion and eat Middle Eastern food"; the combo plates are easily shared, so "go with friends", preferably Wednesday through Sunday, "to watch some belly dancing" and enjoy "a hookah of apricot tobacco" whose aroma adds to the "warm, exotic" atmosphere.

Kate's Kitchen ⊅
23 | 13 | 16 | $15

471 Haight St. (bet. Fillmore & Webster Sts.),
415-626-3984

☑ "Come hungry" to this "kitschy" "erstwhile greasy spoon" "with a Southern flair" serving "gi-normous breakfasts" (till mid-afternoon) that'll make you nostalgic for life "before the low-carb age" (the French Toast Orgy alone is "enough to feed most of the Lower Haight"); "service is sassy" at best and "it couldn't get more crowded on weekends", but a Food score surge suggests it's "better and cheaper than most of the more celebrated spots."

Katia's Russian Tea Room
▽ 21 | 16 | 20 | $29

600 Fifth Ave. (Balboa St.), 415-668-9292;
www.katias.com

■ A "quaint mother-daughter team" prepares and serves "incredible pierogi" and other "lighthearted", "refined" renditions from Russia with love at this "little treasure" in the émigré-dense Inner Richmond; live accordion and guitar music sets the mood on weekend nights.

Khan Toke Thai House   22 | 24 | 19 | $27 |
5937 Geary Blvd. (bet. 23rd & 24th Aves.), 415-668-6654
■ "It's fun to doff your shoes, slide into [cushioned] table pits" and pretend to be "transported" "into a Thai temple" at this "long-established" Outer Richmond "oasis"; the "solid" Bangkok bites "may not be the best in the city, but the atmosphere" – replete with "beautiful wood-carved decor", a "staff dressed in ornate garb", "even a spirit house in the garden" – certainly is; hence, ideal for playing footsie or impressing out-of-towners; P.S. they have Western-style tables for those "not feeling flexible."

King of Thai ⇗   19 | 5 | 14 | $12 |
346 Clement St. (bet. 4th & 5th Aves.), 415-831-9953 ●
639 Clement St. (bet. 7th & 8th Aves.), 415-752-5198 ●
3199 Clement St. (33rd Ave.), 415-831-1301
420 Geary St. (bet. Mason & Taylor Sts.), 415-346-3121 ●
1541 Taraval St. (26th Ave.), 415-682-9958 ●
☑ Noodle dishes served "within minutes of ordering" by "young, energetic Thai-speaking servers" are king at this citywide chain; subjects are sure you'll be satisfied with the "authentic", "delicious" dishes, "and if you aren't – heck, it's not like you emptied your pocketbook"; late hours make it a night-owl's "essential hole-in-the-wall", even if the hostile hiss that housekeeping "is not a high priority."

Koh Samui & The Monkey   21 | 20 | 19 | $25 |
415 Brannan St. (Ritch St.), 415-369-0007
☑ A "well-done industrial-chic" decor and "fancifully presented", "delicately flavored" Siamese food make this SoMa newcomer both "elegant enough for a date and reasonable enough for a weekly work lunch"; though "charming", the "staff is a little slow on the draw"; P.S. the Monkey refers to an attached store where "you can purchase the tableware."

KOKKARI ESTIATORIO ☒   25 | 25 | 23 | $49 |
200 Jackson St. (Front St.), 415-981-0983; www.kokkari.com
■ "High-class Greek goodies" can be found Downtown in this spacious "series of rooms where it always feels as if a party's going on"; amid a "larger-than-life fireplace and dark wood floors", consumers cluster for "lusty" lamb chops and "mmm-moussaka", attended by "servers who could not be friendlier"; "well, it does cost", but whether it's for "a family dinner or to close a deal", nothing beats this bit of Hellenic "heaven"; N.B. the post-*Survey* arrival of chef Erik Cosselmon may outdate the Food score.

Kuleto's   20 | 19 | 18 | $38 |
Villa Florence Hotel, 221 Powell St. (bet. Geary & O'Farrell Sts.), 415-397-7720; www.kuletos.com
☑ "The only place on Union Square that's worth its price" declare Downtowners of this trattoria/wine bar where

self-styled "Cool-eatos" often "eat at the counter to watch" the preparation of "solid if not spectacular" Northern Italian fare; at "peak times" the "service can't keep up with the crowd" (its location makes it "innundated" with tourists), but certainly "you won't insult anyone by bringing him here"; N.B. Kuleto's Trattoria, the Burlingame branch, specializes in wood-burning oven fare.

Kyo-Ya ⊠   25 | 21 | 22 | $54 |
Palace Hotel, 2 New Montgomery St. (Market St.), 415-546-5090; www.kyo-ya-restaurant.com
■ "This most Japanese of SF's Japanese" establishments forgoes "cutesy rolls" in favor of "conservative" sushi and "amazing" kaiseki dinners offered by "cool", "crisp" servers; the "beautifully arranged" food, in fact, "leaves very little to be desired", except, perhaps, the lowering of their "Tokyo-like prices", which don't seem to bother the "executives visiting" Downtown who long for "a bit of home cooking" and a "Zen-like atmosphere."

La Cumbre Taqueria ⊄   21 | 8 | 14 | $10 |
515 Valencia St. (bet. 16th & 17th Sts.), 415-863-8205
☑ "Great-value, super-size burritos" "will keep you full for days" swear Mission mavens who visit this "good ol' standby" of a taqueria "at least once a week"; true, the decor is pure "local dive", but you can always "get the food and run"; N.B. there's now a branch in San Mateo.

La Felce   ▽ 19 | 13 | 17 | $31 |
1570 Stockton St. (Union St.), 415-392-8321
☑ "The owners will make you feel like their favorite relative (*mangia, mangia!*)" at this "old-school" North Beacher that "captures the essence of the Northern Italian–American dining experience"; some "love everything about this place", from the "reasonable prices" to the "down-home" dishes served "family-style", but the disappointed declare it's taken a "step down" of late.

LA FOLIE ⊠   27 | 22 | 25 | $80 |
2316 Polk St. (bet. Green & Union Sts.), 415-776-5577; www.lafolie.com
■ On Polk Street, "passionate" Roland Passot, "with precision and panache", "prepares to perfection" New French fare at this "foodie underground favorite"; within the "whimsical", small but "charming" room, the chef-owner "and his wife, Jamie, go out of their way to make everyone feel welcome"; so, although the "prices are astronomical", the experience "is also out of this world."

La Luna   ▽ 18 | 18 | 19 | $32 |
3126 24th St. (bet. Folsom & Shotwell Sts.), 415-282-7110; www.lalunarestaurants.com
☑ At this "Mission District hideaway" on "one of the grittier parts of 24th Street", Luna-tics are over the moon for

the "warm ambiance" and the "rich" Nuevo Latino food –
"and lots of it" – that "cancels out your last three gym
workouts"; but dissenters deem it "a big disappointment",
despite the "bonus points for live" music on Saturdays.

La Méditerranée   20 15 17 $19

2210 Fillmore St. (Sacramento St.), 415-921-2956
288 Noe St. (bet. Market & 16th Sts.), 415-431-7210
www.cafelamed.com

☑ They're "not the place for a claustrophobic", but most
don't mind rubbing elbows for the "little slice of Med
heaven" (plus "cheap house wine") served by these Upper
Fillmore and Castro "stalwarts"; and even critics who claim
the Middle Eastern meals are "nothing to write home about"
are happy to cart the fare there (they're catering/"takeaway
favorites"); P.S. at the Berkeley branch, sit on the sidewalk
and "watch the College Avenue crowds go by."

La Scene Café & Bar   ∇ 19 17 21 $41

Warwick Regis, 490 Geary St. (Taylor St.), 415-292-6430;
www.warwickhotels.com

■ With a prix fixe that makes it "one of the best price-
performers in SF", audiences applaud this "unpretentious",
"civilized" (you can actually "hear each other talk")
Downtowner that's "great for dinner before the theater";
"friendly servers" deliver the "Med-accented" Cal goods
that are "not fancy but enjoyable", and perhaps most
importantly, they "will get you to the show on time."

Last Supper Club, The   19 17 18 $29

1199 Valencia St. (23rd St.), 415-695-1199;
www.lastsupperclubsf.com

☑ "Kitschy", "crowded and hip", this Mission Californian
is a "fun but loud" locale for a festive night out, especially
given the "awesome drinks"; however, even those who
enjoy the "moderately priced" Italian-inspired cuisine must
confess that it's "not quite Luna Park", its sister nearby,
and it doesn't help that reservations "always run late."

La Table O & CO   20 17 17 $23

(fka Marinette)
3352 Steiner St. (bet. Chestnut & Lombard Sts.), 415-440-9040

☑ The "south of France comes to north of Lombard" at this
Marina Med where "simple" but "exquisitely prepared"
prix fixe dinners are "an excellent value"; but those who
"miss Marinette" moan this successor's servers "haven't
really figured out the whole meal thing yet", making it
harder to "tell if this is a store or a restaurant" (actually, it's
both, and a bakery to boot).

La Taqueria ⊄   24 7 13 $10

2889 Mission St. (25th St.), 415-285-7117

☑ "You'll think you died and went to taco heaven" say
those who tout this "*muy* tasty" taqueria in the Mission,

where "meats marinated in magic", "perfect beans, unadulterated guac and no rice" make for burritos "so good they should be illegal"; "the decor is a little daunting", but luckily the "long lines move quickly" thanks to the "fast" if "cocky" counter staff; N.B. a second branch is South of SF.

La Vie   ▽ 22 | 10 | 18 | $25 |
5830 Geary Blvd. (bet. 22nd & 23rd Aves.), 415-668-8080
■ "When you can't get into Slanted Door", *c'est* La Vie for "both a good value and a culinary treat" declare devotees who "dream of the flaming beef and prawns" and other "dependable" French-Vietnamese victuals; it's a "wonderful neighborhood find" in the Outer Richmond.

Le Central Bistro ⌧   19 | 16 | 19 | $37 |
453 Bush St. (bet. Grant Ave. & Kearny St.), 415-391-2233
⊠ Seems like this "little bistro has been there forever" in Downtown's French Quarter – and "as the chalkboard on the wall will tell you", so has its signature "10,000-day-old cassoulet" (and possibly the "nice" staff as well); all remain "popular with politicians", tourists and Francophiles who hold court at the bar and "add character" to the "authentic Parisian surroundings"; however, some huff this haunt of the ex-mayor rates more "points for photo-ops" than it does for dining.

Le Charm French Bistro   21 | 16 | 19 | $33 |
315 Fifth St. (bet. Folsom & Shipley Sts.), 415-546-6128;
www.lecharm.com
■ "Step in from squalid Fifth Street and you are immediately charmed" by this "prix fixe pleaser", a "perennial favorite" for its "well-executed" "simple French cuisine without all the froufrou stuff"; though the interior's a bit "linoleum palace", the "secret garden patio" complete "with gas heaters for chilly evenings" is definitely "delightful", and service unfailingly "friendly."

Le Colonial   21 | 25 | 19 | $45 |
20 Cosmo Pl. (bet. Post & Taylor Sts.), 415-931-3600;
www.lecolonialsf.com
⊠ Shuttered windows, ceiling fans and an "expansive" porch create a colonial "tropical fantasy" Downtown that "oozes sex (in a good way)"; it can be "difficult to choose among the New French–Vietnamese options", but you can get help from the "personable" if slightly "haughty" servers; of course the "jet-set atmosphere" and "creative" food don't come cheap, so "make sure someone else is paying" or just head with a "hot date" to the "incredibly romantic" upstairs bar, perhaps the "restaurant's best asset."

Le Petit Robert   21 | 18 | 18 | $33 |
2300 Polk St. (Green St.), 415-922-8100; www.lepetitrobert.com
⊠ Fans feel "every neighborhood needs a place" like this "*très* French" bistro on Russian Hill, where "simple" small

plates "perfect for sharing" are "done with flair" in an "adorable" atmosphere that offers "instant transportation to the Paris boulevards"; but malcontents mutter over "mysteriously expensive" tabs, saying this "noisy" scene offers "nothing you will remember – and that includes the conversation that you didn't hear."

Le Soleil
19 | 12 | 16 | $21 |

133 Clement St. (bet. 2nd & 3rd Aves.), 415-668-4848

☑ "Brings a ray of sunshine to the Inner Richmond fog belt" beam boosters of this "hidden Vietnamese" where "you'll have a tough time finding a bad dish"; some countenances cloud over at the decor – "wish the environment matched the food" – but at least the "service is quick."

Le Zinc
18 | 21 | 15 | $32 |

4063 24th St. (bet. Castro & Noe Sts.), 415-647-9400; www.lezinc.com

☑ "A perfect brasserie atmosphere" ("elegant yet homey") plus a "*jardin* out back" makes this sidewalk cafe overlooking the "heart of Noe Valley activity" "one of the most pleasant places to have a leisurely" (read: "slooow"), "buttery brunch"; however, "the waitresses definitely carry their French attitude with them when they serve you" and the "basic" dinners "could be better for the price."

Lhasa Moon
▽ 15 | 12 | 20 | $21 |

2420 Lombard St. (bet. Divisadero & Scott Sts.), 415-674-9898; www.lhasamoon.com

☑ For "something different", see this small site serving specialties from the land of the Dali Lama; while advocates insist the "good but bland" fare is "exactly how Tibetan food is supposed to be", others are "disappointed" that it "doesn't knock your socks off"; still, it's "worth checking out" "for a soothing break from the noisy" Marina scene.

Liberty Cafe & Bakery
22 | 17 | 20 | $29 |

410 Cortland Ave. (Bennington St.), 415-695-8777

■ "The restaurant that put Bernal Heights on the map" 10 years ago continues on its "charming" course with "comforting" American food (e.g. "pot pies that take you home again") and a "welcoming atmosphere"; the "no-reservations policy guarantees a long wait on weekends", but you "can't beat the bakery/wine bar out back" to hang in, and reasonable prices mean "it's a liberating place to escape SF's high food costs."

Limòn
23 | 14 | 20 | $31 |

3316 17th St. (Mission St.), 415-252-0918; www.limon-sf.com

☑ "Peruvian food may be the next haute cuisine", if this "terrific little joint" in the Mission is any indication; "Jardinière-pedigreed" chef Martin Castillo's "upscale" dishes (including "amazingly creative seviches") "can sing", even if "your ears will ring from the noise" bouncing off the citrus-colored walls; "all they need is a larger room", which they'll get in their upcoming move to 524 Valencia Street; the current Mission address will morph into a rotisserie take-out place.

Little Nepal   22 | 19 | 20 | $23
925 Cortland Ave. (Folsom St.), 415-643-3881;
www.littlenepalsf.com
◪ A "nice newcomer to the neighborhood", this Nepalese offers Bernal Heights a "kind of a combination of Indian and Chinese" fare that provides "a spicy kick for the adventurous taste bud"; the service is "conscientious", and, while the space seems "as tiny as the country itself", the "dollar-to-flavor ratio" is Everest-sized.

Liverpool Lil's ◕   16 | 15 | 17 | $24
2942 Lyon St. (bet. Greenwich & Lombard Sts.), 415-921-6664
◪ Marina mavens trolling for a traditional tavern put in a hard day's night at this "locals' hideaway"; make no mistake, it's "a real dive", but it delivers "more than you'd expect" – including "friendly service, strong drinks and a classic menu" of Anglo-American pub grub, including "addictive" hamburger clubs.

L'Olivier ☒   19 | 18 | 21 | $41
465 Davis Ct. (Jackson St.), 415-981-7824;
www.lolivierrestaurant.com
◪ "It's been around for years, but no one knows it's there" – which makes this "quaint" Embarcadero rendezvous reliable for "the older crowd" or anyone seeking "an out-of-the-way liaison"; true, it seems a tad "tired" (especially the "outdated decor"), but while the classic French food and "well-trained staff" seemingly "haven't changed in [almost] 30 years, that can be a good thing."

L'Osteria del Forno ⊄   23 | 13 | 16 | $24
519 Columbus Ave. (bet. Green & Union Sts.), 415-982-1124;
www.losteriadelforno.com
■ Some evenings there seem to be "as many people standing on the sidewalk as sitting" in this "tiny" North Beach Northern Italian; from "sensational roast pork" to "some of the tastiest homemade pasta outside Italia", it's "amazing what they can do" with their single oven; they don't take reservations, which is "a bit of a pain", but given the "great prices", it's "worth the wait."

Lovejoy's Tea Room   19 | 23 | 21 | $19
1351 Church St. (bet. Clipper & 26th Sts.), 415-648-5895
■ "There's always a bridal or baby shower going on" at this "totally girlie" Noe Valley-ite that's "more English than an actual English tearoom", with its "gracious" service and "cluttered, colorful" digs ("don't sneeze or you'll break something"); though "you go for the experience" more than the eats, to adoring Anglophiles "happiness is a

warm scone with clotted cream" and a "bottomless pot" of brewed leaves.

Luna Park   22 | 18 | 17 | $30 |

694 Valencia St. (18th St.), 415-553-8584;
www.lunaparksf.com

☑ Supporters say "there's no such thing as a bad meal" at this Mission Cal-French, which dishes "generous portions" of "posh comfort food"; lunacy reigns at the "terribly small" bar where a mix of "grown-up sorority girls" and "Gen-X hipsters" "spills over" and contributes to the "absurdly noisy" environment; but most maintain the "buzzing scene" and "fabulous food" are "worth the wait (and wait you will, even with reservations)."

Lüx ☒   – | – | – | M |

2263 Chestnut St. (bet. Pierce & Scott Sts.),
415-567-2998

Luke and Kitty Sung have opened this global fusion spot just around a Marina corner from their Isa; since this sleek site with a long zinc bar offers lüx (a Turkish word, pronounced Luke's) not luxe items, diners can expect an eclectic selection of homey Asian- and Med-inspired small plates ranging from truffled cheese fondue to Peking-duck lettuce wraps, all priced well under $20.

MacArthur Park   16 | 18 | 16 | $36 |

607 Front St. (bet. Jackson St. & Pacific Ave.),
415-398-5700

☑ "Crisp" and "club-housy", this "large", "handsome" Downtowner is a destination for "dependable American fare" ("mm-mm, those ribs are the best"); "impressively sized" portions and a "comfortable" noise level make it a "standby" but adventurous eaters say it's "so '80s" and the "food needs a little more magic" to be worth the price and the "hoity-toity" service; N.B. the Palo Alto branch is housed in a Julia Morgan–built historic landmark.

Maki   24 | 16 | 20 | $31 |

Japan Ctr., 1825 Post St. (bet. Fillmore & Webster Sts.),
415-921-5215

☑ "There's a crowd in this tiny" ma-and-pa shop in a Japantown shopping mall that has a bigger selection of sake than seats; still, the "refined" "authentic" "Tokyo-style" eats "presented with care" are as good as any at a "local haunt in Ginza"; critics carp the "miniscule" portions of sashimi are something of a raw deal, but most maintain eating here is "sure to realign your chi."

Mama's on Washington Square ⊅   26 | 15 | 18 | $18 |

1701 Stockton St. (Filbert St.), 415-362-6421

■ "There aren't many places worth waiting in line for breakfast, but this is one of them" ("assuming you don't have babies or toddlers") muse morning risers who "go early" or "skip work" to partake of piles of pancakes or "egg-soaked breads" "just like mama made 'em"; this North Beach pseudo-"country cottage" also offers "homestyle" American lunches before shuttering at 3 PM.

Mandalay   ▽ 22 | 14 | 19 | $19 |
4348 California St. (6th Ave.), 415-386-3895
■ "A recent remodeling has made it a lot more pleasant" at this Burmese bungalow, now bustling with business in the Inner Richmond; also enlarged are the number of "authentic, delicious" dishes at the same "bang-for-the-buck prices"; and should anything cause pause, the staff will "patiently explain the menu."

Mandarin, The   21 | 20 | 20 | $38 |
Ghirardelli Sq., 900 North Point St. (bet. Larkin & Polk Sts.), 415-673-8812
◪ Though some say it ceased being "a leader in Pacific Rim cuisine years ago", this Fisherman's Wharf "old-time favorite still pleases" with its "high-quality Chinese" fare and "elegant decor" overlooking a "beautiful view of the Bay"; P.S. "its Peking duck must be ordered 24 hours in advance, but it's an experience one must have at least once in life."

Manora's Thai Cuisine   ▽ 26 | 17 | 22 | $21 |
1600 Folsom St. (12th St.), 415-861-6224
■ The "best this side of Bangok" declare the few who make a habit of going to this SoMa "surprising find" for its "generous portions" of "fantastically flavored" seafood and soups served by an "attentive" staff in a "homey" space; it's a "phenomenal value" too.

**Mario's Bohemian
Cigar Store Cafe**   19 | 16 | 17 | $16 |
*566 Columbus Ave. (Union St.), 415-362-0536;
www.mariosbohemiancigarstore.com*
■ "Working-class looks" combine with "old-school charm" at this "casual" Northern Italian "neighborhood institution" "next door to Washington Square Park"; though the menu's "very limited" and the food "simple", "great focaccia sandwiches" at "an excellent value" make it "one of North Beach's gems"; but "don't tell the tourists – it's too small" already.

MarketBar   18 | 19 | 16 | $36 |
*Ferry Bldg., 1 Ferry Plaza (Broadway St.), 415-434-1100;
www.marketbar.com*
◪ This Embarcadero newcomer serves "solid" Med fare with "pleasant", if "flaky" service; some chime in "the food is second to the view", but it's saved by the bell (tower) of its Ferry Building location, with "great outdoor people-watching" and a "swank, hip" "bistro atmosphere that's hard to beat."

Marnee Thai
24 | 14 | 16 | $21

2225 Irving St. (bet. 23rd & 24th Aves.), 415-665-9500
1243 Ninth Ave. (bet. Irving St. & Lincoln Way), 415-731-9999
☑ "When you're in the mood for good food", join the crowds at this Outer Sunset staple, one of the top "Thais in town" (and not just because the "large servings" mean "more for your money"); do expect "cramped seating", "quickly turned tables" and the "outspoken owner's" wife to order for you (she's usually right), but hopefully the "new location on Ninth Avenue" will alleviate the "long waits" to get in.

MASA'S ☒
28 | 25 | 27 | $93

Hotel Vintage Ct., 648 Bush St. (bet. Powell & Stockton Sts.), 415-989-7154
■ Celebrated chef Ron Siegel, who restored this legendary Downtowner to "days of glory", has departed post-*Survey*, but the arrival of co-chefs Richard Reddington (ex Auberge du Soleil) and Gregory Short (ex French Laundry) should ensure this "crème de la crème" won't curdle, but will continue the New French cuisine that inspires "transports of delight"; fans feel the front-of-the-house staff will "uphold its reputation" for treating guests "like royalty" in the "hushed", stylishly "updated, urbane" digs.

Massawa
▽ 19 | 8 | 15 | $17

1538 Haight St. (bet. Ashbury & Clayton Sts.), 415-621-4129
☑ In laid-back Haight-Ashbury, this Ethiopian-Eritrean is a "good choice for entertaining out-of-town guests" with the joys of "spicy" "hands-on cuisine" (i.e. you "pick up the food with bread and your fingers"); but don't expect more than plentiful platters: the decor – what there is of it – resembles a "run-down church bingo hall", and service, though "sweet-tempered", is "difficult to draw away from the soccer on TV."

Ma Tante Sumi
24 | 19 | 22 | $38

4243 18th St. (bet. Castro & Diamond Sts.), 415-626-7864
■ Although it's been "serving its own style of East-West fusion food long before fusion became a fad", this "romantic" "respite" remains "somewhat unknown" outside the Castro; but the cognoscenti claim it's "as close as you'll get to fine dining" hereabouts, with "attentive service catering to needs you didn't even know you had" and a "cozy" dining room that, despite an "early-'80s" air, is "quiet enough to hear your companion."

Matterhorn Swiss Restaurant
19 | 18 | 20 | $37

2323 Van Ness Ave. (bet. Green & Vallejo Sts.), 415-885-6116
☑ For "fabulous fondue fun" "with friends", one needn't climb any mountain higher than Van Ness Avenue, where this Swiss miss holds sway; the "hosts clearly care" how you fare within the woody "mountain chalet" ambiance,

but the unmollified mutter it all seems "expensive" "for cheese, bread and a few skewers of meat."

Max's 16 | 13 | 16 | $22

1 California St. (Market St.), 415-781-6297 ⊠
555 California St., concourse level (bet. Kearny & Montgomery Sts.), 415-788-6297 ⊠
311 Third St. (Folsom St.), 415-546-6297
Union Sq., 398 Geary St. (Mason St.), 415-646-8600
601 Van Ness Ave. (Golden Gate Ave.), 415-771-7301
www.maxsworld.com

☑ Supporters say this regional chain is the Bay Area's answer to a NYC "Jewish-style deli", with "large, easily shared portions" of "stick-to-your-ribs" sandwiches and "gooey desserts" served by waiters warbling to live piano (at the Opera branches); but skeptics squawk this "high-scale fast-food place" has seemed "uninspired" of late – "leaden rather than comfort food", "tired" decor – and even "the singing's getting worse."

Maya 23 | 20 | 20 | $37

303 Second St. (bet. Folsom & Harrison Sts.), 415-543-2928;
www.mayasf.com

■ Clearly "not your madre's taqueria", this SoMa site serves "wonderfully inventive Yucátan-inspired cuisine" ("*olé* for the mole") that "adults can enjoy" in "upscale" digs decorated with"dramatic silver serving dishes"; expect grown-up tabs as well, though most feel it's "worth the hefty price."

Mayflower ▽ 22 | 12 | 16 | $22

6255 Geary Blvd. (27th Ave.), 415-387-8338

■ The Outer Richmond teems with Chinese seafooders, but few navigate the seas with the "impeccable Hong Kong style" of this yacht-size site; though dinner is also offered in the "typical, overly bright, noisy surroundings", "dim sum is what they do best", and "for reasonable prices" too.

Maykedah ▽ 23 | 16 | 18 | $29

470 Green St. (bet. Grant Ave. & Kearny St.), 415-362-8286

☑ "A favorite among Iranians" in North Beach for over 20 years, this purveyor of Persian plates is "pricier than other places, but better, too"; reviewers rave over "authentic", "delicate" "dishes not found anywhere else", such as stew-like khoresht; but while patrons praise the "Middle Eastern hospitality", the servers seem "surly" to some.

McCormick & Kuleto's 18 | 22 | 18 | $40

900 North Point St. (Larkin St.), 415-929-1730;
www.mccormickandkuletos.com

☑ All agree that the "marvelous view" of Marin and Alcatraz from this Wharf seafood house "is great, day or night" – "but you can't eat it" sigh surveyors who find the fish dishes "dependable, but unspectacular", served by staffers who basically "bring food and take it away"; still, it's a good place "to bring tourists" to feast on the "huge list of offerings."

Mecca   21 23 20 $42
2029 Market St. (bet. Dolores & 14th Sts.), 415-621-7000; www.sfmecca.com

■ "Still hip" after nine years, this "lively" "industrial chic" supper club on Upper Market remains mecca for "an evening of drinking, dining" and hobnobbing with the "fabulous crowd"; while the "fantastic oval bar" is the "literal and figurative center of the experience", the "*wunderbar*" New American food, "infused with a Southern touch", somehow "manages not to be upstaged"; however, "for maximum comfort", service and acoustics, "snag a booth" in the back.

Mel's Drive-In ◐   13 16 14 $16
3355 Geary Blvd. (bet. Beaumont & Parker Aves.), 415-387-2255
2165 Lombard St. (Steiner St.), 415-921-2867
801 Mission St. (4th St.), 415-227-4477
Richelieu Hotel, 1050 Van Ness Ave. (Geary St.), 415-292-6357
www.melsdrive-in.com

■ "If you're into the whole '50s diner/soda fountain thing", "have a milkshake and soak up the nostalgia" at this retro chain; adorned with "*American Graffiti* memorabilia" and "individual juke boxes at each booth", it's a "standby" for "late-night noshing or hangover breakfasts"; just "stick with the basics" served by the "brightly uniformed staff."

Memphis Minnie's BBQ Joint   20 12 16 $17
576 Haight St. (bet. Fillmore & Steiner Sts.), 415-864-7675; www.memphisminnies.com

☑ "There's a real love of 'cue here and it shows" at this "friendly" Lower Haight smokehouse where the "sweet", "fork-tender" fare is "cheap and messy, the way you want it"; but bear in mind "it's all about the meat here" – not the "mediocre sides" or the "basically take-out joint" decor.

Merenda   23 20 22 $47
1809 Union St. (bet. Laguna & Octavia Sts.), 415-346-7373

■ "Hold a civilized conversation" in this "too-small-but-cozy" Cow Hollow "hangout" where "flexible"-course "prix fixes let you sample your way through a fantastic menu" of "simple" French–Northern Italian dishes, guided by a "knowledgeable staff" and "owners who really take care of you"; P.S. "weekend lunch offerings" are "an extraordinary bargain" at Café Merenda around the corner.

Mescolanza   22 17 22 $27
2221 Clement St. (bet. 23rd & 24th Aves.), 415-668-2221; www.mescolanza.net

■ Taste "all the classics all the time" at this "tiny trattoria in the Outer Richmond"; it's "full of regulars" who flock for the "consistent" cooking ("mm-mm, pasta limone"), "quiet environment" and "pleasant service" at "reasonable prices", so no wonder parking is "difficult."

Michael Mina – | – | – | E
Westin St. Francis, 335 Powell St. (bet. Geary & Post Sts.), 415-397-9222
Michael Mina's new eponymous Downtown dining room features 35-ft. ceilings, Ionic columns and a sea of crème-colored drapery and celadon armchairs, a fitting backdrop for his super-luxe, high-concept New American prix fixe menu built around a single ingredient prepared three ways on the same plate; guests can also choose among the classics from his 11 years at Aqua, along with a 1,000-label wine list overseen by Rajat Parr (ex Fifth Floor).

Michelangelo Restaurant Caffe ⊄ 18 | 15 | 17 | $25
579 Columbus Ave. (Union St.), 415-986-4058
☑ "The Italian food is generic", but at least "you won't leave hungry" when you brave the lines at this North Beacher that's "loud, but fun for families" and "tourists seeking a break from outlandish prices"; service "never keeps you waiting long" in the digs decorated "with various stained-glass lamps, paintings and sculptures"; P.S. the "shared bowl of Gummi Bears" passed around after dinner "brings out the kid" in everyone, except for incorrigible grown-ups who go "gross."

Mifune 17 | 12 | 15 | $17
Kintetsu Bldg., 1737 Post St. (bet. Buchanan & Webster Sts.), 415-922-0337
☑ "Oodles of noodles" are the freshly pulled pull at this "J-town standby" ladling out "big bowls" that "come out almost immediately after you order them"; the "hole-in-the-wall" decor "could use a little spice" and the "indifferent service" a little pep, but "hot soup, cold city" is a "great match" particularly "if time is against you."

Millennium 23 | 21 | 22 | $42
Savoy Hotel, 580 Geary St. (Jones St.), 415-345-3900; www.millenniumrestaurant.com
■ Going "millennia beyond traditional" meatless cuisine, the "eclectic", "high-style" food at this vegan is "so good that [even] meat-eating friends don't mind going" (of course, "the full bar helps"); if the "imaginative", "all-organic" menu leaves you lost, the "great staff will help you understand what to order and why"; its move to "upscale" new Downtown digs, "close to theaters", "is definitely an improvement."

Miss Millie's 21 | 18 | 18 | $24
4123 24th St. (bet. Castro & Diamond Sts.), 415-285-5598
■ Follow the "long lines" of morning hopefuls milling about to find this "definitive Noe Valley brunch destination" cranking out almost "too-generous" helpings of "luscious

lemon ricotta pancakes" and "spectacular" huevos rancheros; while the "homey" interior manages to "make ratty linoleum and beaten-up wooden fixtures seem cozy", the "small back deck is best on a sunny day"; P.S. the "Moosewood-meets–Julia Child" New American dinners (Wednesday–Sunday) "are great as well."

Moki's Sushi & Pacific Grill   22 | 15 | 16 | $28 |
830 Cortland Ave. (Gates St.), 415-970-9336;
www.mokisushi.com
☑ "Inventive" combinations of "classic Pacific flavors" keep this Hawaiian-Japanese with a "surfer motif" hangin' 10 in Bernal Heights; fin-atics "could live off the rolls", and there are "good salads" and "extensive non-sushi items for those who don't like raw fish"; the "ambiance is comfortable", despite "tables that are squeezed in tighter than seaweed around maki" and "inconsistent service."

MoMo's   18 | 18 | 16 | $35 |
760 Second St. (King St.), 415-227-8660; www.eatatmomos.com
☑ Sports fans think they hit a home run with the "good ol' American comfort food" at this South Beach "yuppie heaven" "in the shadow of the ballpark"; but unforgiving umps say they strike out, calling the place "pretentious and overpriced" ("I only go when I'm not paying"); if you want to play ball, "get there very early on game day" when "the bar is buzzing"; otherwise, it's "pretty quiet" and a contender for a "casually elegant evening."

Moose's   21 | 21 | 21 | $42 |
1652 Stockton St. (bet. Filbert & Union Sts.), 415-989-7800;
www.mooses.com
■ "There's a reason why it's always crowded" at this North Beach New American – namely, owner "Ed Moose hasn't lost his touch"; he still offers a "civilized, warm time" "SF-style", "without the attitude", but with "wonderful views of Washington Square Park", "good portions of well-prepared meals", plenty of "beautiful people" at the "happening bar" and "live jazz" to listen to; small wonder that after just 13 years, his namesake is an "established classic."

Morton's, The Steakhouse   23 | 20 | 22 | $59 |
400 Post St. (bet. Mason & Powell Sts.), 415-986-5830;
www.mortons.com
☑ "It may be a chain", but "the formula works" at this Downtown steakhouse known for "tender, juicy" and "huge portions" of porterhouse, "sides that are a meal in themselves" and "service that's to the point, without flair"; some have a cow over the "purely-for-fat-cat" prices and "masculine" decor, but for most the "dimly lit, primal" experience is "just the way a meat eater likes it"; P.S. to management: virtually every surveyor pleads "spare me the Saran wrap" "meat parade."

Mo's 21   11   14 $17
1322 Grant Ave. (bet. Green & Vallejo Sts.), 415-788-3779
Yerba Buena Gardens, 772 Folsom St. (bet. 3rd & 4th Sts.),
415-957-3779
☑ "Awesome hamburgers" – "they grind their own beef" –
are the claim to fame of these two "relaxed places"; "the
decor and service are nothing to write home about", but
watching patties "the size of your face" "rotate on the grill
in North Beach is like watching Food TV", and in SoMa the
"Yerba Buena Gardens view is splendid, especially from
the outside tables."

Naan 'n Curry ● 19   7   10 $12
642 Irving St. (7th Ave.), 415-664-7225
533 Jackson St. (Columbus Ave.), 415-693 0499
478 O'Farrell St. (Jones St.), 415-775-1349
☑ Throughout the town, these "spartan" spots are "hard-
to-beat" "on a cold, foggy night for comfort food" – if you're
comforted by "awesome" and "authentic" Indian and
Pakistani food, that is; though the "almost cafeteria-style"
service is "total chaos" and each outpost has "all the
atmosphere of a Bombay bus terminal", you can't beat the
"bang for the buck"; N.B. a fourth branch is in Berkeley.

Nectar Wine Lounge ⊠ ∇ 17   24   21 $30
3330 Steiner St. (bet. Chestnut & Lumbard Sts.), 415-345-1377;
www.nectarwinelounge.com
☑ This new wine bar in the Marina ("finally!") is "deserving
of the name", with a 600-plus selection of international
bottlings (40 available by the glass or grouped together in
thematic flight) housed in a honeycomb-shaped wine rack
that dominates the "hip, swank" decor; they "still need to
hone the munchies" – just "a few small plates" of Cal-
Fusion fare – but given the "party crowd" already packing
in, chances are the place will "quench your desires."

Nob Hill Café 21   14   18 $27
1152 Taylor St. (bet. Clay & Sacramento Sts.), 415-776-6500;
www.nobhillcafe.com
☑ Nob Hill neighbors go nuts for this "absolutely wonderful
and charming" Italian whose "hilltop location keeps the
tourists away"; "friendly, if overly casual" servers ferry
"homey" food to the regulars (San Francisco Twins Marian
and Vivian Brown are likely "to get the window seat"); and
though some romantics find the "tight quarters" "cozy",
others say "the "sardine-can seating conditions detract."

North Beach Pizza 17   8   13 $16
1310 Grant Ave. (Vallejo St.), 415-433-2444
1499 Grant Ave. (Union St.), 415-433-2444 ●
1649 Haight St. (Belvedere St.), 415-751-2300
4787 Mission St. (bet. Persia & Russia Aves.), 415-586-1400
(continued)

(continued)
North Beach Pizza
*Pier 39 (bet. Grant & Stockton Sts., off The Embarcadero),
415-433-0400*
800 Stanyan St. (Haight St.), 415-751-2300 ◐
3054 Taraval St. (41st Ave.), 415-242-9100
www.northbeachpizza.com
◪This local chain "can vary by location", which may
explain why some locals "love" the "classic, chewy thick-
crust pizza" served by a "prompt" staff, while pickier
pieheads huff over the "too doughy" and "cheesy"
product slung by "servers that couldn't care less"; all
agree, though, it's a "cheap" "cure for the really late-night
munchies"; P.S. though the "original location" – in North
Beach, naturally – "is by far the best", there are branches
throughout the Bay Area.

North Beach Restaurant ◐   21 17 21 $38
*1512 Stockton St. (bet. Green & Union Sts.), 415-392-1700;
www.northbeachrestaurant.com*
■ "Everyone is made to feel like a special guest" by the
"career waiters" at this "traditional trattoria" in North Beach
that's "been here a long time for a reason"; though the
Northern Italian dishes are "straightforward", the "elegant
but not stuffy" setting – particularly the "romantic" wine
cellar – makes this "lesser-known" venue one "to impress."

Olive Bar & Restaurant ◐☒   ▽ 20 22 19 $24
743 Larkin St. (O'Farrell St.), 415-776-9814
■ "Almost hidden from the outside", this "funky, stylish
eatery" is an "oasis in the Tenderloin", where the parched
can quench their thirst with "imaginative" martinis and "a
great selection of wine" served by a "super-friendly" staff;
the combo of Cal "small plates, earthy pizzas and smashing
drinks" make it worth a "trip through the seamier side of
town", and the rotating art exhibits add "a great touch"
to the decor.

One Market ☒   22 22 20 $48
1 Market St. (Steuart St.), 415-777-5577; www.onemarket.com
◪ "Catering to the business crowd" along the Embarcadero,
co-owner Bradley Ogden's "brisk, big-city" "classic"
features "fresh", "robust" and always "reliable" New
American cuisine in an "open, spacious room" (a tad "too
big", some sigh); while many servers "anticipate your
every need", several seem "snooty" – perhaps it depends
on your power-broker quotient; P.S. "if you're alone, sit by
the open kitchen and learn how it's done."

Original Joe's ◐   17 12 17 $27
144 Taylor St. (bet. Eddy & Turk Sts.), 415-775-4877
◪ You'll "feel like you're on the set of *The Godfather*" at this
Italian-American "blast from the past" in the Tenderloin,

where "crusty tux-wearing waiters" dish up "refreshingly plain" food "in a wildly trendy city"; the "old-school" menu – "big portions" of pasta, steak and burgers – is considered "classic" or "dated", depending on your point of view; P.S. the San Jose location, "where it's always 1958", is under different ownership.

Osha Thai Noodles ● 20 | 13 | 16 | $15 |
696 Geary St. (Leavenworth St.), 415-673-2368
819 Valencia St. (19th St.), 415-826-7738 ⌧
■ When you're desperately seeking Siam, either in the gritty Tenderloin or the trendy Mission, these "hip" Thai twins offer a lot of Bangkok for the buck; while the "funky" atmosphere, "pounding dance music" and late-night hours are three good reasons to head there, the "damn good" and "cheap" namesake noodles – stir-fried or in "spicy" soup – served up "wicked fast" are the real draws.

Ozumo 23 | 25 | 19 | $45 |
161 Steuart St. (bet. Howard & Mission Sts.), 415-882-1333;
www.ozumo.com
◪ The "best-looking Japanese restaurant" around – a "stylish", "minimalist" space on the Embarcadero – is the setting for "high-quality sushi" and "inventive" robata items that "pack a ninja-worthy punch"; though service can be "lax" and the tab gets "as steep as Mt. Everest", most think the "transcendental" food and "so-hip-it-hurts" atmosphere worth it, especially "if someone else is paying."

Pacific ▽ 23 | 22 | 21 | $48 |
Pan Pacific Hotel, 500 Post St. (Mason St.), 415-929-2087;
www.panpac.com
■ Ardent admirers are "stunned that no one seems to know about" this "gem inside the Pan Pacific Hotel" where "soothing piano tunes" on weekends offer a welcome "escape from the high-decibel vogue"; the pacific ambiance is backdrop to the "meticulously prepared", "fine" Cal–Pacific Rim food and "friendly, professional staff" that comprise this "tastefully elegant" "retreat."

Pacific Café 21 | 14 | 20 | $29 |
7000 Geary Blvd. (34th Ave.), 415-387-7091
■ "Free wine while you wait in line" renders the long queue "almost pleasant" at the Outer Richmond's "old favorite" fish house; and once in, the "gracious" staff, "cozy" digs and "wonderful" "seafood always reward one's patience"; true, the "menu and style never changes", but perhaps that's why it sets "the gold standard for neighborhood restaurants."

Pacific Catch ⌧ 21 | 12 | 16 | $16 |
2027 Chestnut St. (bet. Fillmore & Steiner Sts.), 415-440-1950;
www.pacificcatch.com
◪ "To-die-for fish tacos", "amazing wasabi bowls" and other permutations of "fresh" seafood at "inexpensive"

prices are the lure at this "almost-fast-food closet in the Marina"; however, the "atmosphere consists of a cramped counter and tiny tables" and "the service can be truly frustrating" ("do they catch it when you order it?"), prompting suggestions that it may be "better for takeout."

Pakwan ⬚   21 | 5 | 9 | $13

501 O'Farrell St. (Jones St.), 415-776-0160
3182 16th St. (bet. Guerrero & Valencia Sts.), 415-255-2440
◪ "Big-taste curries make up for the no-frills" aesthetic at these Tenderloin and Mission Indian-Pakistanis serving "flavorful, rich food at poor-man's prices"; penny-pinchers "love the BYOB policy" (at the 16th Street location there's even "a convenience store living up to its name across the street"); pity that the counter service is "about as unfriendly as it gets"; N.B. a third branch is East of SF.

Palatino   ∇ 22 | 19 | 23 | $28

803 Cortland Ave. (Ellsworth St.), 415-641-8899;
www.palatinosf.com
■ "This authentic Roman trattoria" will have you swearing "Bernal Heights is the eighth hill of Rome", thanks to its charming accented owner, his "excellent" housemade pastas and cracker-thin pizzas and "a wine list that tours the Italian countryside"; "charming copper tables, dark red walls" and a "warm and friendly" staff completes the palatable package.

Palio D'Asti ⊠   20 | 19 | 21 | $38

640 Sacramento St. (bet. Kearny & Montgomery Sts.),
415-395-9800; www.paliodasti.com
■ "A bit like the executive dining room for the Financial District", there's no better place to ciao down on "pricey" but "well-executed", "authentic Tuscan" and Piemonte fare than this weekday Downtowner, serviced by a "superb staff of old-timers"; decorwise, fans "love the flags" and murals of the famed medieval Palio horse race, but the bar brims with refugees of the rat race during the happy-hour offer of a free wood-fired-oven pizza with a two-drink purchase.

Palomino   17 | 20 | 16 | $36

345 Spear St. (bet. Folsom & Harrison Sts.), 415-512-7400;
www.palominosf.com
◪ The "second-to-none" Bay Bridge view from outdoor tables is the main draw of this "colorful" Embarcadero entry; its "reliable" Cal-Med cuisine makes it "a favorite for a business lunch"; however, this horse doesn't run for critics who call the "menu huge but uninspired" and say the place "has the feel of an upscale chain" (which it is).

Pancho Villa Taqueria ◗   23 | 9 | 15 | $10

3071 16th St. (bet. Mission & Valencia Sts.), 415-864-8840
◪ Mexican-food mavens maintain "the best use for $6 in SF" is to buy a burrito at this "perpetually full", "huge,

high-ceilinged taqueria", which stands out among its Mission compadres for its highly "fresh" fare and "rockin' salsa"; the "uncomfortable" seats and "spartan interior" make it "more of a take-out joint", though the occasional "drop-in mariachi" bands help give it "great bang for your buck"; N.B. look for another location South of SF.

Pane e Vino　　23 | 18 | 20 | $35
1715 Union St. (Gough St.), 415-346-2111
■ Since they "moved into new digs on Union Street, there's more room, less wait and food that's just as good as before" at this Northern Italian that never "goes out of style", thanks to "consistent" dishes and "friendly service that reflects the Tuscan spirit"; plus, you can now enjoy the "delicious bread" and other "goodies" on a "delightful patio."

Paragon ⊠　　17 | 21 | 18 | $32
701 Second St. (Townsend St.), 415-537-9020;
www.paragonrestaurant.com
◪ "Knowledgeable bartenders" and "great appetizers" make this "slick" SoMa Californian, located a block from the ballpark, a winner "when you want a drink before or after a Giants game"; many mutter the main menu's "solid, but nothing special" and, of course, the "noise level's much too high"; P.S. at the Berkeley branch, "the dead-on [bridge] view" "outweighs everything else."

Park Chalet　　– | – | – | M
1000 Great Hwy. (bet. Fulton St. & Lincoln Way), 415-386-8439;
www.beachchalet.com
Thanks to its "retractable glass walls that open onto Golden Gate Park", this large "new annex" to the Beach Chalet offers day-trippers and diners a beautiful view to feast on; the bar pours house beers on tap, and there's an affordable brewpub menu with the likes of pizza and shepherd's pie.

Park Grill　　∇ 22 | 19 | 23 | $47
Park Hyatt Hotel, 333 Battery St. (Clay St.), 415-296-2933;
www.hyatt.com
■ "Good food in a hotel? who knew?" – why, those who frequent this "comfortable" New American "where Downtown business is done"; service doesn't "simply shine", it positively "gleams" as they dish up the "delicious" fare; "maybe it lacks the buzz that people seek", but those who think this "quiet spot" is a "surprise treat" wouldn't have it any other way.

Parma ⊠　　21 | 17 | 21 | $27
3314 Steiner St. (bet. Chestnut & Lombard Sts.), 415-567-0500
■ This "family trattoria" in the Marina "hasn't been there for over 20 years for no reason" and that reason is Pietro Elia, "who is direct from a casting call for a restaurant owner in a Fellini movie" with "endless kisses for female diners" and "a glass of wine or two" while you wait for your

table; though "nothing fancy", the "old-fashioned Italian basics" "satisfy cravings" and the "kitschy decor" gets embraced with a ratings rise.

Pasta Pomodoro
15 | 13 | 16 | $18 |

816 Irving St. (9th Ave.), 415-566-0900
2304 Market St. (16th St.), 415-558-8123
1865 Post St. (Fillmore St.), 415-674-1826
4000 24th St. (Noe St.), 415-920-9904
655 Union St. (Columbus Ave.), 415-399-0300
1875 Union St. (Laguna St.), 415-771-7900

☑ "From sophisticated [dishes] for the grown-ups to sure-bet spaghetti and meatballs for the kids", this "standby" chain serves "honest food at honest prices"; they "may not look like anything fancy", and the service and *cucina* may be pure "McPasta", but sometimes "utilitarian Italian" is perfect "when you're too tired to cook" for the *bambini*; P.S. branches are "ubiquitous" throughout the Bay Area.

Pauline's Pizza ☒
24 | 13 | 17 | $22 |

260 Valencia St. (bet. Duboce & 14th Sts.), 415-552-2050

■ "Unique toppings like edible flowers, pesto sauce and fresh, organic vegetables" ("to ease your conscience") come on a "thin, buttery crust" at this "pizzeria for foodies"; not only is each piece a "slice of heaven", but the "salads are fresh and lovely"; despite appearances on the outside (it's on a "dodgy" block in the Mission), it "manages to look classy inside."

paul k
20 | 17 | 19 | $37 |

199 Gough St. (Oak St.), 415-552-7132; www.paulkrestaurant.com

☑ The "unusual blend" of Middle East–meets-West flavors makes this "minimalist" Hayes Valley Med a nice "alternative before ballet or symphony"; supporters suggest "try one of the meze platters to get a sampling" and dine at the bar, which "can be more comfortable than the too-close-together tables"; but many are dismayed by "deafening acoustics" and "small portions"; "the waiter who recites the desserts as soft-porn monologue can be fun, but only if the service is good otherwise."

Pazzia ☒
24 | 15 | 23 | $28 |

337 Third St. (bet. Folsom & Harrison Sts.), 415-512-1693

■ "Gregarious staffers directly from Italy" make you feel like you're "eating on the *piazza*" "among friends" at "the most authentic Tuscan in SF" ("don't go expecting "Cal-Ital"); though the exterior is "unassuming" – it "looks like a strip mall" – the "friendly, lively atmosphere" of SoMa's "hip" "hideaway" ensures it's "always packed."

Pesce
24 | 19 | 21 | $34 |

2227 Polk St. (bet. Green & Vallejo Sts.), 415-928-8025

■ "There is nothing fishy about the things chef-owner Ruggero Gadaldi (also of Antica Trattoria) does with seafood" at this "fun", "lively" slip of a joint "bursting at the gills" on Polk Street; "not your typical small-plates" scene, it features "unusual" "Venetian-style tapas", a "good wine list" and a "staff that goes out of its way for regulars" who appreciate the "reasonable prices."

Picaro   17 | 15 | 13 | $22

3120 16th St. (bet. Guerrero & Valencia Sts.), 415-431-4089
☑ Sangria "like ambrosia", long tables "to accommodate large numbers" and generous portions of "traditional tapas priced the way tapas should be (cheap)" make this "noisy place" – sibling of fellow Missionite Esperpento – "great for groups"; "plenty of vegetarian" options attract herbivores ("you gotta love anything with that much garlic"), even if the service "leaves something to be desired."

Piperade ⌾   25 | 21 | 21 | $43

1015 Battery St. (Green St.), 415-391-2555; www.piperade.com
■ Everyone seems to be "basking in the pleasure" of chef-owner Gerald Hirigoyen's Downtown paean to the Pyrénées, including the "omnipresent" chef himself, "working the room" and making fast friends at the communal table; perhaps they could "use a few more waiters on the floor", but the "haute and folksy Basque cuisine", regional wines that "you won't see anywhere else", "cozy" bistro feel and "easy parking" ensure a "smash hit" here.

Pizzetta 211 ⊅   25 | 16 | 13 | $21

211 23rd Ave. (California St.), 415-379-9880; www.pizzetta211.com
☑ This "teeny-tiny place has a whale of a reputation" for "awesome pizzas" comprised of "crackerlike crusts" and "local" "organic ingredients" "that are worth waiting for even in the Outer Richmond's oceanic weather"; "the overall decor [which rose in ratings] makes you feel like you are in someone's kitchen, but the staff makes you feel like an unwanted guests who've overstayed their welcome."

PJ's Oyster Bed   20 | 16 | 17 | $31

737 Irving St. (9th Ave.), 415-566-7775; www.pjsoysterbed.com
☑ "It's always Mardi Gras in this rockin' Inner Sunset restaurant" where the "staff really gets into the spirit"; "while the party-till-you-drop-atmosphere trumps the dining experience", the "good" "New Orleans–style seafood" comes in "portions to feed all of Louisiana"; sure, it's "noisy, crowded" and not all that authentic – except on the days guest chef "Michael Reese is overseeing the kitchen" – "but you cannot help but leave in a good mood."

Platanos   21 | 17 | 18 | $28

598 Guerrero St. (18th St.), 415-252-9281
■ Reviewers are ready to "jump on the Nuevo Latino bandwagon" at this "truly innovative" Mission Central

American; the "upmarket" dishes, including "delectable small plates", "leave a great taste in your mouth, even though you'll be dropping some coin"; and while the room is "a little cramped", the "nice decor" ("love the floor-to-ceiling windows") and "genuine, warm" service "make it a "neighborhood gem."

Plouf ☒   22 | 16 | 17 | $35

40 Belden Pl. (bet. Bush & Pine Sts.), 415-986-6491;
www.beldenplace.com
☑ At this "loud and lively" "slice of France in the Financial District", "charming waiters" with "dreamy" accents (and sometimes movements) pack you in "like anchovies in a can" for Gallicized seafood, especially mussels "served multiple ways"; "eat outside on a mild night", since "almost sitting in the lap" of your neighbor indoors can be a "no-fun no-no" (unless of course you're into that sort of thing).

PlumpJack Cafe   24 | 21 | 22 | $49

3127 Fillmore St. (bet. Filbert & Greenwich Sts.), 415-563-4755;
www.plumpjack.com
■ "You'll be a little plumper" (though your wallet won't be) after a visit to this "small", "stylish" "high-end joint" in Cow Hollow – "11 years and holding strong"; the "fantastic wine list" famously abstains from "jacked-up prices", the Cal-Med fare is so good it "should be illegal" and the servers are still "dedicated"; skiers even "leave the slopes early" to snag a seat at the Squaw Valley outpost; N.B. at press time, sibling Jack Falstaff was slated to open at 598 Second Street.

Pomelo   21 | 15 | 20 | $20

1793 Church St. (30th St.), 415-285-2257
92 Judah St. (6th Ave.), 415-731-6175
www.pomelosf.com
■ "Fusion noodles and rice plates from around the globe" might not cater to the current "anti-carbohydrate mania", but locals love the "unexpected flavors" found at this open kitchen in the Inner Sunset; the Eclectic, ever-changing menu serves "high-falutin' food at student prices" in a "shoebox-sized" space; N.B. the Noe Valley location is slightly larger with some outdoor seating.

Ponzu   21 | 22 | 19 | $38

Serrano Hotel, 401 Taylor St. (bet. Geary Blvd. & O'Farrell St.),
415-775-7979; www.ponzurestaurant.com
■ "Request a table in the back room" of this "dark and moody" Downtown lounge/eatery, and "you'll feel like you're in Jeannie's bottle"; almost every wish will be granted by the "artistically served" "creative combos" of contemporary Pan-Asian small plates and the "fabulous cocktails" – though they can be "expensive", unless you go during the daily Feng Shui Happy Hour, when low prices and copious appetizers make for a "good pre-theater choice."

Pork Store Café   20 | 11 | 18 | $13
*1451 Haight St. (bet. Ashbury St. & Masonic Ave.),
415-864-6981*
3122 16th St. (bet. Guerrero & Valencia Sts.), 415-626-5523 ⊠
■ Providing dense, deliciously "greasy" Traditional
American breakfasts for the "hungover crowd" through
mid-afternoon, this is the place to "soak up the Haight-
Ashbury experience" and "pig out" on "inexpensive, large
portions" served by "sassy waitresses"; it's "worth the
wait – and you will wait" on weekends – but the "free
coffee while on line" is "bruncholiscious"; N.B. the new
Mission location catches some of the overflow.

POSTRIO   24 | 24 | 23 | $56
*Prescott Hotel, 545 Post St. (bet. Mason & Taylor Sts.),
415-776-7825; www.postrio.com*
◪ Maybe "Wolfgang Puck's SF hallmark" is "not nearly as
hot as it was", "but it still cooks" thanks to the Rosenthal
brothers' "lovely to look at, and even better tasting", New
American eats and a staff that doles out "great treatment";
"nothing beats" "watching the beautiful people making
their entrance down the main stairs", but insiders prefer to
"sit at the bar and enjoy the gourmet pizzas" at lunch or
après-theater, insisting the "overpriced", "noisy" dining
room is so "five minutes ago."

Public, The ⊠   23 | 22 | 19 | $33
*1489 Folsom St. (11th St.), 415-552-3065;
www.thepublicsf.com*
◪ Blessed with a "cool" "loft space", this recent addition
to the SoMa scene is "the place to go, if you're young and
hip", to savor a "short menu" of Cal "down-home food with
a flair" ("two words: rabbit sugo") "without breaking the
bank"; but some dub the "servers who act hipper than they
are" "public enemy" number one.

Puerto Alegre   17 | 10 | 13 | $16
546 Valencia St. (bet. 16th & 17th Sts.), 415-255-8201
◪ "While the food is good" at this Mission sit-down Mexican
place that's "a step or two up from a taqueria", "no one
really remembers it", mainly because of "the miraculous
margaritas"; they "take the edge off" the "really noisy"
interior packed with "urban hipsters, rowdy partyers and
lost yuppies", but don't mitigate the "burdensome wait
times", which have caused the Service score to slip.

Q   19 | 15 | 16 | $20
225 Clement St. (bet. 3rd & 4th Aves.), 415-752-2298
◪ "Q is for the quirky ambiance" of this "funked-up
American BBQ" joint in the Inner Richmond, where hipsters
play with alphabet magnets and toys while reliving their
childhood over "mac 'n' cheese topped with tater tots"
and frosty beer; foes "love to hate" its "long lines" and

"rude staff", "but all too often they find the meatloaf beckoning", and queue up all over again.

Quince
25 | 23 | 25 | $55 |

1701 Octavia St. (bet. Bush & Pine Sts.), 415-775-8500; www.quincerestaurant.com

■ Lindsay and Michael Tusk's "pricey" "hot" "newcomer" in a converted Pacific Heights apothecary "is earning some stripes"; "she makes customers feel special" in the "refined", albeit "noisy", 15-table dining room, while his startling "simple", yet "superlative" Italian-French multicourse menu of seasonal, "edible shrines to a few good ingredients" "in the style of Paul Bertolli and Alice Waters" (the duo's training ground) "leave you wanting more" – and not just because "the portions are small."

Ramblas
18 | 17 | 16 | $27 |

557 Valencia St. (bet. 16th & 17th Sts.), 415-565-0207; www.ramblastapas.com

☑ "One of the hippest, most desirable hangouts" in the Mission (with the "loud" noise level to prove it) is this "easygoing" "Barcelona-style" tapas destination that "quickly serves up" Spanish small plates that are "well done, but largely ordinary"; still, it's "not too hard on the wallet", and besides, "after the sangria, do you care if they serve food?"

R & G Lounge
23 | 13 | 15 | $27 |

631 Kearny St. (bet. Clay & Sacramento Sts.), 415-982-7877; www.rnglounge.com

☑ R & G could stand for Refresh and Go at this "mammoth" Chinatown stop where the Cantonese dishes and seafood specialties are "the real thing" and the staff will "serve you fast and get you out the door"; you might not want to linger anyway, as the "overlit" "upstairs has some ambiance, but downstairs has none."

Restaurant LuLu
20 | 19 | 18 | $39 |

816 Folsom St. (bet. 4th & 5th Sts.), 415-495-5775; www.restaurantlulu.com

☑ "Huge portions" in a "huge space" with a "huge noise" (the buzz comes partially from the "bar scene" vibe) sums up this SoMa specialist in spit-roasted meats and "iron skillet–baked mussels"; diners deal with the rotisserie racket "because everyone is having fun" feasting on the French fare they serve "family-style"; but be aware that "you may smell like the brick oven smoke-filled air afterwards."

Rica Restaurant & Bar ☒
– | – | – | M |

1838 Union St. (bet. Laguna & Octavia Sts.), 415-474-3773; www.ricasf.com

Michael Schwab (of the shuttered Charlie's) has hooked up with the team behind Sushi Groove to transform this Cow Hollow space into a hip, new Spanish-Mexican small plates emporium; a hipster crowd lounges in front of plasma screens flashing Spanish art, knocking back fresh-fruit-puree cocktails and zoning out to ambient music.

Ristorante Bacco   23 | 19 | 21 | $36

737 Diamond St. (bet. Elizabeth & 24th Sts.), 415-282-4969

■ Tucked away on a bacco street, this "under-the-radar gem in Noe Valley" is "becoming well known" for "mostly traditional", universally "delicious" Italian eats, like a made-from-scratch risotto that'll "make a grown man cry"; the "real-trattoria" ambiance is as "authentic as the servers", whose "pleasing" efforts charm most.

Ristorante Ideale   ▽ 20 | 17 | 18 | $35

1309 Grant Ave. (Vallejo St.), 415-391-4129

◪ Of all of the establishments in North Beach, locals admire that this "Italian bistro is run by real Italians" – Maurizio and Shanna Bruschi, who provide "clockwork service" and feature "wine at close-to-retail prices"; their rustic food can be "uneven" but "great when it's on"; however, the decor is "struggling", even after a recent remodel.

Ristorante Milano   24 | 16 | 23 | $33

1448 Pacific Ave. (bet. Hyde & Larkin Sts.), 415-673-2961; www.milanosf.com

◪ "The waiters' romantic accents are worth the visit alone", but this "tiny neighborhood institution" in Russian Hill dishes out "exceptional Italian" food – the lasagna and veal favorites for almost 15 years – served by a "charming, knowledgeable owner and host"; its one pinch is the "tight quarters", giving one an unwelcome kinship to the "wonderful sardine appetizer."

Ristorante Umbria ⊠   18 | 15 | 19 | $29

198 Second St. (Howard St.), 415-546-6985

◪ Northern Italian eats can be difficult to come by in SoMa, but "if you're in the area", "good if unimaginative" "basics" are available at this address, particularly if you don't mind dealing with the "crampy space"; to its credit, most agree that it's "a good value" and that the staff "makes you feel like family."

RITZ-CARLTON DINING ROOM ⊠   27 | 27 | 28 | $86

Ritz-Carlton Hotel, 600 Stockton St. (bet. California & Pine Sts.), 415-773-6198; www.ritzcarlton.com

■ "For truth in advertising, they could have named it" the "technically perfect" dining room fawn fanciers of this "formal" Nob Hill address, offering a "privileged" experience in the "grand European tradition"; the setting's "splendor" is outranked only by the "first-class" staff – rated the *Survey*'s No.1 – that serves from "so many carts, you lose count"; the Food score doesn't reflect the arrival of chef Ron Siegel (ex Masa's) who's expected to add slight Asian influences to the "heavenly" New French menu.

Ritz-Carlton Terrace　　24　24　25　$51
Ritz-Carlton Hotel, 600 Stockton St. (bet. California & Pine Sts.), 415-773-6198; www.ritzcarlton.com

■ "Be sure to bring sunglasses when dining on the terrace courtyard" at this "Ritz road less traveled" – "both for the sun and to keep from letting on that you're staring at all the who's-who who are sitting next to you"; the decadent Sunday jazz brunch "in an enchanting garden atmosphere" is the preferred place to "impress out-of-town relatives", but "for those watching the bank account, the weekday Med lunch is an unbelievable deal", especially since it stars the same "spectacular service."

RNM ⬚　　23　24　20　$39
598 Haight St. (Steiner St.), 415-551-7900; www.rnmrestaurant.com

◪ Touted as a "New York lounge" in the "grungy Lower Haight", this sophomore is "more than just another trendy place", thanks to its "inventive", "edgy" New American small plates; the chainmail-lined "living-room atmosphere" attracts a "see-and-be-seen crowd" that "feels a little out of place" for the area – certainly the "downright snooty service" is.

Roe ◗⬚　　－　－　－　M
651 Howard St. (Hawthorne St.), 415-227-0288

Although owner Ben Chu's dad brought Burmese food to the Bay Area two decades ago with Nan Yang Rockridge, this swanky SoMa venue is definitely not his father's restaurant; scattered among the classics are sushi, French fusion ditties like curry-scented lobster bisque and, of course, several types of caviar; but the most radical departure is the ambiance of the bi-level brick building, which rocks with live jazz in the downstairs dining room, while a DJ spins in the upstairs bar.

RoHan Lounge ◗　　▽　19　19　16　$22
3809 Geary Blvd. (bet. 2nd & 3rd Aves.), 415-221-5095; www.rohanlounge.com

■ "The food is just a sidebar to the main course – the soju cocktails" at this "way cool" Inner Richmond lounge, SF's first "bar to be wholly dedicated" to the "Korean vodkalike" drink; still, the "specialty small plates" have Seoul-searchers swearing "Asian fusion never tasted so good", especially when served "in such a subtle, sexy scene."

ROSAMUNDE SAUSAGE GRILL ⊅　　26　10　20　$8
545 Haight St. (bet. Fillmore & Steiner Sts.), 415-437-6851

■ Brat-packers have this "sausage bar's" phone number "programmed into their cell phone", because while it "only does one thing", it does it right; for "the best quick meal in the city", and the *Survey's* Top Bang for the Buck, order "a German, Italian or Californian-style" variation, grab one of the eight stools "or take it to the bar next door" and "pair it with a beer"; the "friendly counter staff" will bring it over and "even put the condiments on for you"; P.S. also serves "fabulous hamburgers on Tuesdays."

Rose Pistola
21 | 20 | 19 | $41 |

532 Columbus Ave. (bet. Green & Union Sts.),
415-399-0499

☑ Still hot as a pistola, this "North Beach staple" is "great for out-of-towners and locals" alike who seek "authentic Ligurian dishes"; though the thorny-tongued feel the menu has a few withered petals, the "snappy surroundings" and "surprisingly good service" alleviate the "extremely noisy" digs; N.B a recent chef departure may affect the Food score.

Rose's Cafe
20 | 18 | 18 | $27 |

2298 Union St. (Steiner St.), 415-775-2200

☑ In Cow Hollow, this "Rose Pistolalike" site (same owners) is a popular "place to mingle" for "tasty" Northern Italian cuisine amid a "yellow-tinted decor"; but it really bursts into bloom at weekend brunch, with "mouthwatering French toast", breakfast pizzas and "good crunchy bacon" – all of which is "made even better when you score an outside table."

Rotee
– | – | – | I |

400 Haight St. (Webster St.), 415-552-8309; www.roteesf.com

Authentic Pakistani-Indian food in an edgy atmosphere is the come-on at this stylish Lower Haight neophyte; while the menu and prices are characteristic of the city's curry shacks, you're also treated to electronica music while you break bread (or rather roti) in a mod, tangerine-tinged interior inspired by the glitzy restaurants found on Bollywood back lots.

Rotunda
20 | 24 | 20 | $36 |

Neiman Marcus, 150 Stockton St. (Geary St.), 415-362-4777;
www.rotundarestaurant.com

☑ "First, shop till you drop, then drop in for the lobster club sandwich" or "ever-so-elegant afternoon tea" in seats surrounding the "splendid stained-glass windows" at this New American inside Neiman Marcus; it's a "must-do for all tourists", given the "beautiful" "Union Square view", but locals "love it too, especially at Christmastime."

Roy's
22 | 22 | 21 | $44 |

575 Mission St. (bet. 1st & 2nd Sts.), 415-777-0277;
www.roysrestaurant.com

☑ While travelers insist "no Roy's can come close to the Honolulu one", this SoMa "mainland clone" is "one of the better branches", with "amazing" Hawaii Regional seafood, "pastel-colored cocktails" and "genuinely hospitable servers" who will "transport you to the islands for the evening"; while the menu looks to the sea, prices "continue to reach for the sky", but there is a "great prix fixe" that "includes their signature chocolate-soufflé cake."

Rubicon ☒   23 | 20 | 23 | $57 |

558 Sacramento St. (bet. Montgomery & Sansome Sts.), 415-434-4100; www.sfrubicon.com

■ Oenophiles happily "cross this Rubicon" just to get a little "tableside education" from Larry Stone, aka "the king of wine"; while his "famous list" of 1,600 labels "rules the roost", there is an "excellent" Cal–New French fine "restaurant attached to it", sporting an "old-school-men's club-meets-California-chic" air and attracting an "A-list" and "business-suit crowd" with its "smart service"; N.B. scores may not reflect chef Stuart Brioza's arrival.

Ruth's Chris Steak House   24 | 20 | 21 | $53 |

1601 Van Ness Ave. (California St.), 415-673-0557; www.ruthschris.com

☑ "The food and atmosphere sizzle" at this Van Ness version of the national steakhouse chain; consumers craving "a nice hunk of grass-munching bovine, drenched in butter" and "generous" sides come for "a guilty pleasure"; some bristle at the gristle of its "old-fashioned, expense-account attitude" and prices, but all admit that the "quality of the meat is fabulous."

Samovar   ▽ 17 | 25 | 18 | $15 |

498 Sanchez St. (18th St.), 415-626-4700; www.samovartea.com

☑ An "impressive variety of international teas", "from vintage to custom blends", is on hand at this "New Age-y" salon, "the Castro's first"; leaf-lovers find the selection and the international array of "light" eats "tea-rific", though pessimists pout it's pretty "pricey for a pot."

Sam's Grill &   21 | 16 | 19 | $37 |
Seafood Restaurant ☒

374 Bush St. (bet. Kearny & Montgomery Sts.), 415-421-0594

■ One feels "hundreds of deals have been done" in the booths by the "old-school" business clientele that patronizes this Downtown seafood house – the first in the city; as befits a place founded in 1866, they "make a virtue of consistency", with sand dabs that still "can't be beat"; and if "the waiters all remember Truman better than your order", "that's part of the charm" of this haven of "SF's halcyon days."

Sanraku Four Seasons   23 | 14 | 18 | $29 |

Sony Metreon Ctr., 101 Fourth St. (Mission St.), 415-369-6166
704 Sutter St. (Taylor St.), 415-771-0803
www.sanraku.com

☑ Satisfied surveyors smile on these sister Japanese joints, whose menu "ranges from the obvious (gyoza) to the obscure (fish cheeks)"; while the SoMa shop is "convenient if you're in the Metreon for a movie", most prefer the "calm" of the "Sutter Street location"; neither has "a lot of atmosphere", but "for the price, one can't complain much."

Savor   18 16 17 $19
3913 24th St. (bet. Noe & Sanchez Sts.), 415-282-0344
◪ Savoring savory and sweet crêpes on the "large backyard patio" or in front of the fireplace is the raison d'être for long weekend lines at this Noe Valley Med, a "kid-friendly" hangout where "even the pickiest eaters will find something that appeals"; "they wouldn't recognize these crêpes in Paris" (smoked salmon is the signature), but "they sure are tasty", as are the "luscious entree-size salads" at dinner.

Scala's Bistro ◕   22 20 20 $41
Sir Francis Drake Hotel, 432 Powell St. (bet. Post & Sutter Sts.), 415-395-8555; www.scalasbistro.com
◪ For "bustling big-city atmosphere", "locals and tourists alike" head Downtown to the Drake Hotel for "ample portions" of "familiar" but "delightful" Northern Italian–Southern French dishes served "pre- or post-theater" by "pleasant personnel"; "everyone seems to be having a good time" – maybe almost too good ("*mamma mia*, is it noisy").

Scoma's   21 17 19 $39
Pier 47, 1 Al Scoma Way (bet. Jefferson & Jones Sts.), 415-771-4383; www.scomas.com
◪ "Feel like a fish in a school of tourists" at this "casual" Fisherman's Wharf seafooder, a "longtime standard-bearer" for "well-prepared", "generous portions" of "the freshest" fish; landlubbers lament that with "too long a wait" and "spotty service", "you pay for the experience" and the sight of "sparkling city lights reflecting off the Bay", but even they are still "suckers for the old place"; P.S. "the Sausalito spin-off has a great view" too.

Seasons   25 25 26 $59
Four Seasons Hotel, 757 Market St. (bet. 3rd & 4th Sts.), 415-633-3838; www.fourseasons.com
◼ "Sure to impress both your palate and your guests", this "true winner" "located in the Four Seasons Hotel" works all year round providing "more-than-exquisite" "Cal-French comfort food", "amazing" city views and "impressive decor" that are second only to a staff that "pampers you to the max" (like "replacing the white napkins with black if you're wearing black"); "bring two credit cards" because it's "expensive – but worth it."

Shalimar/Shalimar Gardens   23 4 9 $14
532 Jones St. (Geary St.), 415-928-0333 ◕⇛
417 O'Farrell St. (bet. Jones & Taylor Sts.), 415-447-4041
1409 Polk St. (Pine St.), 415-776-4642 ⇛
www.shalimarsf.com
◪ "Naan from the gods" and "top-notch tandoori" headline at this trio of cheapo BYOB Pakistani-Indians where fans

overlook "flies buzzing around" and "blank" atmosphere ("decor? what decor? service, ditto") at smoke-filled O'Farrell Street because "the food and spices make your eyes water with delight"; but "a couple bucks more" buys you "alfresco dining" and "table linens" at the Polk and Jones Street branches; N.B. a fourth is in Fremont.

Shanghai 1930
20 | 23 | 18 | $40
133 Steuart St. (bet. Howard & Mission Sts.), 415-896-5600;
www.shanghai1930.com
◪ Taste a "fine" "style of Chinese food not found in many area Chinese" at this "sexy" SoMA "supper club"–cum–"speakeasy" with "real (not smooth) jazz" in the "classy" bar and a "cigar lounge – hooray"; "it's best to go with a few friends or colleagues so you can share hot dishes that are just that"; "service can be off-putting sometimes", and prices might be "a little precious" for "small portions", but the prix fixe lunch is "an unbeatable deal."

Silks
24 | 25 | 25 | $62
Mandarin Oriental Hotel, 222 Sansome St.
(bet. California & Pine Sts.), 415-986-2020;
www.mandarinoriental.com
■ "The ultimate in elegance", this "underutilized" room in the Mandarin Oriental Hotel offers "imaginative" Asian-Cal haute cuisine, "polished service" and "low sound levels" ("you can have a conversation in here!") to those seeking a "self-indulgent" experience without "having to battle a throng of hipsters for a table"; and if that makes it seem "a bit stuffy" to some, scores side with those who smile it's "smooth on everything (but your wallet)."

SLANTED DOOR, THE
26 | 20 | 21 | $40
Ferry Bldg., 1 Ferry Plaza (Market St.), 415-861-8032;
www.slanteddoor.com
◪ There's almost "nothing askew" now that Charles Phan's "mom-and-pop organization" has relocated to "ultrachic" Ferry Building digs (a move the scores may not fully reflect); it's "the paragon of Southeast Asian dining" ("no phooling") where an "eager-to-please wait staff" proffers "intriguing" "modernized Vietnamese" chow and "a hugely innovative" wine list; a few opponents opine it's "overrated and overpriced", but most folks "have never been disappointed, except when they can't get a reservation."

Slow Club
22 | 19 | 19 | $29
2501 Mariposa St. (Hampshire St.), 415-241-9390;
www.slowclub.com
◪ "Show out-of-towners that you're in-the-know" by bringing them to this intimate Mission "industrial hideaway" "that looks like a welder's dream"; the New American menu "offers nice variety" – "whatever sounds the strangest is probably the most delicious", e.g. Gorgonzola dolce latte –

and the "beautifully tattooed staff" are "the hottest", though they sometimes embody the establishment's name.

Sociale ☒ 23 | 21 | 22 | $39 |
3665 Sacramento St. (bet. Locust & Spruce Sts.), 415-921-3200
■ "Everything just works" at this "adorable" Italian "that serves its purpose with flair"; it becomes quite a sociale scene, as converts converge on its Presidio Heights "hidden courtyard" for "intimate" meals chosen from an "eclectic menu", steered by "friendly, informed servers."

South Park Cafe ☒ 23 | 18 | 20 | $34 |
Jack London Sq., 108 South Park St. (bet. 2nd & 3rd Sts.), 415-495-7275
■ "While it doesn't have the hustle and bustle it did during the dot-com days", this "enduring", *très petit* French bistro opposite "quiet, sunny South Park" "stays its course"; "locals" say *oui* to the "charming style" of its "polite, down-to-earth service", "summer sidewalk patio" and most of all its "quick (or not so quick) informal meals" of "delicious no-frills food in a super-frills town."

Stinking Rose, The 15 | 17 | 16 | $30 |
325 Columbus Ave. (bet. Broadway & Vallejo Sts.), 415-781-7673; www.thestinkingrose.com
☑ T-shirt–buying tourists are drawn to the perfume of this "garlic-lover's paradise" in North Beach, where every "breathtaking" (literally) Cal–Northern Italian dish contains the namesake; but unfortunately there's also an unsavory aroma of "service and quality that are lacking"; in short, everyone should "go and be garlic-ized" once – but "once is enough."

STRAITS CAFE 22 | 20 | 18 | $33 |
3300 Geary Blvd. (Parker Ave.), 415-668-1783; www.straitsrestaurants.com
■ In the Inner Richmond, surveyors head strait for "the ultimate in Pan-Asian", Singapore-style, which means "flavor-packed" "interestingly spicy" "small-plate dining", plus "cocktails that are not to be overlooked" in a "nicely appointed setting"; perhaps the service needs a little straitening out, but that's a minor quibble for a place that "doesn't screw up the fusion theme like others do"; P.S. there are several venues South of SF, including San Jose's "hot, trendy Santana Row."

Street Restaurant 22 | 16 | 19 | $30 |
2141 Polk St. (Vallejo St.), 415-775-1055; www.streetonpolk.com
☑ "It's worth the wait" for "simple, New American" comfort food "like mom makes" ("save room for the bread pudding") in this "dark", "cramped" Polk Street Gulch "neighborhood joint"; the "noise level can be really disruptive" but "the owner treats you right", providing "well-priced" "ample

portions" that taste "great on a drizzly SF evening", "once you finally get in the door" ("no reservations taken").

Suppenküche　　21 16 18 $28
601 Hayes St. (Laguna St.), 415-252-9289; www.suppenkuche.com
■ "It's Oktoberfest" in Hayes Valley, so "bring your appetite" for "heavy and hearty" "home cooking, German-style" (which means "enough for lunch the next day"), and "boots full of beer"; "be prepared to be social" because "it's virtually impossible to hold a normal conversation" at the "shared, long, wooden tables" in the "bare-bones" room; for service, just "bang your tankard."

Sushi Groove　　23 20 17 $35
1516 Folsom St. (bet. 11th & 12th Sts.), 415-503-1950 🖻
1916 Hyde St. (bet. Green & Union Sts.), 415-440-1905
■ Finatics "crave the Groove" for "great quality" sushi with "imagination" and "attitude" at "two locations with very different feels": the Russian Hill spot is "a great date place" with low lighting, while its "sexier" sibling to the south "feels like SoHo in SoMa"; both are "surprisingly cool" (if somewhat "pretentious") hangs for "beautiful people" that are "pricey for a reason" – i.e. "solid" fare that's "worth dealing with the horrible parking situation" and "cramped quarters."

Swan Oyster Depot 🖻⊄　　25 11 22 $26
1517 Polk St. (bet. California & Sacramento Sts.), 415-673-1101
■ "Slurp down" "heaven on a half-shell" at this "historic" cash-only oyster bar on Polk Street serving up "the freshest seafood" ("any fresher and you'd be eating underwater") "and not much else"; it's "not as cheap as its decor suggests", and you can expect to "stand in line to sit on wobbly, uncomfortable stools at an ancient marble counter", but the "fabulous" fare and the "charming" brothers preparing it make it worthwhile; N.B. the take-out counter and bar closes at 5:20 PM.

Tablespoon　　21 18 19 $37
2209 Polk St. (Vallejo St.), 415-268-0140
■ From a highly pedigreed pair of owners, chef Robert Riescher (ex Erna's Elderberry House) and manager John Jasso (ex Gary Danko), this "brilliant, noisy and narrow" New American is an "up-and-comer" on the "Polk Street scene"; though it retains the same "sleek" look as its predecessor Spoon, the "interesting menu" and "well-thought-out wine list" are "outstandingly original" and the service is "sublime"; "if it weren't so hard to book or impossible to park", most would "return in a heartbeat."

Tadich Grill 🖻　　21 17 18 $36
240 California St. (bet. Battery & Front Sts.), 415-391-1849
■ A "SF tradition for fish lovers", "California's oldest restaurant" "still charms", with "gruff waiters" serving

"huge portions" of "old-school grill classics" ("the cioppino can't be beat") in "spartan" Downtown digs sporting "cramped booths", a "bustling counter" and an ambiance "akin to a dry martini"; fans say "no trip is complete without it", but advise "going for lunch" only, since it's "packed every night with tourists" and a "convention crowd."

Taiwan
17 | 6 | 11 | $14

445 Clement St. (6th Ave.), 415-387-1789
See review in East of San Francisco Directory.

Takara
▽ 22 | 14 | 19 | $27

22 Peace Plaza (bet. Laguna & Webster Sts.), 415-921-2000
■ Among the sea of restaurants in Japantown, this one stands out for an "unusual selection" of "harder-to-find" "homestyle" dishes besides sushi, such as rice cooked in an "iron pot", shabu-shabu and sukiyaki prepared tableside by Japanese matrons who are wont to "boss you around"; some yen-watchers yelp "it seems a bit pricey", but for many the "combo dinners and lunches" are a "great value."

Tallula
23 | 23 | 19 | $38

4230 18th St. (bet. Collingwood & Diamond Sts.), 415-437-6722;
www.tallulasf.com
■ Groupies gush this "sexy" Castrolite is "the most exquisite restaurant to show up in years", offering "the latest twist on the small-plates craze", a "memorable" marriage of "Indian and French cuisines", served by a "knowledgeable staff"; the "romantic" converted tri-level Victorian is divided into a "labyrinth" of opulently colored dining rooms and a "cute bar area" where a "beautiful crowd" can be seen sipping "clever" sake cocktails.

Tao Cafe
▽ 20 | 21 | 18 | $27

1000 Guerrero St. (22nd St.), 415-641-9955; www.taocafe.com
■ Run by a "French-Vietnamese woman who has stories to tell", this "adorable" colonial-looking corner cafe in the Mission is "much nicer than most", offering a menu of "mostly hits" made with "very fresh ingredients"; though some grouse the "service moves like a speeding glacier", most agree that "dining here is a real pleasure" and wonder why this "sleeper" doesn't get "more press."

Taqueria Can-Cun ●⊄
23 | 7 | 14 | $8

1003 Market St. (6th St.), 415-864-6773
2288 Mission St. (19th St.), 415-252-9560
3211 Mission St. (Valencia St.), 415-550-1414
☑ "What appears to be just another taqueria" chain with "rock-bottom prices" is home to what amigos attest is the "paramount burrito", which leaves "all others humbled"; "the keys are the grilled tortillas, avocado chunks" and "two kinds of [spicy] salsa" that give it "that added textural experience", while "festive murals and streamers transform it into a little Mexican pueblo."

Tartare 🅾️ — — — E
550 Washington St. (bet. Montgomery & Sansome Sts.),
415-434-3100; www.tartarerestaurant.com
Chef George Morrone (ex Fifth Floor) is back wowing
Downtowners at this smart New French newcomer whose
menu may be half-baked – it's built around five tartares
(including ostrich, fruit and ahi versions), two carpaccios
and raw oysters, along with heated entrees – but is hardly
un-thought-out; the small, cozy rectangular dining room
features warm, wood-toned walls and a black-leather-
lattice arched ceiling.

TARTINE BAKERY 26 15 13 $13
600 Guerrero St. (18th St.), 415-487-2600; www.tartinebakery.com
☑ Sugar-happy habitués "drool all over the pastry displays"
brimming with "the best" baked goods "this side of
anywhere" and fab Frenchified sandwiches at this "hotter-
than-hot" Mission bakery/cafe, and "never leave without a
full belly and bag for later"; though cynics get a good
"laugh" at the "scattered", "snooty staff", "ridiculously
long lines and lack of seating", they admit they "keep
coming back" nonetheless.

Taylor's Automatic Refresher 22 14 16 $15
Ferry Bldg., 1 Ferry Plaza (Market St.), 866-328-3663;
www.taylorsrefresher.com
See review in North of San Francisco Directory.

Ten-Ichi 20 14 19 $28
2235 Fillmore St. (bet. Clay & Sacramento Sts.), 415-346-3477;
www.tenichisf.com
☑ An Upper Fillmore "neighborhood institution" for more
than 25 years, this "low-key" shop is "more than a sushi"
joint (though it's known for its "infamous" Indian Summer
roll), serving "all the great Japanese favorites" like sukiyaki
and udon "for those who like their food cooked"; however,
"shopworn decor" and uneven service limit its appeal.

Thai House 21 14 20 $20
2200 Market St. (bet. 15th & Sanchez Sts.), 415-864-5006
151 Noe St. (Henry St.), 415-863-0374
■ These Siamese twins purvey "the best Thai in the Castro"
according to fans, though in less-than-identical settings:
while Noe Street is more of a "cozy" "neighborhood
townhouse", its more visible Market Street sibling, dubbed
"ThaIHOP" for its "pancake-house" look, offers "a window
on the world" and outdoor seating; neither one is "too
pricey" or presents "too much reservation hassle."

Thanh Long 25 16 19 $41
4101 Judah St. (46th Ave.), 415-665-1146; www.anfamily.com
☑ "Like its more expensive sister, Crustacean", "roasted
crab" "cooked so many ways" "is king" at this "laid-back"

but still "pricey" Outer Sunset Vietnamese, and the "famous garlic noodles" are "to die for"; stick to those items and "you can't go wrong", for the rest of the menu isn't "worth the trip to the boondocks" advise insiders, who also suggest you get cracking about making reservations and "don't bring the nice clothes", because it can get "messy."

Thep Phanom Thai Cuisine   25 | 17 | 19 | $26
400 Waller St. (Fillmore St.), 415-431-2526
☑ "Thep Phenomenal" is what pad-estrians call this "remarkable" Lower Haight spot that's "one of the best" "in a city with a Thai joint on every corner", thanks to "outstanding", "flavorful" fare served by a "welcoming staff" in a "living room" setting; it's "always crowded" and the "cramped" layout "makes you feel like you're in Bangkok – among 20 million people", which is why "reservations are a must" (or else "arrive early") and some "good parking karma" helps, too.

Three Seasons   22 | 19 | 17 | $31
3317 Steiner St. (bet. Chestnut & Lombard Sts.), 415-567-9989;
www.threeseasonsrestaurant.com
☑ "It's swank, it's cheap, it's moan-with-pleasure delicious" gush groupies of this "energetic, noisy" Marina Vietnamese about its "excellent variety" of "awesome spring rolls and potstickers" and other small and large plates "with way more than three seasons to tempt the taste buds"; while the service can be "spotty", the staff is "always welcoming"; P.S. the "beautiful dining room" at the Palo Alto location has boosted the Decor score, but the Walnut Creek branch is new and unrated.

Ti Couz   21 | 15 | 15 | $21
3108 16th St. (Valencia St.), 415-252-7373
☑ "SF's original" "design-your-own" crêperie is "still the place for an economical" meal while you "watch the world" of the Mission; the galettes are "deceptively filling" and "you want to make sure you have room" for the "aphrodisiacal dessert" varieties, or other Bretagne fare and Celtic beers; razzers rap the "way too long waits" and "snooty" service, but many "keep coming back" for "delectable food for a pittance."

Tita's hale 'aina 🖾   ▽ 19 | 14 | 19 | $18
3870 17th St. (bet. Noe & Sanchez Sts.), 415-626-2477;
www.titashaleaina.com
■ Savvy surveyors swear there's "*no ka oi* (no finer place)" for "a taste of the islands in SF" than this "quirky" "mom-and-pop" shop in the Castro, where the "fantastic Kalua pig" with "two scoops" of rice and "plate lunches" are "better here than at most places in Hawaii"; "don't expect too much atmosphere" in the "tired" looking room, but "dis is da place for great brunch" at "reasonable prices";

N.B. there's a luau with live entertainment on the last Friday of every month.

Tokyo Go Go   23 | 21 | 18 | $33
3174 16th St. (bet. Guerrero & Valencia Sts.), 415-864-2288; www.tokyogogo.com
■ A "hipper-than-thou" Japanese *izakaya* with "pop sensibilities", this Mission spot offers "pristine piscine creations" and "creative" Pan-Asian apps ("to-die-for miso-marinated sea bass") that "far surpass" the offerings of many "other hipster sushi joints", at "more affordable" prices; "loud" "club music" fills the "modern room" where "hot waitresses" attend to a "good-looking" "trendy" crowd.

Tommaso's   24 | 14 | 17 | $24
1042 Kearny St. (bet. Broadway St. & Pacific Ave.), 415-398-9696
■ "Cue up *The Godfather* theme" because you'll be "treated like family" at this "old-school" North Beach Southern Italian hidden in "what appears to be a cellar" where thin-crust pizzas baked in a "wood-fired brick oven" (circa 1935) and "standards made the right way" are served with pitchers of "house red" at a "long table"; its location "amid the strip clubs" may "not be the best for families with kids", and "no reservations" can add up to "long waits."

Tommy Toy's Cuisine Chinoise   23 | 23 | 23 | $55
655 Montgomery St. (bet. Clay & Washington Sts.), 415-397-4888; www.tommytoys.com
◪ Don your jacket and tie and pretend to be "an emperor for the evening" at this "star-studded" "fancy Chinese" ("with a French accent") known for its "Asian glitz" and "constantly over-the-shoulder service"; admirers advise "the tasting menu is clearly the way to go", be it for a "businessman's lunch" or to "celebrate a birthday", but cynics warn "don't get Shanghaied" by the "extravagant" experience that requires "a mortgage at the end to pay for it all."

Tonga Room   11 | 25 | 14 | $36
Fairmont Hotel, 950 Mason St. (California St.), 415-772-5278; www.fairmont.com
◪ "If you missed the Tiki Room at Disneyland", fans tout this "gleefully kitschy" Pan-Asian "theme bar" and restaurant in the Fairmont Hotel, where "umbrella drinks", "fake indoor monsoons" and a "cheesy" Polynesian "band on a boat" in a pond await; though surveyors "wouldn't say much about the food" except that it's "overpriced", for many it's a "classic place to take" a "large goofy group" for happy hour, when the "foo foo drinks" "are actually affordable."

Ton Kiang   25 | 13 | 16 | $25
5821 Geary Blvd. (bet. 22nd & 23rd Aves.), 415-387-8273; www.tonkiang.com
■ "You'd think this is the only dim sum place in town" judging from the "lines stretching around the corner" on

weekends, as shu mai mavens flock to this Outer Richmond spot for "fresh, inventive", "amazing dumplings" "rolling your way" "all day long" in a "plain" but "clean, well-lit room"; it might be pricier "than most others" in the area, but it's one of the "best in the city", and "one of the few that serves Hakka cuisine" at dinner; P.S. insiders advise "going before 11 AM."

Tonno Rosso
– | – | – | M

Hotel Griffon, 155 Steuart St. (bet. Howard & Mission Sts.), 415-495-6500; www.tonnorosso.com

There's nothing fishy going on at the Hotel Griffon's replacement to Red Herring, which features regional Italian cuisine overseen by chef Ryan Johnston (ex Bouchon); the dining room has been transformed into an Italianate beauty replete with antique mirrors, ornate chandeliers and a tile-decorated hearth for cooking meats, but still sports its predecessor's exhibition kitchen and Bay Bridge views.

Town Hall
23 | 21 | 20 | $45

342 Howard St. (Fremont St.), 415-908-3900; www.townhallsf.com

◪ Rub elbows with "politicos and socialites" and tuck into "creative" "New Orleans–influenced" New American cuisine and "upstaging desserts" at this "new new thing" in SoMa from chef-brothers Mitchell and Steven Rosenthal (who continue to share the toque title at Postrio) and "quintessential host Doug Washington"; though critics cavil about the "acoustically challenged" "exposed-brick" interior and service "jitters" that "need to be worked out", most agree the "food is worthy of a repeat."

Town's End Restaurant & Bakery
22 | 15 | 18 | $24

South Beach Marina Apts., 2 Townsend St. (The Embarcadero), 415-512-0749

■ "Scrambled eggs, venture capital deals" and pre-game tailgaters "mix together in one of SF's best see-and-be-seen brunch hangouts", a New American eatery located "right on the Embarcadero" ("get there early because it's packed by 9 AM"); "the basket of mini-muffins" "served before your food arrives" is "reason enough to go", but so is the outdoor seating where you can "enjoy the Bay and sunshine on a nice day", and the "hugely economical" prix fixe dinner on Tuesdays.

Trattoria Contadina
24 | 17 | 22 | $32

1800 Mason St. (Union St.), 415-982-5728

■ "Be with the locals" and "watch the cable car go by" at this "down-home, funky traditional" North Beach Italian "off the beaten path", where organic vegetables and fresh meat and fish go into "classic cuisine done very well", "without any unnecessary flash", and the staff is always "eager to please"; the "tight" space is usually "crowded", so "get there early or make reservations."

Tre Fratelli
18 | – | 19 | $31

(fka I Fratelli)

Del Monte Cannery, 2801 Leavenworth St. (Beach St.),
415-474-8240

◪ This "solid, family-style" "neighborhood Italian" has "survived the test of time" (25 years!) with "reasonably priced" if "standard" fare and a "staff that is super-nice" – "if you're a local"; its new, larger digs in the Cannery boast French doors and a menu that features fresh fish from nearby Wharf vendors.

Truly Mediterranean
23 | 6 | 14 | $10

3109 16th St. (Valencia St.), 415-252-7482
627 Vallejo St. (Columbus St.), 415-362-2636
www.trulymed.com

■ "A great break from burritos" in the Mission can be found at this "truly great grab-and-go" Middle Eastern emporium that "takes pride in the food"; "no-frills good chow" like falafel and schwarma comes at "bargain-bin prices", but seats are few and decor is almost nonexistent; N.B. there are branches in North Beach and Berkeley.

Tsunami Sushi & Sake Bar ●☒
▽ 22 | 21 | 20 | $32

1308 Fulton St. (Divisadero St.), 415-567-7664;
www.tsunami-sf.com

◪ Riding the wave of hipster raw-fish joints, this dimly lit Western Addition Japanese with a '70s aesthetic stands out with its "impressive" selection of "premium sakes" (45) and "tremendously helpful" staff; while purists sniff that it's "more of a drinking bar with a sushi menu", finatics laud the fin fare as "some of the freshest around"; N.B. the kitchen serves until midnight, while the bar stays open until 2 AM.

Tu Lan ☒⌀
23 | 2 | 10 | $11

8 Sixth St. (Market St.), 415-626-0927

◪ "Saigon meets Sixth Street" at this Vietnamese "dive" in an "iffy neighborhood" of SoMa, but "the food rocks", particularly the imperial rolls (registering a substantial jump in its Food score), so enthusiasts urge "don't let the scary location keep you away"; a recent remodeling has improved the decor "from minimal to tolerable" and the staff works with "unworldly efficiency."

2223 Restaurant
21 | 19 | 20 | $35

2223 Market St. (bet. Noe & Sanchez Sts.), 415-431-0692

■ "Still going strong after all these years", this "boisterous" "no-name" New American with "an easy-to-remember address" "right on the Market Street trolley line" reigns as the "classiest in the Castro"; its "atmospheric" scene is always "hopping with" the "queer" eye along with the "straight" guy (or couple) tucking into "inventive comfort food", "heavenly weekend brunch" and "killer cocktails" delivered by "flirty" "waiters as pithy as juice."

Universal Cafe
22 16 18 $32

2814 19th St. (bet. Bryant & Florida Sts.), 415-821-4608

◪ The "eclectic clientele" "comes back for seconds" of "fresh, imaginative" New American "comfort food, gourmet style" at this Mission "gem", where the menu changes with each rotation of the Earth; the "light-filled hi-tech space" is "a combination of hip and intimate", but "don't expect much privacy" in the "busy, cramped" environs.

Valentina Ristorante
▽ 18 15 16 $27

419 Cortland Ave. (Bennington St.), 415-285-6000

◪ This "cute little" Northern Italian on the main drag of Bernal Heights is a "lovely neighborhood spot for homey Italian food", including lots of "Ligurian specialties" and vegetarian options; the staff is "welcoming" but occasionally "spacey", while the space, with its walls airbrushed to resemble a sunset and other decorative touches, is "interesting."

Venticello
24 21 22 $40

1257 Taylor St. (Washington St.), 415-922-2545;
www.venticello.com

■ "Take your valentine" to this "very romantic" Nob Hill trattoria where you can "sit by the fireplace and stare into your lover's eyes" over "consistently excellent" Northern Italian dishes (for an extra dose of romance, "take the cable car to get there; it stops right in front"); the servers not only "know what they are doing" but they also "seem to enjoy it."

Vicolo
19 8 11 $17

201 Ivy St. (bet. Franklin & Gough Sts.), 415-863-2382;
www.hayesstreetgrill.com/vicolo

◪ Pennywise pie-zanos looking for a pre-symphony repast are pleased by the pizzas with the "crisp cornmeal crust" at this "casual, order-at-the-counter" spot in Hayes Valley; add a "fresh salad" and a glass from the "tiny but imaginative wine list" and you've got a "fast meal in the performing arts neighborhood", even if the service is "not that organized or gracious"; now if only they would "bring back dessert."

Vivande Porta Via
22 14 16 $33

2125 Fillmore St. (bet. California & Sacramento Sts.),
415-346-4430; www.vivande.com

◪ Carlo Middione offers "consistently fine, creative" Italian fare ("why can't anyone else do fettuccine like this?") at his "easily missed, but not to be overlooked" restaurant and gourmet shop on Fillmore; while the tightly packed rows of tables near the deli counter and "hectic" service gives it the aura of an authentic "Roman trattoria", that also makes many "pick up" a bag of "expensive" goodies and "*mangia*" elsewhere.

Walzwerk ⊠   ▽ 19 17 17 $27

381 S. Van Ness Ave. (bet. 14th & 15th Sts.), 415-551-7181;
www.walzwerk.com

■ "Feel as if you are in a Berlin living room where your
friends have rustled you up some schnitzel" at this "funky
Mission District hole-in-the-wall" where the "delightful
East German food defies unpleasant stereotypes" and the
"amazingly friendly staff" "takes good care of everyone";
the setting is a bit "stark" (think "behind the iron curtain"),
but *die freunden* find it "arty" and "absolutely fabulous."

Wasabi & Ginger   ▽ 22 13 19 $29

2299 Van Ness Ave. (Vallejo St.), 415-345-1368

☑ "You would never know from the exterior" or "drab"
"bad '70s" decor of this "unassuming" Marina "gem" that
it serves such "fantastic, fresh" raw fin fare, which is why
some call it the "unsung hero of the SF sushi scene"; "get
friendly with the chef and sit at the bar" recommend
regulars who always appreciate the "free edamame and
red bean ice cream."

Washington Square Bar & Grill   18 18 19 $34

1707 Powell St. (bet. Columbus & Union Sts.), 415-982-8123

☑ "A refreshing change from über-trendy space-age sushi
restaurants", this "happy throwback" serves "solid"
New American–Northern Italian cuisine in an "attractive
room" with a "lively atmosphere" and "jazz playing in the
background" nightly; while some suspect that it's "living
on its reputation" as Herb Caen's beloved 'Washbag',
you can always "meet some real characters at the bar"
"pontificating on the world's problems."

Watercress   21 18 19 $31

(fka Watergate)

1152 Valencia St. (bet. 22nd & 23rd Sts.), 415-648-6000

☑ Since moving its "more pricey predecessor" Watergate
to Nob Hill, the owners of this Mission spot are "embracing
economizing with cheaper" Cantonese-French fusion fare
in a "very pretty" "boîte that gives the feeling of a much
more expensive venue"; "lots of people on first or second
dates" flock here for the prix fixe dinner that "gets you any
three courses for $19.95", but "beware the [high] corkage
fee" and service that swings from "friendly" to "rude."

Waterfront Restaurant & Cafe   17 23 17 $43

Pier 7, The Embarcadero (Broadway St.), 415-391-2696;
www.waterfrontsf.com

☑ "When the weather is perfect", "the view of the Bay
Bridge and San Francisco Bay" "approaches the divine"
extol enthusiasts of this Embarcadero establishment that
"serves both basic and dressed up" "fresh seafood" and
Cal fare in a dining room with "graduated table tiers" and
a "glass-protected" "outdoor patio"; cynics sniff that it

might be a contender "with improved food" and service that wasn't so "snooty."

Watergate　　22　17　19　$43
1177 California St. (bet. Jones & Taylor Sts.), 415-474-2000;
www.watergaterestaurant.com
☑ Fans insist "it's worth the crawl through the lobby" of a Nob Hill high-rise to enter this French-Asian production, and while "the move from the Mission made for a change of clientele" and "the prix fixe has gone up a few bucks", aficionados are still "awed by the food"; deep-throated detractors deride the "tired '70s decor", "weak wine list" and "slow service", but by "fine dining" standards, it's an "unbelievably good deal."

Woodward's Garden ⌧　　24　17　22　$42
1700 Mission St. (Duboce St.), 415-621-7122;
www.woodwardsgarden.com
☑ "Perfect for an intimate special occasion or date", this "cute" little Mission "gem" offers "impeccably prepared New American cuisine" and "wonderful" service in a "quaint", "homey interior" with "soft lighting"; killjoys find the "strange layout" "small" and a bit "depressing" (even though it's brighter since a nearby section of the freeway was torn down) and suggest management "hire a painter."

XYZ　　19　21　18　$43
W Hotel, 181 Third St. (Howard St.), 415-817-7836;
www.xyz-sf.com
☑ The arrival of star chef Malachi Harland has "brought new life" to this SoMa New American housed "in the hip W Hotel", where many have been "pleasantly surprised by the food and knowledgeable waiters"; cynics, however, feel the "distressingly average" fare and "ultra-pompous" service don't match the "sophisticated surroundings", sniffing that "it's overrated by the 'in'-crowd."

Yabbies Coastal Kitchen　　23　18　21　$39
2237 Polk St. (bet. Green & Vallejo Sts.), 415-474-4088;
www.yabbiesrestaurant.com
☑ This "little-known gem on Polk Street" is "crowded for a reason" – or several, namely, its menu of "delicious fish and shellfish" (the tuna poke in particular "floats the boat" of many finatics), "excellent wine list", "accommodating staff" and "sophisticated" decor; a few wonder "what all the fuss is about", but for many it's a "reliable standard."

YANK SING　　25　17　18　$32
Rincon Ctr., 101 Spear St. (bet. Howard & Mission Sts.),
415-957-9300
49 Stevenson St. (bet. 1st & 2nd Sts.), 415-541-4949
www.yanksing.com
■ "Yum yum dim sum" "is the name of the game" at this Downtown dumpling duo where an "endless parade" of

"ever-circulating carts" delivers "delectable tidbits" "piping hot and fresh" in an "upscale setting"; the service is solid and "nobody goes away hungry", "but oh boy, can the bill get out of control" if you're not careful; P.S. "they take reservations, bless them."

Yianni's ▽ 16 | 15 | 19 | $24
1708 Church St. (29th St.), 415-647-3200;
www.yiannisgreekcuisine.com
☑ "For a nice change of pace", this "traditional" homey Hellenic in Noe Valley warms the spirit "on a cold night" with a "friendly" staff and plenty of ouzo on offer; while it's a "big step up from gyros on a stick", purists pooh-pooh the "inconsistent" fare that "seems to be a blend of Cal-Greek and doesn't excel in either category", and decor that's "nothing special."

Yuet Lee ●⊄ 20 | 5 | 13 | $17
1300 Stockton St. (Broadway St.), 415-982-6020
■ "Don't be deterred by the decor" or "intense fluorescent lights" at this Chinatown "greasy spoon" and "late-night ramen savior" lest you miss the "wonderful seafood" and "no-frills" Cantonese grub served until 3 AM by an "efficient" staff; "how does something brought out in five minutes taste so good?" marvel fans of the "killer" salt-and-pepper squid and "fish pulled straight from the tank."

Yukol Place Thai Cuisine ▽ 21 | 12 | 20 | $20
2380 Lombard St. (bet. Pierce & Scott Sts.),
415-922-1599
☑ "Wonderful people, wonderful food" win applause for this Thai serving "innovative" dishes and "consistently good curries", whether you "eat in" or "take out"; "the only shame is that the location" (smack on Lombard Street) "lacks charm."

Yumma's 20 | 10 | 16 | $10
721 Irving St. (bet. 8th & 9th Aves.), 415-682-0762
☑ "Get your fix of Middle Eastern flavors" – from a "good selection of wraps" to "lamb kebabs that melt in your mouth" – at this Inner Sunset spot "popular with the UCSF crowd", not least because it's "fast and cheap"; the "small garden out back" is more appealing than the interior, and it's always "great for takeout"; N.B. all meats are organic.

Zante's Pizza & Indian Cuisine 20 | 7 | 12 | $17
3489 Mission St. (Cortland St.), 415-821-3949;
www.zantespizza.com
☑ The "multi-culti" curry pizza at this Bernal Heights Indian "sounds strange" but it's "tough to beat", especially "when your wallet is running low" attest aficionados; "hot and fast delivery" makes it an even more appealing option, though, since "the decor leaves something – well, everything – to be desired" and "service is shoddy."

Zao Noodle Bar   15 | 12 | 14 | $16

2406 California St. (Fillmore St.), 415-345-8088
2031 Chestnut St. (Fillmore St.), 415-928-3088
3583 16th St. (bet. Market & Noe Sts.), 415-864-2888
www.zao.com
☑ "Fast food with a healthy twist" can be found at this Pan-Asian noodle chain that offers "large, flavorful servings" to "the college crowd"; though the fare's "not very authentic" and the service is "variable", it's "reliable", "quick and cheap"; N.B. there are additional branches in Palo Alto and Emeryville.

Zaré ☒   23 | 22 | 23 | $44

568 Sacramento St. (bet. Montgomery & Sansome Sts.),
415-291-9145; www.zarerestaurant.com
■ "Varied, semi-exotic and plentiful" Mediterranean fare awaits at this "country inn in the middle of Downtown" where chef-owner Hoss Zaré makes you "feel like a guest in his home" with little touches such as roses for female patrons; the "small but comfortable dining room" attracts a clientele "in their 40s" who find the "wonderful food" and "sexy surroundings" "a delight to the senses."

Zarzuela ☒   23 | 16 | 20 | $32

2000 Hyde St. (Union St.), 415-346-0800
■ For a "nice dash of Spanish cuisine in Russian Hill" "without breaking the bank", amigos approve of this Iberian specializing in "delicately spiced" tapas and "lethal" sangria; the staff is "charming" and "caring" and the intimate dining room is equally "fantastic" for a date or "to bring a group of friends", but "be prepared to wait for a table."

Zazie   21 | 18 | 18 | $23

941 Cole St. (bet. Carl St. & Parnassus Ave.), 415-564-5332
☑ Tucked into Cole Valley, this "sweet" French bistro is "the neighborhood's most popular brunch spot", and an "excellent choice for every meal of the day"; "expect to wait", especially for the "lovely outdoor patio when the fog's not rolling in", but you'll be rewarded with "delicious" fare, "quiet conversation" and "warm, friendly service."

ZUNI CAFE ◐   24 | 20 | 20 | $43

1658 Market St. (bet. Franklin & Gough Sts.), 415-552-2522
☑ "One of the great SF dining parties" takes place nightly at Judy Rodgers' perennially hot boîte, where the "who's who" "meet and eat" "till the wee hours" in the "fab glass-walled" space "with a Market Street view"; after 25 years, "she may be tired of making the roasted chicken and bread dish, but that's too darn bad", because it's so darn good — as is the "perfect burger" and Med dishes "cooked over an open fire"; "service is sometimes snooty, but if you can overlook that", you'll have a "phenomenal" time.

East of San Francisco

Top Ratings

Except where indicated by a ∇, top lists exclude places with low voting.

Top Food

27 Chez Panisse
   Erna's Elderberry
   Rivoli
   Chez Panisse Café
26 Bay Wolf
   Kirala
   Dopo
   Lalime's
25 Zachary's Pizza
   Oliveto

   Vik's Chaat
24 Wente Vineyards
   Jojo
   PlumpJack
   À Côté
   Soizic
   Cafe Esin
   Uzen
   Tratt. La Siciliana
   Soi 4

By Cuisine

American
24 Cafe Esin
22 Lark Creek
   Rick & Ann's
   Bette's Oceanview
21 Mama's Royal

Californian
27 Chez Panisse
   Chez Panisse Café
24 Wente Vineyards
   PlumpJack
   Soizic

Chinese
22 Shen Hua
   Great China
21 Rest. Peony
19 Little Shin Shin
   Jade Villa

French
27 Erna's Elderberry
24 Jojo
   À Côté
   Citron
23 Café Fanny

Indian
25 Vik's Chaat
23 Ajanta
   Shalimar
21 Pakwan
   Breads of India

Italian
26 Dopo
25 Oliveto
24 Tratt. La Siciliana
23 Prima
22 Postino

Japanese
26 Kirala
24 Uzen
22 O Chamé
21 Grasshopper
18 Yoshi's

Mediterranean
27 Chez Panisse
   Rivoli
   Chez Panisse Café
26 Bay Wolf
   Lalime's

Mexican/Pan-Latin
24 Doña Tomás
23 Fonda Solana
21 Cactus Taqueria
   Picante Cocina
17 Juan's Place

Southeast Asian
24 Soi 4
23 Le Cheval
21 Grasshopper
20 Battambang
19 Plearn Thai

By Special Feature

Breakfast/Brunch
27 Erna's Elderberry
25 Oliveto
24 Wente Vineyards
   PlumpJack
23 Café Fanny

Late Night
23 Fonda Solana
   Koryo BBQ
20 Everett & Jones
19 Caspers Hot Dogs
17 Taiwan

Newcomers (Rated/Unrated)
26 Dopo
23 La Rose Bistro▽
– Eccolo
– Pearl Oyster Bar
– Va de Vi

Outdoor Seating
26 Bay Wolf
25 Oliveto
24 Wente Vineyards
   À Côté
   Doña Tomás

People-Watching
27 Chez Panisse Café
24 À Côté
23 César
21 Grasshopper
   downtown

Romance
27 Chez Panisse
   Erna's Elderberry
26 Lalime's
24 Wente Vineyards
   Citron

Small Plates
24 À Côté
   Soi 4
23 Fonda Solana
21 Grasshopper
   OnoMazé

Winning Wine Lists
27 Chez Panisse
   Erna's Elderberry
   Chez Panisse Café
23 César
   Prima

By Location

Berkeley
27 Chez Panisse
   Rivoli
   Chez Panisse Café
26 Kirala
   Lalime's

Oakland
26 Bay Wolf
   Dopo
25 Zachary's Pizza
   Oliveto
24 Jojo

Top Decor

28	Ahwahnee		Trader Vic's
26	Erna's Elderberry		O Chamé
25	Wente Vineyards		Zax Tavern
	Postino		Garibaldis
24	Bridges Rest.		Bay Wolf
	Chez Panisse		Blackhawk Grille
23	Skates on Bay	*21*	Prima
	Rivoli		Fonda Solana
22	Chez Panisse Café		Venezia
	Oliveto		Yoshi's

Top Service

27	Erna's Elderberry	*22*	Zax Tavern
25	Chez Panisse		Prima
24	Lalime's		PlumpJack
	Bay Wolf		Soizic
	Chez Panisse Café		Jojo
	Rivoli	*21*	Bridges Rest.
23	Wente Vineyards		Oliveto
	Dopo		Postino
	Citron		Ajanta
	Cafe Esin		Vic Stewart's

Top Bangs for the Buck

1.	Caspers Hot Dogs	11.	Bette's Oceanview
2.	Cactus Taqueria	12.	Barney Hamburger
3.	Truly Med.	13.	Zachary's Pizza
4.	Caffe 817	14.	Naan 'n Curry
5.	Vik's Chaat	15.	Blackberry Bistro
6.	Mama's Royal	16.	Jimmy Bean's
7.	Fenton's Creamery	17.	FatApple's
8.	Picante Cocina	18.	Juan's Place
9.	Café Fanny	19.	Rick & Ann's
10.	Asqew Grill	20.	Blue Nile

East of San Francisco

F	D	S	C

À Côté
24 | 21 | 19 | $34

5478 College Ave. (Taft St.), Oakland, 510-655-6469;
www.citron-acote.com

☑ "It's the little things that make life sweet" and there's plenty of them at this Rockridge "destination", "among the original, and now the epitome", of "*petit plats* places" – one "tightly packed" "with beautiful young hipsters" "trading tastes" of tapas with "French flair" in a "dark", "buzzing atmosphere"; although the no-reservations policy means "go early or wait forever" and "service gets worse as the crowds get bigger", you can "dull the pain with a snazzy cocktail" or hold out for the "peaceful" outdoors.

AHWAHNEE DINING ROOM, THE
18 | 28 | 19 | $48

Ahwahnee Hotel, 1 Ahwahnee Rd., Yosemite National Park,
209-372-1489; www.yosemitepark.com

☑ "With a view like this" – "floor-to-ceiling windows" "framing the waterfalls and glacial peaks" of Yosemite Valley – "they could feed you twigs and berries" joke happy hikers about this "historic" "regal dining room"; the "good" but "pricey" Cal dinners and Sunday brunches "can't compete with the amazing atmosphere", and the "amateurish" "service doesn't even try", but "the grandeur of the hotel and park more than makes up for it"; just remember to "pack a decent outfit" or "you won't get in."

Ajanta
23 | 18 | 21 | $24

1888 Solano Ave. (bet. The Alameda & Colusa Ave.),
Berkeley, 510-526-4373; www.ajantarestaurant.com

■ "The aristocrat's answer" to your typical Berkeley "curry shop", this "high-end" Indian is "one of the best" "this side of Mumbai" thanks to "small but nicely presented portions" of "consistently excellent" fare on a "monthly changing menu" that "spotlights different regional" dishes; foodwise, the staff will accommodate "your desired degree of hotness"; in terms of ambiance, the copies of the Ajanta Cave "R-rated" "naked women murals" may well "make your date more interesting."

Albany Bistro
– | – | – | M

1403 Solano Ave. (Carmel Ave.), Albany, 510-528-1237;
www.albanybistro.com

Chef-owner King Wong, who won the hearts and bellies of Danville diners with the late 301 Bistro, has launched this newcomer in colorfully appointed digs in the thick of Solano Avenue's Restaurant Row; here he continues to prepare his signature East-meets-West dishes (but at slightly lower prices than his last place), along with Eclectic twists on staples.

Asqew Grill   18 | 12 | 14 | $13
5614 Bay St. (Shellmound St.), Emeryville, 510-595-7471; www.asqewgrill.com
See review in City of San Francisco Directory.

Balboa Cafe   18 | 17 | 17 | $31
1995 Squaw Valley Rd. (Squaw Peak Rd.), Olympic Valley, 530-583-5850; www.plumpjack.com
See review in City of San Francisco Directory.

Barney's Gourmet Hamburger ⊅   19 | 12 | 14 | $14
1600 Shattuck Ave. (Cedar St.), Berkeley, 510-849-2827
1591 Solano Ave. (Ordway St.), Berkeley, 510-526-8185
5819 College Ave. (Chabot Rd.), Oakland, 510-601-0444
4162 Piedmont Ave. (Linda Ave.), Oakland, 510-655-7180
www.barneyshamburgers.com
☑ "So little time, so many burgers" – "all fixed a myriad of ways" at this "family-friendly" ground chuck chain; you'll "definitely want fries with that" ("the best spicy curlies on the planet") as well as their "phenomenal milkshakes"; pity the "staff is less alert than a cow" and the "no-frills" decor creates a less-than-happy moo-d; N.B. there are also branches in SF proper.

Battambang ⧄   20 | 11 | 17 | $18
850 Broadway (9th St.), Oakland, 510-839-8815
☑ Badda bing, Battam bang, this "Cambodian diner" "in the heart of Oakland's Chinatown" "has to be one of the best bangs for the buck in the East Bay"; and while the "officelike decor" and "AC transit buses on Broadway" roaring by may "spoil your Siem Reap moment", "cheerful service" and "flavors that sing" "fulfill the craving" for most.

BAY WOLF   26 | 22 | 24 | $44
3853 Piedmont Ave. (Rio Vista Ave.), Oakland, 510-655-6004; www.baywolf.com
■ "One of the original Californian cuisine staples", this Oakland "classic", situated in a "cute converted home", "continues to shine" (and even increase its Food score) after 30 years, thanks to chef/co-owner Michael Wild's "clever", "continually shifting, seasonal" Cal-Med menu; "while duck is the dish of renown", "old-timers also swear by" the "fine wine list", mercifully "quiet" interior and "transporting patio"; the "excellent service" is "less pretentious than many of its peers."

Bette's Oceanview Diner   22 | 15 | 17 | $16
1807 Fourth St. (Hearst St.), Berkeley, 510-644-3230
☑ Offering "upscale" "down-home American" lunches and "just about the best breakfast in Berkeley", this "packed"

"Fourth Street institution" "is everything a diner should be, down to the jukebox" and "brusque" but "hip" waitresses; but while the food may be manna "from heaven", "the wait for a table is hell" and "the prices aren't retro like the atmosphere" (which has "no ocean view", either); N.B. for the time-challenged, the adjacent Bette's To Go is the way to go.

Bistro Liaison   21 | 19 | 21 | $32

1849 Shattuck Ave. (Hearst Ave.), Berkeley, 510-849-2155; www.liaisonbistro.com

◪ For "a bit of Paris in Berkeley", locals love to liaise at this "intimate", "upbeat" Gourmet Ghetto Gulch corner for "reliable", "satisfying" portions of "real French food", "warm service" and "charming" "authentic" atmosphere ("down to rubber-stamping the dessert menu on the paper tablecloth"); however, sensitive types wince it's "*trop* noisy" and "*trop* crowded", "even by bistro standards."

Blackberry Bistro   21 | 16 | 15 | $17

4240 Park Blvd. (Wellington St.), Oakland, 510-336-1088; www.blackberrybistro.com

◪ Early birds cheer "the return of the great Oakland breakfast" at this "brunch place" whose "impeccable" "imaginative" American morning and midday meals "never fail to perk up the day"; still, some snap the "food isn't quite enough" to atone for "annoying waits" and servers that seem "both impatient and slow."

Blackhawk Grille   21 | 22 | 19 | $41

The Shops at Blackhawk, 3540 Blackhawk Plaza Circle (Camino Tassajara), Danville, 925-736-4295; www.calcafe.com

◪ Suitably set in an "upscale" shopping mall, this "dress-up" creekside Californian attracts "the usual chichi Blackhawk crowd" "hobnobbing" in its "*Saturday Night Fever* does deco" dining room; despite playing musical chefs of late, it remains a "safe place" with "solid" food "nicely presented and served" doves declare; but critics say "overinflated egos" and prices send this blackhawk down, and they suggest you stick to "cocktails on the patio" near the man-made lake.

Blue Nile   19 | 16 | 17 | $18

2525 Telegraph Ave. (Dwight Way), Berkeley, 510-540-6777

■ "It's like entering a different world when you step off Telegraph Avenue" and "behind the beaded curtains" into this budget Ethiopian where "eating with your hands" and quaffing "carafes of wonderful honey wine" "has never been such fun"; purists pout the tastes are "toned-down", but their blues are belied by a rise in the Food score (and Service too).

Bo's Barbecue ⊄   21 │ 9 │ 14 │ $19 │
3422 Mt. Diablo Blvd. (Brown Ave.), Lafayette, 925-283-7133

☑ "Bo knows barbecue" – and brisket and links – at his "down-home yuppie" rib joint in Lafayette "where locals slobber over their food just like regular class" folks; the "superb selection of red wines by the glass" and "upscale sides" "make up for the grade-school-cafeteria decor" and equally unsophisticated service; but if you don't want to "fight for a table", "eat on the charming patio or take 'em to go."

Breads of India & Gourmet Curries ⊄   21 │ 9 │ 14 │ $18 │
2448 Sacramento St. (Dwight Way), Berkeley, 510-848-7684

☑ "The longest bread line in Berkeley" can be found outside this no-naansense subcontinental, dubbed "the Chez Panisse of Indian food" for its use of "local organic ingredients" and "sustainably raised meat and poultry" on the "ever-changing menu"; however, "absurd waits", "rushed service, forced communal tables" and "cafeteria"-like decor fail to curry favor with the less-enthralled.

Bridges Restaurant   22 │ 24 │ 21 │ $47 │
44 Church St. (Hartz Ave.), Danville, 925-820-7200; www.bridgesrestaurant-bar.com

☑ A "quintessential special-occasion spot" for Danville denizens who "don't feel like driving into the city", this bistro offers the whole shebang – a "beautiful setting", "fine" French–"Asian fusion cuisine" and "nice service"; still, some sigh it "just doesn't knock your socks off", possibly because "it's easy to drop more than a C-note here and still leave hungry."

Bucci's ⊠   20 │ 19 │ 19 │ $28 │
6121 Hollis St. (bet. 59th & 61st Sts.), Emeryville, 510-547-4725; www.buccis.com

■ "Not what you'd expect in the middle of industrial Emeryville", this "large warehouse" featuring "cool art", "witty chalkboard sayings" and an "airy" patio is a "welcome change from the chain-filled" area; maybe "matriarch" Amelia Bucci herself is its "best asset", but the varied menu, from "scones and coffee in the morning" to "reasonably priced" Cal-Med dishes at night, is "always worth a try."

Cactus Taqueria   21 │ 14 │ 15 │ $11 │
1881 Solano Ave. (The Alameda), Berkeley, 510-528-1881
5642 College Ave. (Keith Ave.), Oakland, 510-658-6180

☑ "There's no better place to get fast, tasty" Cal-style Mexican than at these two East Bay taquerias known for their "absolutely addictive" "free-range-chicken" tacos and "the best gourmet burritos" this side of the Mission; despite "cafeteria decor" and "self-serve" service, they're perennially "packed and noisy" with "soccer moms", their rowdy broods and BART commuters grabbing it to go.

Cafe Cacao   ▽ 19 | 20 | 16 | $17

Scharffen Berger Chocolate Maker Factory, 914 Heinz Ave. (7th St.), Berkeley, 510-843-6000; www.cafecacao.biz
☑ "Heavenly aromas" abound at this new cafe set in an "atmosphere seething with chocolate" (a candy factory) that would make Willy Wonka proud; with its "to-die-for desserts" and quirky New French–American savories fashioned from the company's confections (chocolate pasta, anyone?), it has the potential to be a "delicious new addition" to Berkeley, but currently the food and service suggest it's still "a work-in-progress."

Cafe Esin ⌧   24 | 17 | 23 | $36

2416 San Ramon Valley Blvd. (Crow Canyon Rd.), San Ramon, 925-314-0974; www.cafeesin.com
☑ Although "located in a shopping center (what isn't in this part of suburbia?)", this "unassuming" San Ramon Med–New American run by a husband and wife reveals "SF qualities" in its "fresh, uncluttered" fare and "short but thoughtful" wine list for prices that are "more reasonable" than across the Bay; alas, "sterile" decor doesn't match up to the "helpful" staff or the eponymous pastry chef's "sublime desserts" that are the "most memorable things on the menu."

Café Fanny   23 | 13 | 15 | $15

1603 San Pablo Ave. (Cedar St.), Berkeley, 510-524-5447
☑ "Happy 20th birthday" cheer loyal morning and midday "crowds" who "belly up to the bar" of Alice Waters' "quintessential" Berkeley cafe that dispenses "perfect eggs", "fabulous" bowls of "café au (organic) lait" and Franco-Italian sandwiches made with "the best possible ingredients"; however, not everyone can "forgive" the "uncomfortable" "parking lot" seating, "precious portions" and "overblown prices" that make you feel "you're paying for the cachet."

Café Rouge   21 | 19 | 18 | $34

Market Plaza, 1782 Fourth St. (bet. Hearst Ave. & Virginia St.), Berkeley, 510-525-1440; www.caferouge.net
☑ "Smack dab in the middle" of the "Fourth Street scene" is this "meat-oriented" French-Med bistro-cum-butchery whose "open, airy" space and "fabulous" zinc bar host those hungry for "housemade" charcuterie, "wonderful burgers", "terrific roast chicken" and a "good raw bar", all complemented by a "well-selected wine list"; while cynics are "disappointed" by "shrinking" portions and "amateurish" service, optimists avow "it's getting better."

Caffe 817 ☒   20 | 16 | 15 | $13

817 Washington St. (bet. 8th & 9th Sts.), Oakland, 510-271-7965;
www.caffe817.com

☑ For a taste of "Rome on the sidewalks of Oakland", this
"always hopping" daytime "cafe/art gallery" run by a
"charming Italian host" is a "great place to meet a friend"
over "great coffee", delectable "polenta and poached egg"
breakfasts and "European-style sandwiches", even if it
seems service has "declined" over the years.

Caffé Verbena ☒   18 | 19 | 18 | $32

(fka Verbena)

Walter Shorenstein Bldg., 1111 Broadway (11th St.),
Oakland, 510-465-9300; www.caffeverbena.com

☑ Local "business leaders flock for lunch" to this "grown-
up" Italian-inflected Californian that's "a badly needed oasis
in Downtown Oakland"; despite sometimes "indifferent"
service and bumps in the kitchen, it's a "pleasant" spot for
"drinks after work" or a quiet "early dinner" "before an
event" (it closes at 9 PM).

Carrara's   ▽ 19 | 12 | 15 | $19

2735 Broadway (27th St.), Oakland, 510-663-2905

☑ "Only in Oakland" would you find a breakfast and lunch
"destination" housed in an "auto showroom" say bemused
boosters who praise chef Paul Carrara's "imaginative, fresh
and beautifully presented" Mediterranean fare; but while
some say "it's a shame" he doesn't serve dinner, foes fume
it's hard to ignore the "dreary" staff who've perhaps inhaled
too much of that "overwhelming new-car smell."

Casa Orinda   18 | 16 | 18 | $31

20 Bryant Way (Moraga Way), Orinda, 925-254-2981

☑ When the "hankering for some of the Bay Area's best
fried chicken" strikes, saddle up the mini-van and take the
family to this Orinda "institution" that has "Wild West
decor" complete with rifles and branding irons on the
walls; but sharper shooters snap it's merely for a "martini
before going elsewhere for dinner" since service is
"spotty" and the "old-time" Italian steak menu recalls that
of "a high-priced Sizzler."

Caspers Hot Dogs ⇗   19 | 7 | 14 | $7

545 San Pablo Ave. (bet. Brighton Ave. & Garfield St.),
Albany, 510-527-6611
5440 Telegraph Ave. (55th St.), Albany, 510-652-1668
6998 Village Pkwy. (Dublin Blvd.), Dublin, 925-828-2224
951 C St. (bet. Main St. & Mission Blvd.), Hayward, 510-537-7300
21670 Foothill Blvd. (bet. Cotter Way & Kimball Ave.), Hayward,
510-581-9064 ●
1240 First Ave. (International Dr.), Oakland, 510-465-5058
6 Vivian Dr. (Contra Costa Blvd.), Pleasant Hill, 925-687-6030
2530 Macdonald Ave. (Civic Center St.), Richmond, 510-235-6492

(continued)
Caspers Hot Dogs
*1280A Newell Hill Pl. (San Miguel Dr.), Walnut Creek,
925-930-9154*
☑ Lifelong East Bay residents wax enthusiastic over the
"pop-when-you-bite-'em hot dogs", "steamed buns" and
"fresh condiments" dispensed by this family-owned
"institution", as many have been eating them "since they
were kids"; if decor and service aren't anything to write
home about, they're still destinations for "the best of the
würst" on the "cheap."

César   23 | 21 | 19 | $29
*1515 Shattuck Ave. (bet. Cedar & Vine Sts.), Berkeley,
510-883-0222; www.barcesar.com*
■ "Constantly packed and roaring with life", this "bit of
Barcelona in sleepy Berkeley" is "one of the best places in
the East Bay for drinks and tapas with friends", as those
small, "salty" plates have "bold flavors" ("don't miss the cod
spread" or "heavenly fries") that marry well with "dynamite"
cocktails or "great wine and sherry"; but "watch out": the
"stylish, tiled" room is "very loud" and those "tantalizing
treats" "add up" to a "deceptively expensive" tab.

Cha Am Thai   19 | 13 | 16 | $18
1543 Shattuck Ave. (Cedar St.), Berkeley, 510-848-9664
See review in City of San Francisco Directory.

CHEZ PANISSE ☒   27 | 24 | 25 | $69
*1517 Shattuck Ave. (bet. Cedar & Vine Sts.), Berkeley,
510-548-5525; www.chezpanisse.com*
■ "The culinary gene pool of great chefs nationwide",
Alice Waters' "legendary Berkeley" establishment "still
packs them in" with its "distinctively" "simple" Med-
inspired meals that let the "meticulously selected" Cal
products "shine through" in an "Arts and Crafts setting
that suits" the "subtle" cuisine; you just have to "get past"
the "like-it-or-not" set menu and the "expert" staff's "this-
is-mecca" 'tude – because while it's "no longer cutting-
edge", this "grande dame" has "aged like a fine wine."

CHEZ PANISSE CAFÉ ☒   27 | 22 | 24 | $43
*1517 Shattuck Ave. (bet. Cedar & Vine Sts.), Berkeley,
510-548-5049; www.chezpanisse.com*
■ Alice Waters' "more boisterous version of foodie heaven"
"is no longer the consolation prize for not getting into" her
"flagship" prix fixe downstairs; in fact, it's the preferred
choice of "Berkeley intellectuals and tourists in shorts"
who come seeking that "Chez Panisse mystique without
breaking the bank"; not only do they recieve the same
"marvelous" Med-influenced "farm fresh" fare, funky "Arts
and Crafts interior" and "impeccable" wine-savvy staff,
they get "lots of choice" on the menu.

Chow/Park Chow 19 15 18 $21
La Fiesta Sq., 53 Lafayette Circle (Mt. Diablo Blvd.), Lafayette, 925-962-2469
See review in City of San Francisco Directory.

Citron 24 20 23 $47
5484 College Ave. (bet. Lawton & Taft Aves.), Oakland, 510-653-5484; www.citron-acote.com
☑ On Rockridge's Restaurant Row, "À Côté's big brother" is "an oasis of calm elegance", an "intimate" under-celebrated, special-celebration site where the staff is "well educated" ("a rarity these days") about the "scintillating wine list" and the "limited, rotating" seasonal New French–Cal menu that's "consistently excellent"; some "sour"-pusses pout it's not worth the "dent in the wallet", but "sitting out back on warm nights", most "don't really mind."

Doña Tomás ☒ 24 19 18 $29
5004 Telegraph Ave. (bet. 49th & 51st Sts.), Oakland, 510-450-0522
☑ "High-end Mexican" is a rarity in Oakland, so locals go loco over this "sophisticate's" "fresh" fare from an "inspired", "innovative" menu; regulars recommend the "romantic outdoor courtyard" over the often "brashly loud" interior, and scold "servers too hip for their own good"; still, the overall experience "brings a new perspective" to supping south of the border–style.

Dopo ☒ 26 19 23 $27
4293 Piedmont Ave. (Echo St.), Oakland, 510-652-3676
■ Though "they hate to share it", Oaklanders with the inside dopo know it's worth waiting "in the rain under umbrellas" to get into this "hot new" trattoria, given its "amazing Italian food [and wine] at amazing prices" ("only one bottle over $30"); a "professional" staff negotiates the "tiny" space with aplomb, and while the "daily changing", "not-for-the-carb-conscious" menu is "limited", "who needs 50 mediocre options when you have five extraordinary ones?"

downtown 21 21 20 $39
2102 Shattuck Ave. (Addison St.), Berkeley, 510-649-3810; www.downtownrestaurant.com
☑ A "welcome" presence on the "Berkeley theater district dining scene", this "ambitious and swanky" Cal seafooder is center-stage for "applause-worthy", "creative dishes" that "will get you to the show on time", thanks to the "civilized" servers; still, pessimists pout it's "pricey for an experience" that just "doesn't wow."

Duck Club, The 20 21 20 $42
Lafayette Park Hotel & Spa, 3287 Mt. Diablo Blvd. (Pleasant Hill Rd.), Lafayette, 925-283-3700; www.lafayetteparkhotel.com
See review in South of San Francisco Directory.

Eccolo   – – – M
1820 Fourth St. (Hearst Ave.), Berkeley, 510-644-0444;
www.eccolo.com
If you're looking for the Next Big Thing in Berkeley, *eccolo!*
(this is it): a new trattoria from longtime Chez Panisse
alums Christopher Lee and wife Janet Hankinson that's
Northern Italian in inspiration (lots of homemade *salumi,* or
cured meats) and Northern Californian in ingredients, with
wines from The Boot; although the duo has transformed
the former Ginger Island space into an isle of rustic chic
with Tuscan yellow and blue walls and exposed wood
beams, they've retained its retractable roof.

ERNA'S ELDERBERRY HOUSE   27 26 27 $76
48688 Victoria Ln. (Hwy. 41), Oakhurst, 559-683-6800;
www.elderberryhouse.com
■ Tucked away "in the Yosemite boonies", this "enchanted"
forest hideaway offers an extravagant "fine dining"
"experience out of *Lifestyles of the Rich and Famous*",
where lavish six-course Cal–New French menus "with
wine enhancing each dish" are paraded by a staff trained
to make you "feel like a princess in a fairy tale"; unless
you're en route to the park or plan to "spend the night at
the château" next door, it's "not on the beaten path – but
it's worth beating a path to" elder platesmen proclaim.

Everett & Jones Barbeque   20 10 12 $17
296 A St. (Myrtle St.), Hayward, 510-581-3222 ●⇱
126 Broadway (2nd St.), Oakland, 510-663-2350
2676 Fruitvale Ave. (bet. Davis & 27th Sts.), Oakland,
510-533-0900
3415 Telegraph Ave. (34th St.), Oakland,
510-601-9377 ⇱
◪ For over 30 years ("consistency is the highest praise you
can give a BBQ joint"), this family-owned franchise has kept
East Bayers in ecstasy at the "religious experience" of
eating "fall-off-the-bone ribs" with "out-of-this-world
sauce" and "good gravy-soppin' soul food"; but frequent
'cue-ers warn "not to expect much more than the excellent"
eats, as the service is "scary" and there's "zero ambiance."

FatApple's   18 13 15 $15
1346 Martin Luther King Jr. Way (bet. Berryman & Rose Sts.),
Berkeley, 510-526-2260
7525 Fairmount Ave. (bet. Colusa & Ramona Aves.), El Cerrito,
510-528-3433
◪ They should be called "PhatApple's" smile supporters
of this East Bay pair of "well-oiled factories" that are
perpetually "busy" with those craving the "ordinary
greatness" of their burgers, pies and olallieberry shakes;
"this comfort food is a little less comfortable on the wallet"
for some, "but it does what it's got to do: fill you up and
leave you feelin'" phat and happy.

Faz
17 | 18 | 17 | $33

600 Hartz Ave. (School St.), Danville, 925-838-1320
Four Point Sheraton Hotel, 5121 Hopyard Rd. (bet. Gibraltar &
Owens Drs.), Pleasanton, 925-460-0444
www.fazrestaurants.com
See review in City of San Francisco Directory.

Fenton's Creamery
18 | 15 | 14 | $13

4226 Piedmont Ave. (Entrada Ave.), Oakland, 510-658-7000;
www.fentonscreamery.com
☑ After a fire shuttered it for a spell, this "sentimental favorite" in Oakland is once again scooping out "heaping portions" of "homemade ice cream" that "licks the competition any day"; while the "savory options will leave you cold", service is "scattered" and "prices higher" since the remodel, legions still "line up" for "bigger-than-your-head" sundaes, like the signature "off-the-charts" black-and-tan.

Fonda Solana ☻
23 | 21 | 20 | $31

1501 Solana Ave. (Curtis St.), Albany, 510-559-9006;
www.fondasolana.com
■ As a "refreshing" beacon of cool in suburban Albany, this "popular" Latin American delights with a seasonal selection of "artful" small plates, "spot-on service" and a "fantastic cocktail menu" that nurtures a permanent "happy-hour" vibe; depending on your appetite, the portions mean either "lite dining" or an "expensive" bill, but nocturnal types are thrilled to have "somewhere to go after midnight."

Garibaldis
22 | 22 | 20 | $40

5356 College Ave. (Manila Ave.), Oakland, 510-595-4000
See review in City of San Francisco Directory.

Grasshopper
21 | 19 | 18 | $29

6317 College Ave. (Claremont Ave.), Oakland, 510-595-3559;
www.grasshoppersake.com
☑ A Pan-Asian "multicultural mecca" in Rockridge, this "grasshopper keeps hopping to higher culinary heights" with "offbeat and interesting" small plates (regulars recommend "anything on a skewer"), an "excellent selection of sake" and "unrushed service"; "incredibly small" portions, though, bug some who say "you'll go away hungry or broke."

Great China
22 | 9 | 11 | $16

2115 Kittredge St. (Shattuck Ave.), Berkeley, 510-843-7996
☑ The "Peking duck is fabulous" and "everyone loves the walnut prawns" at this "hole-in-the-wall", one of "Berkeley's best options" for Chinese eats; but while fans find the "distinctive" dishes at "cheap" prices "worth the long wait", "frustratingly slow" and even "extremely rude"

service amid "crowded, noisy" digs is a price foes aren't willing to pay.

IL FORNAIO
| 19 | 20 | 18 | $34 |

1430 Mt. Diablo Blvd. (bet. Broadway & Main St.), Walnut Creek, 925-296-0100; www.ilfornaio.com
See review in City of San Francisco Directory.

Jackson's Canvas
▽ | 18 | 16 | 17 | $36 |

(fka Canvas)
5761 Thornhill Dr. (Grisborne St.), Oakland, 510-339-7400
◪ Nicknamed the Yellow Submarine for its marigold-colored walls and large port hole windows, this "unpretentious" locals lair in Montclair is a bit like "the little restaurant that could", given chef/co-owner Peter Jackson's "imaginative" market-driven New American menu; but it could go even further and warrant its "city prices" "if it could polish up the service."

Jade Villa
| 19 | 10 | 13 | $19 |

800 Broadway (bet. 8th & 9th Sts.), Oakland, 510-839-1688
◪ "Dim sum is the star" at this Downtown Oakland "stalwart" that converts claim is "just what such places should be – big, loud, full of carts"; but dissident decorators declare "it's time for a remodel", while those weary of "the big waits on weekends" wonder "service? what service?"

Jimmy Bean's
| 20 | 11 | 15 | $15 |

1290 Sixth St. (Gilman St.), Berkeley, 510-528-3435; www.jimmybeans.com
◪ With "all the right foods for the morning cravings", breakfast and brunch at this "basically self-serve" Berkeley coffee shop are "terrific" – "just ask the dozen people in line before you"; doubters ding the "dingy" digs ("it's a community experience, with the community about six inches from each elbow"), but cravers of its Cal cuisine cry "if only it were open for dinner."

Jojo ⑤
| 24 | 18 | 22 | $40 |

3859 Piedmont Ave. (bet. 40th St. & Macarthur Blvd.), Oakland, 510-985-3003; www.jojorestaurant.com
■ In Oakland, this "jewel box of a French bistro" is a "labor of love" for chef-owners Curt Clingman and his "pastry-wizard wife", Mary Jo Thoresen, who produce a "limited menu" of "sensual", "seasonal food with flair", including desserts "so good they bring a tear to your eye"; "warm" service contributes to a "totally charming" time, despite the "shoebox" setting ("could this place be any tinier?").

Jordan's
▽ | 20 | 25 | 22 | $49 |

Claremont Resort & Spa, 41 Tunnel Rd. (Claremont Ave.), Berkeley, 510-549-8510; www.claremontresort.com
◪ As a strong Decor score attests, a "sweeping panoramic view of the Bay makes for splendid dining" at this "classic

Berkeley" hotel, whose "attentive" service and "stately, dignified" ambiance are "perfect for a parental visit or anniversary"; "though the setting is better than the food", the Cal–Pacific Rim fare is "pretty good", especially at the "extensive Sunday brunch" – even if the "array of genres (roast beef, pancakes *and* dim sum) is like a cruise ship on dry land."

Juan's Place   17 | 12 | 16 | $15 |
941 Carleton St. (9th St.), Berkeley, 510-845-6904
◪ A "Berkeley institution" that's "been around forever" (actually 1972), this honky-tonk is popular with "poor college students" who come to "feast on more homestyle Mexican food than you'll be able to finish"; "service varies greatly" and the "schlocky" "Baja ambiance" "isn't exactly stunning", but most "merrymakers" are content just to down "pitchers of sangria and let it all hang out."

KIRALA   26 | 17 | 17 | $33 |
2100 Ward St. (Shattuck Ave.), Berkeley, 510-549-3486;
www.kiralaberkeley.com
◪ "At the risk of increasing the already insane lines outside", reviewers rave about the sushi "so fresh it could have dived off the table" and "unique robata" selections at this Japanese that "sets the bar" in Berkeley; true, the "no-reservations policy is annoying" and service can range from "efficient" to "indifferent", but none of that dampens the "lively scene."

Koryo Wooden Charcoal BBQ ☻   23 | 8 | 12 | $21 |
4390 Telegraph Ave. (Shattuck Ave.), Oakland, 510-652-6007
◪ In Oakland's "powerhouse of Korean BBQ", carnivores keep the fires burning for "marinated meats" cooked at your own "wobbly, bingo hall"–like table in a "bare-bones", "folding-chair-and-fluorescent-light" interior; "service can be downright surly", but "the food is worth the attitude"; P.S. "wear clothes that you don't mind infusing with smoke odors."

Lalime's   26 | 21 | 24 | $42 |
1329 Gilman St. (bet. Neilson St. & Peralta Ave.), Berkeley, 510-527-9838; www.lalimes.com
■ For almost 20 years, this "long-lived Berkeley institution" has offered "brilliant", "continually inventive" Cal-Med fare that "never fails to satisfy the palate" of "vegetarians and meatlovers" alike; the "marvelous service" makes "it feel like going to visit friends" – ones living in a "quiet neighborhood" house with a "plain white front and vines" outside, an "old-fashioned Euro feel" inside.

La Méditerranée   20 | 15 | 17 | $19 |
2936 College Ave. (Ashby Ave.), Berkeley, 510-540-7773;
www.cafelamed.com
See review in City of San Francisco Directory.

La Note　　22　21　17　$21
2377 Shattuck Ave. (bet. Channing Way & Durant Ave.),
Berkeley, 510-843-1535
☑ "One more glass of wine and I could be convinced I
was in Provence" attest *amis* of this "charming" cafe
in Downtown Berkeley, where even the "servers have
mastered the French air of boredom"; though "pleasant",
the accordion-serenaded weekend dinners play second
fiddle to the "addictive" "bistro-style breakfasts and
brunches" (the latter the raison d'être for the "long lines");
but "drinking café au lait on the back patio" is an earthly
delight "worth waiting for."

Lark Creek　　22　20　20　$37
1360 Locust St. (Mt. Diablo Blvd.), Walnut Creek, 925-256-1234;
www.larkcreek.com
☑ "As American as apple pie – and that's on the menu
too" – owner Bradley Ogden's Walnut Creek tributary
"sets a new level of dining in the community", offering
suburbanites the "dressed-up comfort food" "that mom
never made" and born-in-the-USA wines, proffered by
"dependable servers"; while "it's not as good as the mother
ship" in Larkspur (some quip the food "appeals to Omaha,
not the Bay Area"), it's "more affordable" and a heck of "a
lot closer to home."

La Rose Bistro　　▽　23　17　22　$29
2037 Shattuck Ave. (bet. Addison St. & University Ave.),
Berkeley, 510-644-1913
■ The bloom is definitely on this rose, a "hard-to-find" but
"exciting" new Berkeley bistro; chef-owner Vanessa Dang
(ex Bridges) "always comes out to greet the guests" before
preparing "extraordinarily creative" Cal-French dishes with
some Indochine influences; colorful, "cozy and charming",
it's a "class act" all 'round.

La Salamandre　　▽　21　22　22　$46
267 Hartz Ave. (Diablo Rd.), Danville, 925-837-2000;
www.lasalamandre.net
☑ "In the heart of Danville", this "*très français*" spot is for
East Bayers yearning for a taste of the City of Lights without
the city; admirers acclaim the "attentive, accented service"
and "quaint surroundings"; however, while "it's called
a bistro", "it leans more toward a restaurant in prices",
causing detractors to deem it "disappointing for the dollar."

Le Cheval　　23　15　16　$21
1007 Clay St. (10th St.), Oakland, 510-763-8495
☑ This perennially packed Vietnamese daily "swallows up
hundreds of hungry diners" who hurry in for "heaping plates
of excellent, authentic" fare at near-"bargain prices"; the
patronage is "quintessential Oakland" – "movers and
shakers of diverse ethnicities", "with a sprinkling of cops",

enjoying the bar topped with vats of infused "snake wine"; the "aging" "banquet hall–sized" room gets pretty "noisy", but the "slam-bam-thank-you-ma'am service" ensures you won't linger.

LEFT BANK   20 | 21 | 18 | $36
60 Crescent Dr. (Monument Blvd.), Pleasant Hill, 925-288-1222; www.leftbank.com
See review in North of San Francisco Directory.

Legendary Palace ●   ▽ 20 | 16 | 12 | $21
708 Franklin St. (7th St.), Oakland, 510-663-9188
☑ "Bright enough for brain surgery, this purple palace" serves "superb dim sum"and "ok dinners" in "Oakland's Chinatown"; several cite "language barriers" with some of the servers, which optimists say "adds to the mystique", but leaves pessimists "wondering if being a round eye gets you the fish eye", like the ones "staring at you from the tanks."

Little Shin Shin   19 | 9 | 15 | $19
4258 Piedmont Ave. (bet. Echo & Entrada Aves.), Oakland, 510-658-9799
☑ OK, so the the food's only "slightly above ordinary" ("corn starch is not a necessary ingredient, honest"), but a "convenient location on Piedmont Avenue" makes this Chinese vet a "favorite family joint"; however, the combination of "crazy parking", "lousy seating" and "rude service" suggest you should "do as the locals do" and go for takeout.

LoCoCo's Restaurant & Pizzeria   20 | 13 | 19 | $21
1400 Shattuck Ave. (Rose St.), Berkeley, 510-843-3745
4270 Piedmont Ave. (Echo Ave.), Oakland, 510-652-6222 ⊄
www.lococospizzeria.com
☑ An "omnipresent line says it all" at these East Bay Sicilian siblings where "sated diners sing paeans to their penne and meatballs", "chewy" crusted pizzas and other "authentic" Southern Italian dishes; however, while "friendly service" and an "inviting neighborhood feel" make up for the "small" space, oenophiles suggest you "bring your own wine rather than suffer their list" (easily done in Oakland, which waives the corkage fee).

Mama's Royal Cafe ⊄   21 | 14 | 16 | $13
4012 Broadway (40th St.), Oakland, 510-547-7600
■ The only place for morning meals "outside my own mama's kitchen" conclude ravenous "hipsters" who also give this Oakland American with the "kitschy interior" their vote for "best diner coffee" and "best staff tattoos"; the menu may be "full of your usual breakfast suspects", but the "hearty, fresh ingredients" and "superb" execution make it "worth the wait"; arrive early "to beat the bohemians" regulars suggest.

Marica
▽ 21　19　21　$33

5301 College Ave. (Bryant Ave.), Oakland, 510-985-8388

■ A "must-eat for all lobster fans", Oakland's "low-key local seafooder" lures neighborhood devotees of "well-prepared" swimming delicacies; the "homey service" makes you "comfortable" in a "small" but "soothing" shell.

Max's ⊠
16　13　16　$22

Oakland City Ctr., 500 12th St. (bet. Broadway & Clay St.), Oakland, 510-451-6297; www.maxsworld.com

See review in City of San Francisco Directory.

Mezze
22　21　20　$32

3407 Lakeshore Ave. (bet. Hwy. 580 & Mandana Blvd.), Oakland, 510-663-2500; www.mezze.com

■ "Shockingly good" Sicilian fare (which has risen in the ratings) in a "quaint" "European" setting makes this Oakland Cal-Med the "upscale" "star of the neighborhood" near Lake Merritt; although it's "off the beaten path", it's a "multi-visit destination" for the "bargain prix fixe" and staffers who "make you feel like you're home."

Naan 'n Curry ⊅
19　7　10　$12

2366 Telegraph Ave. (bet. Channing Way & Durant Ave.), Berkeley, 510-841-6226

See review in City of San Francisco Directory.

Nan Yang Rockridge
20　14　19　$23

6048 College Ave. (Claremont Ave.), Oakland, 510-655-3298

◨ "Take a chance on Burmese food – it pays off" boast boosters of this "one-of-a-kind" Oakland eatery where "warm and comforting curries" share the menu with "more exotic dishes" ("noodles never had it so good"); longtimers lament "some dishes lack the punch" of yore, but the "demure" decor works well for "a second or third date."

Nizza La Bella
19　17　19　$30

825-827 San Pablo Ave. (bet. Solano & Washington Aves.), Albany, 510-526-2552

◨ "Feel like you're on the French-Italian border for the evening" at this "casual" Albany bistro; but while many are happy to keep the "*belle* bouillabaisse" and "warm atmosphere" "a well-kept secret", others tattle this "tantalizing" place "looks great, but doesn't quite deliver."

North Beach Pizza ●
17　8　13　$16

1598 University Ave. (California St.), Berkeley, 510-849-9800; www.northbeachpizza.com

See review in City of San Francisco Directory.

O Chamé ⊠
22　22　20　$30

1830 Fourth St. (Hearst Ave.), Berkeley, 510-841-8783

■ "Zen" palates find religion on "trendy Fourth Street" in the form of "distinctive" Japanese "dishes beautifully

prepared and presented in a spare, appealing way";
"timeless, artistic decor" and a "casual but competent
staff" augment the "sensuous experience"; it's all perhaps
"a bit precious, but it can please."

OLIVETO CAFE & RESTAURANT   25 22 21 $47
5655 College Ave. (Shafter Ave.), Oakland, 510-547-5356;
www.oliveto.com
☑ "Great on a normal night and amazing" on a "special
themed one" attest acolytes of Oakland's "casually
elegant" "temple to chef/co-owner Paul Bertolli's"
"heartfelt", "handcrafted" "take on Northern Italian" fare
("order anything on the spit" and the "dreamy" "homemade
salami"); however, heretics huff over the "absurdly small
portions" and the "staff takes itself oh-so-seriously";
accord is reached at the downstairs cafe that all agree is
"wonderful" "at a fraction of the price."

OnoMazé   21 19 19 $36
1616 N. Main St. (Civic Dr.), Walnut Creek, 925-945-1120;
www.onomaze.com
■ There's "a little bit of Hawaii" "right in Walnut Creek",
where "small plates" of Cal-French fare with "mildly exotic
Pan-Asian" tastes are prepared with "creativity" and
served by a "friendly" staff; a "modern", "richly darkened room"
and "sidewalk-cafe setting" also make it "something out
of the ordinary" for "girls' night out" or a "romantic" meal.

Pakwan ⊅   21 5 9 $13
26617 Mission Blvd. (Sorenson Rd.), Hayward,
510-538-2401
See review in City of San Francisco Directory.

Paragon   17 21 18 $32
Claremont Resort & Spa, 41 Tunnel Rd. (Domingo St.),
Berkeley, 510-549-8585; www.paragonrestaurant.com
See review in City of San Francisco Directory.

Pasta Pomodoro   15 13 16 $18
5614 Shellmound St. (Powell St.), Emeryville,
510-923-1173
5500 College Ave. (Lawton Ave.), Oakland, 510-923-0900
See review in City of San Francisco Directory.

Pearl Oyster Bar & Restaurant ☒   _ _ _ M
5634 College Ave. (bet. Keith Ave. & Ocean View Dr.),
Oakland, 510-654-5426
This sleek new *poisson* palace, located across from the
Rockridge Market Hall, takes an aquatic twist to the tapas
craze with chef Mark Lusardi (founding chef of Yabbies
Coastal Kitchen) preparing a dozen or so cold and hot small
seafood plates; while recycled glass and steel gives the
small dining room a sleek, urban look, the staff maintains
a neighborly vibe.

P.F. Chang's China Bistro | 18 | 19 | 17 | $27 |
Broadway Plaza, 1205 Broadway Plaza (Mt. Diablo Blvd.),
Walnut Creek, 925-979-9070; www.pfchangs.com
See review in South of San Francisco Directory.

Phoenix Next Door 🗷⇗   ∇ | 23 | 13 | 17 | $16 |
1788 Shattuck Ave. (Delaware St.), Berkeley,
510-883-0783
■ Locals plead "don't publicize" this little Italian – a
"delicious side project from the owners of Phoenix, the
fresh pasta supplier to better Bay Area restaurants" – for
fear they'll have to wait even longer to get in; there's "not
much decor" and "service can be downright awful", but
who cares when there's "fabulous handcrafted" noodles
with "an ever-changing menu of enticing sauces" and
"warm olive bread" to sop 'em up with.

Piatti | 18 | 19 | 18 | $34 |
100 Sycamore Valley Rd. W. (San Ramon Valley Blvd.),
Danville, 925-838-2082; www.piatti.com
See review in North of San Francisco Directory.

Picante Cocina Mexicana | 21 | 13 | 14 | $14 |
1328 Sixth St. (bet. Camelia & Gilman Sts.), Berkeley,
510-525-3121
☑ The line often "reaches to the door" at Berkeley's
"innovative", "California-inspired" "fresh Mex" where
you get "upscale food at peasant prices"; the "noisy",
"cafeterialike" interior is so popular with the little ones
that "you can feel like you're in a day care center", but that
doesn't deter those hollering "hooray for their handmade
corn tortillas" and boosting the Food score.

Pizza Rustica | 20 | 11 | 15 | $17 |
5422 College Ave. (bet. Kales & Manila Aves.), Oakland,
510-654-1601
6106 La Salle Ave. (Warren Fwy.), Oakland, 510-339-7878
www.caferustica.com
☑ They got "fresh" "nouveau toppings", they got "fabulous
corn meal crust" "and they deliver" – these Oakland
pizzerias are "everything you want from a local" pie shop,
plus "good rotisserie chicken" too; if dining in, take heed:
"service is friendly but spotty" and the interior "dumpy",
so "the best thing is taking it upstairs to the Conga Lounge
Room" (on College Avenue); otherwise, if "you want
ambiance, take it home."

Plearn Thai Cuisine | 19 | 14 | 16 | $17 |
2050 University Ave. (bet. Milvia St. & Shattuck Ave.),
Berkeley, 510-841-2148
☑ "A real pioneer in Thai food" (open since 1982), this
"spacious" Berkeley standby remains "packed with UCal
students" who find it a "good place to get a reliable pad

Thai" – "they actually give you spicy if you want it" – that "doesn't break the bank"; but when "there is so much better out there, why settle for this?" demand the disappointed.

PlumpJack Cafe 24 | 21 | 22 | $49 |

PlumpJack Squaw Valley Inn, 1920 Squaw Valley Rd. (Hwy. 89), Olympic Valley, 530-583-1576; www.plumpjack.com
See review in City of San Francisco Directory.

Postino 22 | 25 | 21 | $40 |

3565 Mt. Diablo Blvd. (Oak Hill Rd.), Lafayette, 925-299-8700; www.postinorestaurant.com
☑ "If you want a romantic setting, this is the place to go" advise advocates of this "beautiful" "old post office that's now an Italian eatery", complete with "fantastic garden" patio; but while the "interior is seductive", Lafayette locals "would love to see the food and service match it", murmuring the menu, while "nicely done", is "more for the country-club set than the gourmet", and the service is "sometimes good, other times exasperating."

Prima 23 | 21 | 22 | $43 |

1522 N. Main St. (bet. Bonanza St. & Lincoln Ave.), Walnut Creek, 925-935-7780; www.primaristorante.com
■ In Walnut Creek, this "buzzing" Southern Italian's specialties are created with "fresh regional ingredients, and served with aplomb"; but while the "knowledgeable staff" and the food are draws, it's the "unsurpassed" 1,600-label, global cellar that makes this a "special-occasion place"; the prima seats are on the *loggia,* an enclosed patio "away from the fray" and "right out of Tuscany."

Purple Plum, The 21 | 17 | 18 | $28 |

4228 Park Blvd. (Wellington St.), Oakland, 510-336-0990; www.thepurpleplum.com
☑ "Sunday suppers at grandmother's house" can be had at this "charming" Oakland "joint" servin' up "Southern food by way of California" that'll "comfort anyone's soul" ("have the fried chicken once before you die"); however, "amateur service and long waits" in a room that has "too small an area to wait in" detract from the fruits of the kitchen's labor.

Restaurant Peony 21 | 14 | 13 | $23 |

Pacific Renaissance Plaza, 388 Ninth St. (bet. Franklin & Webster Sts.), Oakland, 510-286-8866
☑ "The few non-Chinese patrons who find" this "Hong Kong–style" "garage" hidden "in the midst of Oakland's Chinatown are in for a real treat" – namely, "much more authentic" dim sum than at your typical shu mai shop and multicourse "white tablecloth set dinners"; "however, get there early on weekends" or face "fighting with the crowds to get seated", followed by efforts to "catch the server's eye so you might get fed."

Rick & Ann's 22 16 18 $19
2922 Domingo Ave. (bet. Ashby & Claremont Aves.), Berkeley, 510-649-8538; www.rickandanns.com

☑ For American "home-cooked food, only better", Berkeley has been stopping by this "staple" for 15 years; the "deliciously crafted" weekend brunch "brightens the morning" – "if you can get in"; indeed, the "one-to-two-hour waits" make the comfort food less comfortable critics cry.

RIVOLI 27 23 24 $42
1539 Solano Ave. (bet. Neilson St. & Peralta Ave.), Berkeley, 510-526-2542; www.rivolirestaurant.com

■ "It would be a perfect world if all neighborhoods had neighborhood restaurants this good" fantasize fanciers of Wendy Brucker's near-"perfect" Cal-Med whose ambiance, "expressive, straight-shootin'" fare and "gracious" service are "comparable to the best SF haunts but at Berkeley prices"; the "snug" dining room, with its "windows overlooking a peaceable garden" lets you watch what the "local wildlife" eats for dinner, even as you enjoy yours; P.S. "the bar is a great place for a quick bite."

Saul's Restaurant & Delicatessen 18 15 15 $17
1475 Shattuck Ave. (bet. Rose & Vine Sts.), Berkeley, 510-848-3354; www.saulsdeli.com

☑ "If it weren't for all the Birkenstocks, you'd swear you were on the Lower East Side", not Berkeley, at this Jewish "kosher-style" deli "duplicating the food and ambiance" of a traditional "knish shop"; critics kvetch over the "barn"-like digs, service that's "responsive to waves" only and "oy, the prices"; but for "pastrami piled high", "it's the only game in town", and besides, "New York is so far away."

Shalimar/Shalimar Gardens ⌀ 23 4 9 $14
3325 Walnut Ave. (Paseo Padre Pkwy.), Fremont, 510-494-1919; www.shalimarsf.com

See review in City of San Francisco Directory.

Shen Hua 22 19 18 $21
2914 College Ave. (bet. Ashby Ave. & Russell St.), Berkeley, 510-883-1777

☑ "An East Bay stronghold" – "just look at how crowded the place is every day" – this Berkeleyite offers "addictive" Mandarin dishes and "sleek decor" that are "a step above" the usual "downtrodden Chinese-restaurant path"; it's "conducive to all sorts of occasions", except perhaps romantic ones, as critics cavil over the "worst acoustics" and "efficient" yet "curt" service.

Skates on the Bay 16 23 17 $34
100 Seawall Dr. (University Ave.), Berkeley, 510-549-1900

☑ For two decades, this Berkeleyite has skated on its "beyond-perfect" view of the Bay Area's three bridges; but "you can't eat atmosphere" and the belligerent bellow "it's a little overpriced", considering the "nothing-special seafood" and New American eats; best bet: "sit at the bar, have appetizers" and "wave at the passengers on the boats cruising so close."

Soi 4   24 | 21 | 19 | $28
5421 College Ave. (bet. Kales & Manila Sts.), Oakland, 510-655-0889; www.soifour.com
☑ When they want "trendy" fare that is "full of flavor", connoisseurs come to this Oakland original for "small portions" of "Bangkok street food" "cooked to perfection" and complemented by "creative, delicious drinks" amid a "lovely minimalist interior"; all told, it offers a "sleek, chic and [relatively] cheap" time – although the service has some skeptical types fit to be Thai-ed ("the staff is barely acquainted with time").

Soizic   24 | 21 | 22 | $35
300 Broadway (3rd St.), Oakland, 510-251-8100; www.soizicbistro.com
■ Ok, so the exterior lacks a little "curb appeal" ("looks like a cross between a bail bondsman's office and a shark tank"), but this Cal "favorite" "just a block from Jack London Square" is where "the glitterati of Oakland, such as they are, go to unwind"; the secret lies in the "unusual combinations of food, artfully presented" ("exquisite ginger custard") that "please a variety of tastes" from "simple to sophisticate"; "the staff's super-friendly", and the inside is actually "warm and arty."

Spenger's   13 | 15 | 15 | $29
1919 Fourth St. (bet. Hearst & University Aves.), Berkeley, 510-845-7771; www.spengers.com
☑ Ahoy, mateys, for a sea-faring voyage to Berkeley's "classic" "favorite family" fish house; while old salts salute the "fresh seafood prepared the old-fashioned way", skeptics snap the menu walks the plank for "trying to do far too much" (likewise the "rushed servers"); the real hook is the "schmaltzy, kitschy" nautical atmosphere that's "dark, sea-shantyesque" and "full of history."

Tacubaya   ▽ 20 | 16 | 14 | $14
1788 Fourth St. (bet. Hearst Ave. & Virginia St.), Berkeley, 510-525-5160
☑ A "cute little" daytime spot "from the owners of Doña Tomás", named after a town near Mexico City, this casual upscale taqueria in Fourth Street's "chichi" shopping complex prepares authentic "mouthwatering" Mexican breakfast and lunch fare with a California "twist" (organic ingredients, "sustainably raised poultry and meat"); "shamefully high prices" for "tweezers-size portions", however, rankle rebels as *loco*.

Taiwan ☻   17   6   11 $14
2071 University Ave. (Shattuck Ave.), Berkeley,
510-845-1456
☑ "Watching them roll your potstickers" "in the front of the restaurant" "before they're steamed to order" is a highlight at this "late-night spot" popular with Berkeley students for "good, cheap" "homestyle" Chinese – "definitely try the Taiwanese specialties"; it's the "place to go for good food, but not atmosphere" or "sophistication of decor"; N.B. the SF branch serves dim sum all day.

Three Seasons ⊠   22   19   17 $31
1525 N. Main St. (Bonanza St.), Walnut Creek, 925-934-4831
See review in City of San Francisco Directory.

Tomatina   18   14   16 $18
1338 Park St. (Encinal Ave.), Alameda, 510-521-1000
1325 N. Main St. (Mt. Diablo Blvd.), Walnut Creek, 925-930-9999
www.tomatina.com
See review in South of San Francisco Directory.

Townhouse Bar & Grill ⊠   21   19   19 $29
5862 Doyle St. (bet. 59th & Powell Sts.), Emeryville,
510-652-6151; www.townhousebarandgrill.com
■ It may look like a "run-down dive", but this "funky" Emeryville "roadhouse" housed in "an authentic Prohibition speakeasy" is a "charming", "first-class" bar and grill run by a "professional, friendly staff" serving "delicious", "consistent" Cal fare; "if it's warm enough", you'll find locals and "power-lunchers" "on the deck" sipping the bartender's infamously "minty mojitos."

Trader Vic's   17   22   18 $41
9 Anchor Dr. (Powell St.), Emeryville, 510-653-3400;
www.tradervics.com
☑ "Go for the views and the fantastically kitschy South Seas decor" at Emeryville's "venerable", "expensive" "Polynesian paradise" where you can "make a full night of scorpions, navy grogs and pupu platters" at "the bar overlooking the water"; "skip the food", though, counsel critics who also warn of waiters who can be as prickly as "porcupines"; P.S. the upscale Palo Alto branch is also noted for its "great primitive artworks" on display, and a new branch is slated to open in SF in 2004.

Trattoria La Siciliana ⌿   24   18   18 $26
2993 College Ave. (Ashby Ave.), Berkeley, 510-704-1474
☑ "Amazingly delicious" garlic-heavy red-sauce fare has garnered a "loyal clientele" for this Southern Italian place "in Berkeley's quaint village of Elmwood", and some sprucing up has improved the Decor score; still, the service can be "highly inconsistent", and *amici* advise "be prepared to be bossed around while ordering."

Truly Mediterranean 23 6 14 $10
1984 Shattuck St. (University Ave.), Berkeley, 510-540-9997;
www.trulymed.com
See review in City of San Francisco Directory.

Udupi Palace ∅ ∇ 22 8 16 $14
1901-1903 University Ave. (Martin Luther King Way), Berkeley,
510-843-6600
941 Bluebell Dr. (Springtown Blvd.), Livermore, 925-960-1942;
www.udupipalaceca.com
■ Pros proclaim "the selection is immense and the quality
is high" at these "bargain" Berkeley and Livermore South
Indians; the vegetarian cuisine is so "addictive" that
"even die-hard meat eaters don't complain", about that or
the "simple storefront settings" ("keep your eyes closed
and your mouth open and you'll be thrilled"); P.S. South of
SFers "think the one in Sunnyvale is the best."

Uzen ⊠ 24 16 18 $30
5415 College Ave. (bet. Hudson St. & Kales Ave.), Oakland,
510-654-7753
☑ Maki mavens make their way to this Oakland Japanese
for "well-prepared" "large portions" of "extremely fresh
sushi" "classics – not fancy rolls with silly names"; the digs
are "tiny" and the "new-wave '80s decor" strikes some as
"stale", but the service is "efficient"; P.S. for small parties,
request the "no-extra-charge, almost-secret room upstairs."

Va de Vi – – – M
1511 Mt. Diablo Blvd. (Main St.), Walnut Creek,
925-979-0100; www.va-de-vi-bistro.com
With an international list of over 100 bottles (half of 'em
available by the glass or taste), this new Walnut Creek wine
bar lives up to its name, which translates into 'It's About
Wine' in the Catalan dialect; the kitchen cranks out Eclectic
small plates served in a narrow, dark dining room lined with
racks, or on the patio out back; N.B. reservations aren't
accepted, but you can call ahead to get on the waiting list.

Venezia 19 21 19 $27
1799 University Ave. (Grant St.), Berkeley, 510-849-4681
☑ At this Berkeley Italian, a "big, open" "dining room done
up to look like a Venetian street with laundry hanging and
[faux] pigeons perching above" "sets the stage" for
"hearty", "delicious" fare and "friendly", if somewhat
"slow", service; it's a "good place for groups or kids",
which means it can get "noisy."

Venus 21 17 18 $21
2327 Shattuck Ave. (Durant Ave.), Berkeley, 510-540-5950;
www.venusrestaurant.net
■ A change of pace from "places that serve pretty much
the exact same eight dishes" at brunch, this "adorable

jewel box" in Berkeley serves "creative", "reasonably priced" Cal cuisine made mostly from "fresh organic produce and free-range meats"; the atmosphere is "laid-back", and while "you have to wait on weekends" for the "sublime" breakfast, it usually "isn't overcrowded" at dinner.

Vic Stewart's　　21　21　21　$45

850 S. Broadway (bet. Mt. Diablo Blvd. & Newell Ave.), Walnut Creek, 925-943-5666

☑ Carnivores crow "if you love beef, you'll love" this "old-school steakhouse" in Walnut Creek where "melt-in-your-mouth meat" is served by an "attentive" staff in "remodeled railroad cars" (it's housed in a "former station"); while most find the setting "cozy and romantic", the "train motif doesn't do it for everyone", and razzers rail that it's "overhyped and overpriced", "especially the wine list."

Vik's Chaat Corner　　25　5　10　$10

726 Allston Way (bet. 4th & 5th Sts.), Berkeley, 510-644-4412; www.vikdistributors.com

☑ At this "Berkeley staple", "monumental" portions of "flavorful", "rich" Indian fare served on "flimsy" paper plates make up for "long lines" and a "chaotic" system ("you'll have to hover for a table" after ordering and have your "name butchered over the loudspeaker"); though the "warehouse" has the "atmosphere of an airplane hangar" and "there is no such thing as service", "you can't beat the food or prices"; P.S. "go early", because it closes at 6 PM.

Vi's ⌷　　∇　20　10　17　$14

724 Webster St. (bet. 7th & 8th Sts.), Oakland, 510-835-8375

■ A "wide variety of Vietnamese fare", including "absolutely the best pho in the area" awaits at "Oakland's best-kept secret", and "one of the best deals in town" according to phonatics; the "spartan" surroundings are "not in the least bit swanky", but the service is "consistently good."

Wente Vineyards　　24　25　23　$47

5050 Arroyo Rd. (Wetmore Rd.), Livermore, 925-456-2450; www.wentevineyards.com

■ "The setting, the wine, the food . . . ah, the food" rhapsodize those who make the trek to this "fabulous destination" in Livermore where the "gorgeous" patio "with vineyard views", a "splendid" Cal-Med menu that "changes daily" and "fantastic wines" create a "wonderful setting for a romantic dinner"; "every detail is taken care of" by the "skilled staff", leaving fans nothing to wish for except that "it were closer to home."

Yoshi's at Jack London Square　　18　21　18　$33

Jack London Sq., 510 Embarcadero W. (Washington St.), Oakland, 510-238-9200; www.yoshis.com

☑ Japanese and jazz make a "great combo" at this "very hip" club in Oakland, an "unbeatable" "date place" where a "dinner of succulent sushi or tempting tempura is the ticket" to getting the best seats to live performances; downbeat detractors, though, declare it's "a little pricey", with "so-so" service and food that "could be much, much better."

ZACHARY'S CHICAGO PIZZA ⊅   25 | 12 | 15 | $16 |
1853 Solano Ave. (The Alameda), Berkeley, 510-525-5950
5801 College Ave. (Oak Grove Ave.), Oakland, 510-655-6385
www.zacharys.com
◪ Boosters boast the "deeply satisfying deep-dish pizzas" at this pie pair in Berkeley and Oakland "are better than Chicago-style pizza in Chicago", with their "crunchy, soul-satisfying crust" and "juicy, flavorful tomatoes" – "what more could you want?"; "I suppose a shorter line" respond regulars who know that "takeout is the only way" to avoid the "punishing wait" and "noisy" dining room "chock-full of college students."

Zao Noodle Bar   15 | 12 | 14 | $16 |
5614 Bay St. (Shellmound St.), Emeryville, 510-595-2888;
www.zao.com
See review in City of San Francisco Directory.

Zax Tavern ⊠   23 | 22 | 22 | $39 |
2826 Telegraph Ave. (bet. Oregon & Stuart Sts.), Berkeley,
510-848-9299; www.zaxtavern.com
■ "Outstanding" Euro-Med fusion cuisine ("the goat cheese soufflé still tops the list"), "amazing drinks" and a "nice wine list", "patient, informed" service and a "very pretty decor" of mahogany and marble add up to a "great Berkeley dining experience"; "reasonable prices" and "easy access and parking" are added pluses, but while the scene is usually "calm", the room is "always full."

North of San Francisco

Top Ratings

Except where indicated by a ▽, top lists exclude places with low voting.

Top Food

28 French Laundry
27 Farmhouse Inn▽
Sushi Ran
Cafe La Haye
La Toque
Fork
26 Rest. at Stevenswood
Terra
Bistro Jeanty
Auberge du Soleil

Lark Creek Inn
25 Manka's Inverness
Cole's Chop Hse.
Madrona Manor
Martini Hse.
Willi's Seafood
Hana Japanese
24 Tra Vigne
Bistro Don Giov.
Mustards Grill

By Cuisine

American
28 French Laundry
26 Terra
Lark Creek Inn
25 Madrona Manor
Martini Hse.

Asian
27 Sushi Ran
25 Hana Japanese
24 Royal Thai
21 Gary Chu's
20 Robata Grill

Californian
27 Farmhouse Inn▽
Cafe La Haye
Fork
25 Manka's Inverness
24 Cafe Beaujolais

French
27 La Toque
26 Bistro Jeanty
Auberge du Soleil
24 El Paseo
22 Angèle

Italian
24 Tra Vigne
Bistro Don Giov.
zazu
Santi
23 Della Santina's

Mediterranean
26 Rest. at Stevenswood
Auberge du Soleil
23 Insalata's
Ledford Hse.
22 Manzanita

Mexican/Spanish
24 LaSalette
23 Villa Corona
Zuzu
21 Las Camelias
19 Joe's Taco

Seafood/Steakhouses
25 Cole's Chop Hse.
Willi's Seafood
21 Scoma's
19 Izzy's Steak
18 Yankee Pier

By Special Feature

Breakfast/Brunch
26 Auberge du Soleil
   Lark Creek Inn
24 Bouchon
   John Ash & Co.
23 MacCallum Hse.

Newcomers (Rated)
26 Sonoma Saveurs▽
25 Willi's Seafood
22 Cinq▽
21 Père Jeanty
   Poggio Rist.

Outdoor Seating
26 Bistro Jeanty
   Auberge du Soleil
   Lark Creek Inn
25 Martini Hse.
23 Julia's Kitchen

People-Watching
26 Bistro Jeanty
25 Martini Hse.
24 Tra Vigne
   Bistro Don Giov.
   Mustards Grill

Romance
27 Farmhouse Inn▽
   La Toque
26 Rest. at Stevenswood
   Terra
25 Manka's Inverness

Small Plates
27 Fork
25 Willi's Seafood
24 Willi's Wine Bar
23 Zuzu
22 Cindy's Backstreet

Tasting Menus
28 French Laundry
27 La Toque
   Fork
26 Terra
   Auberge du Soleil

Winning Wine Lists
28 French Laundry
27 La Toque
26 Terra
25 Martini Hse.
22 Meadowood Grill

By Location

Marin County
27 Sushi Ran
   Fork
26 Lark Creek Inn
25 Manka's Inverness
24 Royal Thai

Mendocino County
26 Rest. at Stevenswood
24 Cafe Beaujolais
23 MacCallum Hse.
   Albion River Inn
   Little River Inn

Napa County
28 French Laundry
27 La Toque
26 Terra
   Bistro Jeanty
   Auberge du Soleil

Sonoma County
27 Farmhouse Inn▽
   Cafe La Haye
25 Madrona Manor
   Willi's Seafood
   Hana Japanese

Top Decor

27 Auberge du Soleil
Madrona Manor
El Paseo
26 French Laundry
Martini Hse.
Alexander Valley
Farmhouse Inn▽
25 Tra Vigne
Lark Creek Inn
Domaine Chandon

John Ash & Co.
Poggio Rist.
24 Rest. at Stevenswood
Manka's Inverness
La Toque
Terra
Napa Valley Train
23 Caprice, The
Dry Creek Kit.
Pinot Blanc

Top Service

27 French Laundry
La Toque
26 Rest. at Stevenswood
Farmhouse Inn▽
25 Terra
Cafe La Haye
Auberge du Soleil
24 Madrona Manor
Little River Inn
Meadowood Grill

Lark Creek Inn
Domaine Chandon
LaSalette
23 John Ash & Co.
El Paseo
Albion River Inn
Martini Hse.
Fork
Cole's Chop Hse.
Ledford Hse.

Top Bangs for the Buck

1. Downtown Bakery
2. Jimtown Store
3. Emporio Rulli
4. Villa Corona
5. Taylor's Automatic
6. Joe's Taco
7. Alexis Baking Co.
8. Amici East Coast
9. Dipsea Cafe
10. Royal Thai
11. Pasta Pomodoro
12. Lotus Cuisine
13. Las Camelias
14. Pizzeria Tra Vigne
15. Gira Polli
16. Cafe Citti
17. Gordon's
18. Max's
19. Gary Chu's
20. Christophe

North of San Francisco

	F	D	S	C

Albion River Inn 23 | 22 | 23 | $47
3790 North Hwy. 1 (Albion Little River Rd.), Albion, 707-937-1919;
www.albionriverinn.com
■ "For a quick getaway", head to this "dreamy, romantic spot perched atop a cliff overlooking the ocean" in Albion where you can "watch a pod of whales play" and the "sunset during dinner"; while the "excellent" Cal coastal cuisine "rarely breaks new ground (or should that be water?)", the wine list is "mind-boggling" and the service "convivial"; and should you consume a little too much "rare scotch" from their "spectacular collection", you can always stay the night.

ALEXANDER VALLEY GRILLE 21 | 26 | 20 | $38
(fka Chateau Souverain Café at the Winery)
400 Souverain Rd. (Hwy. 101, Independence Ln. exit),
Geyserville, 707-433-3141; www.chateausouverain.com
■ With "incredible views" "overlooking the vineyards" and "proprietary" "vino suggestions with each entree", this Geyserville winery/eatery offers "the consummate wine-country experience" ("it's where we take guests when we want to make them envious of where we live"); while the "fine Cal-French cuisine" and "attentive service" "don't match the setting", "drunk or sober", "you can't beat it in the summer" on the "beautiful outdoor patio" or "in the cold of winter when the fireplaces are aglow."

Alexis Baking Company 22 | 11 | 14 | $16
(aka ABC)
1517 Third St. (School St.), Napa, 707-258-1827;
www.alexisbakingcompany.com
☑ It "wouldn't be Saturday without" a visit to this Downtown Napa "institution" crammed with bakery devotees who find it "worth the wait in line" for "excellent coffee drinks", "creative breakfast offerings" ("of note: the huevos rancheros"), "divine cakes" and "down-home" New American lunches; however, don't expect much from the "disinterested" staff.

All Season's Cafe & Wine Shop 22 | 16 | 20 | $38
1400 Lincoln Ave. (Washington St.), Calistoga, 707-942-9111;
www.allseasonsnapavalley.com
■ Offering "no-nonsense" "seasonal" Cal–New French fare "paired with the fine wines" found in "the shop next door" (served *sans* markup), this "totally unpretentious" Calistoga eatery is where "all the local vintners" and

families dine; while the "fantastic food" and "knowledgeable staff" are "worthy of celebratory evenings", the "casual" "converted-storefront" ambiance may work better for lunch after winery-hopping.

Amici's East Coast Pizzeria 21 12 16 $18
1242 Fourth St. (C St.), San Rafael, 415-455-9777; www.amicis.com
See review in City of San Francisco Directory.

Angèle 22 22 21 $41
540 Main St. (3rd St.), Napa, 707-252-8115; www.angele.us
☑ Although "the tourists haven't found their way" into this "simpatico bistro" – yet – locals insist it's "one of the best" in "Napa's emerging restaurant scene", where "comfortable" "country-style French" food, an "adorable bar", "attentive service" and "romantic" "riverside dining" "equal a winning combination"; however, most prefer the "lovely patio" over the somewhat "spartan", "wood-beamed" interior.

Antidote _ _ _ E
201 Bridgeway (2nd St.), Sausalito, 415-331-9463; www.anti-dote.com
Former Domaine Chandon chef Eric Torralba's Sausalito newcomer showcases a 'deconstructed' French menu – e.g. 'Like a Sardine Touched for the Very First Time' (pristine fillets layered with tomatoes) and 'The Apricot's Problem' (the fruit treated six ways); dinner can begin in the lounge with a free glass of bubbly before progressing into the dining room dotted with oversized tables, bowls of goldfish and picture windows overlooking SF and the Bay.

Applewood Inn & Restaurant ▽ 24 20 21 $46
13555 Hwy. 116 (River Rd.), Guerneville, 707-869-9093; www.applewoodinn.com
■ Nestled in a "beautiful inn near the Russian River", this "quiet" "romantic" is "about as cozy as you'll find with two fireplaces" and "nice forest views", but even more dazzling is what's on the table; the "great new chef (ex Zazu) is really strutting her stuff" whipping up "excellent" locally driven Cal cuisine, while "informative waiters" are on hand to pair something from their "great wine list"; P.S. "Sunday-Monday Italian nights are screaming bargains."

AUBERGE DU SOLEIL 26 27 25 $69
Auberge du Soleil, 180 Rutherford Hill Rd. (Silverado Trail), Rutherford, 707-967-3111; www.aubergedusoleil.com
■ "Few experiences are more romantic" than this "exclusive Rutherford resort" where you "overlook a picture-postcard view" while sampling something off the "unbelievable" wine list and being "pampered by the staff"; while "even a frozen dinner would taste great" here, the "luscious" French-Med prix fixe is "so worth the price tag" – though locals "suggest stopping for lunch" for "better

vistas at half the price"; N.B. the arrival of chef Joseph Humphrey (ex Fifth Floor) postdates the Food score.

BayLeaf Restaurant   ▽ 19 22 19 $44
2025 Monticello Rd. (Vichy St.), Napa, 707-257-9720;
www.bayleafnapa.com

◪ The jury is still out on this "romantic" Napa newcomer, an unapologetically "old-fashioned" kind of place, with "a tuxedoed host", valet parking and American "food from another era" (think beef Wellington); its "fan club" appreciates the "elegant" warren of rooms and atmospheric outdoors, but modernists moan this "pretentious", "pricey" place "just doesn't work in the Valley."

Belle Arti   ▽ 19 19 18 $31
1040 Main St. (bet. 1st & Pearl Sts.), Napa, 707-255-0720;
www.bellearti-napa.com

◪ This "*belissimo*" bistro boasts a "lovely setting" "next to the river in Downtown Napa" and "straightforward" "authentic" Sicilian *cucina* that's "a welcome change from the standard Italian"; but while "good prices and friendly service" have made it into a real "locals' spot", bellicose tourists counter "competition is too tough" for an often "uneven" and "unmemorable" experience.

BISTRO DON GIOVANNI   24 22 22 $42
4110 Howard Ln. (bet. Oak Knoll & Salvador Aves.), Napa,
707-224-3300; www.bistrodongiovanni.com

■ It's "no wonder the parking lot's always full" at this "consummate" "wine-country bistro" "in the heart of Napa"; the "hearty food" tastes "as if California mated with Tuscany", "the servers are in overdrive" and the "stylish", "boisterous" room is "always packed" with an "exuberant" mix of tourists, vintners and locals; "you'd be hard-pressed to find a better scene" partisans pronounce, particularly "sitting on the patio looking out over the vineyards."

BISTRO JEANTY   26 21 23 $45
6510 Washington St. (Mulberry St.), Yountville, 707-944-0103;
www.bistrojeanty.com

■ Featuring "scrumptious", "soul-satisfying" "classic French bistro cuisine", "quaint" "farmhouse decor" and "*très bien*" service, Philippe Jeanty's "wine-country 'in' spot" "makes you feel" like "you could be in Paris" "right here in Yountville"; *oui*, it's "noisy and cramped", but in the chef-owner's "expanding culinary empire, it remains the stalwart" and "well worth" "*le détour*" – "even if you aren't going to the wineries"; P.S. spontaneous types can "just sit at the bar" or the "communal table for drop-ins."

Bistro Ralph 🖾   22 17 20 $39
109 Plaza St. (Healdsburg Ave.), Healdsburg, 707-433-1380

■ Despite a myriad of newcomers to Healdsburg, Ralph Tingle's boisterous, busy little bistro, located just off the

"Rockwell-esque town square", remains a "longtime favorite" among acolytes who relish the "excellent New American" menu made with "fresh Sonoma Valley products" and a varietal "list heavily weighted to local entries"; and while the "friendly" servers "know more about wine than a sommelier", they also proffer a martini "big enough to swim in."

Bistrot La Poste   ▽ 25 15 20 $41
599 Broadway Ave. (Patton St.), Sonoma, 707-939-3663; www.bistrotlaposte.com

☑ "Be prepared to have a good time" and make "new *amis*" at this "cheerful", "casual" "postage-stamp–size bistro" in Sonoma, "since it's like you're all sitting around having dinner together"; while the "cramped space" "could be a little difficult" for claustrophobics, it helps that the textbook French food and wine are "wonderful" and the service "boisterous and sincere."

Boonville Hotel   ▽ 22 21 19 $40
Boonville Hotel, 14050 Hwy. 128 (Lambert Ln.), Boonville, 707-895-2210; www.boonvillehotel.com

■ In the midst of "the Anderson Valley viticultural region", this "nicely restored old hotel" is a "great place to stop on your way to or from Mendocino", offering a daily changing selection of "simple" but "well-executed" Cal–New American eats and "friendly service" in the "lovely" Shaker-style dining room and bar; however, despite it being "way off the beaten path", expect interstate prices.

Bouchon ●   24 22 21 $46
6534 Washington St. (Yount St.), Yountville, 707-944-8037; www.frenchlaundry.com

☑ "French bistro fare as good as any in Paris" and "a happening late-night scene" make this Thomas Keller creation a "welcome consolation" "to those who can't get in, or just refuse to pay" for his "more famous" Yountville place; yes, "tables are tight" (lots of "patron interaction") and the "room's loud, but it's still a great wine-country experience", especially if you sit at the "awesome" zinc bar with chefs and other "interesting folks from town and beyond"; P.S. they've got a "bakery next door."

Brannan's Grill   20 21 20 $37
1374 Lincoln Ave. (Washington St.), Calistoga, 707-942-2233; www.brannansgrill.com

☑ Departing from the "quintessential charm of Calistoga", this "lively" lair evokes an "East Coast feel" with "heavy wood" "intimate lighting and cozy booths"; it's a go-to place when you're hankering for "hearty" New American fare and a "wonderful wine selection" "without the Napa Valley prices"; but critics carp it "looks better than it tastes" – or treats guests ("the servers may as well be in Vallejo").

Brasserie de la Mer
▽ 19 | 16 | 17 | $40

Vineyard Creek Hotel, 170 Railroad St. (W. 3rd St.), Santa Rosa, 707-636-7388

◪ "A fine selection" of seafood, a good value of an "early-bird prix fixe" and a "romantic, cozy fireplace bar" ("tip: ask to be seated" there) all make this Santa Rosa French bistro "better than the usual convention-center restaurant"; however, the "Denny's-like" "look detracts from the dining experience", as does an unseasoned staff that "needs some love."

Brix
21 | 22 | 20 | $44

7377 St. Helena Hwy./Hwy. 29 (Washington St.), Yountville, 707-944-2749; www.brix.com

■ Although it's "not as famous as some", this "casual" Yountviller "holds its own amid some tough wine-country competition" with its "glamorous" venue of "unobstructed views of the hills, vineyards and gardens" – the latter providing produce for the "creative" Cal cuisine; all allow the "Sunday brunch is a dream-come-true for any local or tourist", but views diverge on the adjacent wine/gift shop ("commercial" vs. "nice").

Bubba's Diner
▽ 20 | 14 | 19 | $19

566 San Anselmo Ave. (Magnolia St.), San Anselmo, 415-459-6862; www.bubbas-diner.net

■ There's "always a crowd" of Marinites munching meatloaf or "not-to-be-missed" breakfast all day at this "time-honored" diner that's back after "changing hands last year"; its "new owners" have made the place "a little more spiffy" with a "retro" '50s look – "they even have jukeboxes."

Buckeye Roadhouse
23 | 22 | 20 | $39

15 Shoreline Hwy./Hwy. 1 (west of Hwy. 101), Mill Valley, 415-331-2600; www.buckeyeroadhouse.com

■ Though it's located "off an on-ramp to 101", this Mill Valley "mainstay" is "hardly a roadhouse" – just look at the "line of Beamers valet-parked out front"; further proof's provided by the menu of "American favorites" "elevated to new levels" (like the "the best brisket outside the Lone Star state"), "great wines by the glass" and a "hunting-lodge" atmosphere that's "cozy on a rainy night"; P.S. "if you're looking for a pal for around the campfire, one can be found in the bar's" "divorced-yuppie singles scene."

Cafe Beaujolais
24 | 20 | 21 | $48

961 Ukiah St. (School St.), Mendocino, 707-937-5614; www.cafebeaujolais.com

■ "Still one of the best on the North Coast", this "charming bungalow" with lovely gardens and rustic bakery out back is always "buzzing" with the "easygoing Mendo crowd" and savvy tourists who "drive three hours from SF" just to savor the "wonderful breads" and Cal-French menu that's "simplicity rediscovered"; some still pine for "the old days" under original owner Margaret Fox, but most find the "relaxed feel" and "attentive" staff "live on."

Cafe Citti   20   11   16 $21
9049 Sonoma Hwy./Hwy. 12 (Shaw Ave.), Kenwood, 707-833-2690
☑ "A locals' favorite", this "informal" family-friendly "roadhouse" serving "awesome rotisserie chicken" and "wonderful" "Northern Italian trattoria food" at "budget-conscious" prices is a "good place to fill up" en route to or from "your favorite winery" in Kenwood; just "forget the atmosphere" (or lack thereof) and concept of service (as you "order from a counter").

CAFÉ LA HAYE   27   20   25 $40
140 E. Napa St. (bet. 1st & 2nd Sts.), Sonoma, 707-935-5994; www.cafelahaye.com
■ "It's unbelievable what chef John McReynolds creates in his tiny kitchen" at this "always fun" Cal–New American that he co-owns with Saul Gropman, who oversees the "compact", "art"-oriented room and "lovely" service; many feel it's "one of the best in Sonoma", as well as a "value", because the food based on "fresh items from local markets and farms" is "outstanding" and the wine list "worthy" of the locale.

Cafe Lolo ☒   23   17   21 $40
620 Fifth St. (Santa Rosa Ave.), Santa Rosa, 707-576-7822; www.cafelolo.com
☑ "A real Santa Rosa favorite", this "small" New American is "a standby" for locals thanks to consistently "solid" fare, "great wine" and "friendly" service; but some sense "it's getting tired" and "needs to get its winning energy back"; in particular, a "remodeling" would tame the "noise level."

Calistoga Inn   19   18   18 $30
Restaurant & Brewery
Calistoga Inn, 1250 Lincoln Ave. (Cedar St.), Calistoga, 707-942-4101; www.calistogainn.com
☑ "Hip restaurants have come and gone", but this "folksy" Calistoga brewpub has been a steadfast "fixture", supplying "straightforward", if "inconsistent", Cal fare and "crafty" "homemade beers"; but everyone agrees "the best thing" about the joint is not the "dark, uninviting dining room" but the "creek-side" patio that's "sublime on summer evenings."

Caprice, The   20   23   21 $45
2000 Paradise Dr. (Mar West St.), Tiburon, 415-435-3400; www.thecaprice.com
☑ The "main reason to go" to this address "perched over a Tiburon cove" is its "smashing" vista of San Francisco Bay and Angel Island that makes for a "special evening out" with either a "romantic" interest or grandma; but those who crave more than scenery alone say "why can't

the Californian-Continental food match the view?"– even if a few assert that, like the service, it's "improved over the last year or two."

Carneros   ▽ 23 | 19 | 20 | $43 |

The Lodge at Sonoma, 1325 Broadway (Leveroni Rd.), Sonoma, 707-931-2042; www.thelodgeatsonoma.com
☑ Set in a Sonoma hotel, this Californian offers a "splurge night out in the wine country" with a menu that makes "excellent use of the area's bounty" and plenty of vintages from the region; not everyone warms to the "somewhat corporate setting", and some add that while it's a "solid" choice, "there are better in the area"; N.B. a recent chef change may outdate the Food score.

Celadon   22 | 20 | 22 | $40 |

Napa Mills, 500 Main St. (5th St.), Napa, 707-254-9690
■ Greg Cole's "hidden treasure" in the Napa Mill complex serves New American fare that "we're all familiar with" but adds "special touches and creative pairings", plus an "interesting wine list", "to keep it fresh and worth repeat business"; service is "attentive but not obtrusive" and if the decor leaves some "feeling cold", the patio with an "outdoor fireplace is incredibly romantic."

Cena Luna 🖾   – | – | – | M |

241 Healdsburg Ave. (Matheson St.), Healdsburg, 707-433-6000; www.cenaluna.com
This 68-seat newcomer in Healdsburg is an exercise in simplicity, thanks to a weekly changing menu that offers a dozen or so regional Italian dishes (half of which feature housemade pasta) and a wine list heavy on local Sonoma picks; the dining room is old-world chic with handsome dark-cherry-wood wainscoting and a myriad of mirrors.

Chapter and Moon   ▽ 18 | 15 | 15 | $25 |

32150 N. Harbor Dr. (Shoreline Hwy.), Fort Bragg, 707-962-1643
☑ Although "hidden behind a trailer park", this newish "sweet spot on Noyo Harbor" in Fort Bragg has "nice water views" and "former Mendocino Hotel chef Colleen Murphy at the helm", cooking American "comfort food dressed up for a formal outing"; critics note the menu's "a little ambitious and should be simplified", but concede it's "needed" in these parts, especially since "you can't beat the prices."

Charcuterie   21 | 16 | 19 | $31 |

335 Healdsburg Ave. (Plaza St.), Healdsburg, 707-431-7213
■ The "decor is all pigs – and you'll feel like one after you leave" this "quaint" corner offering "locals and tourists alike" a "limited" but "well-executed" menu of French "comfort food" classics (think duck confit, salade niçoise) and "a simple wine list to match"; throw in a "friendly staff", and it all seems reminiscent of a "Paris bistro", even though it's smack dab "in the heart of Healdsburg."

Chez Felice   _ _ _ M
716 McClelland Dr. (Windsor Town Green), Windsor,
707-836-9922
Run by the owners of nearby Château Felice Winery, this
casual new bistro/tasting bar/retail shop sits on the
Windsor Town Green; chef Laurie Souza (who's cooked at
sundry wineries, most recently Kenwood) prepares a Med-
inspired menu that includes a 'Flights of Fancy' section,
pairing small plates with wines, from Felice's own vintages to
a collection of older French and California 'library' bottles.

Christophe   22 18 22 $32
1919 Bridgeway (Spring St.), Sausalito, 415-332-9244;
www.christopherestaurant.com
■ "When you are next to broke, but want to go to France",
join the "older folks" and wallet-watchers who visit this
"unapologetically French" Sausalito stalwart that "pleases
the palate as well as the pocketbook"; "while it's a tight
squeeze" in the "quaint" "one-room" space, "you won't
be disappointed" with the "never outrageous", "truly
authentic" "traditional bistro fare" and unauthentic
service (that is, "they're friendly").

Cindy's Backstreet Kitchen   22 19 19 $35
1327 Railroad Ave. (bet. Adams & Hunt Sts.), St. Helena,
707-963-1200
■ "Similar Cal–New American comfort food" given
"the Napa touch" to chef-owner "Cindy Pawlcyn's sister
restaurant" prompts patrons to dub her "re-created" "St.
Helena hot spot" "Mustards Grill North" – minus the "tourist
glitz"; there's "good cheer all around" the "quaint" digs –
"even the waiters seem to be having fun" – especially if
you join the "local wine crowd" "out on the garden patio."

Cinq ⊠   ▽ 22 17 19 $42
60 Corte Madera Ave. (Redwood Ave.), Corte Madera,
415-945-9191; www.cinqrestaurant.com
◪ "A nice addition to the Marin dining scene", this "tiny",
"casual" Corte Madera newcomer's "limited" monthly
changing menu showcases simple French classics – each
plate containing no more than five flavors – that you can
really "cinq your teeth into"; however, "service can be
uneven" and the "no-reservations policy frustrating": once
you're in, after a "long wait", "the crowds outside watch
your every move" as they hope for theirs.

Cole's Chop House   25 23 23 $52
1122 Main St. (bet. 1st & Pearl Sts.), Napa, 707-224-6328
■ If they need "to offset all that fancy wine-country"
cuisine, carnivores corral at this "*Gunsmoke*"-esque site
(think "wooden bar and rock walls"); though it specializes
in "steaks the size of an Oldsmobile", it also appeals to
non-meatheads with "some of the best seafood around";

beefy prices save it "for expense accounts and power dinners with winemakers", but with "friendly servers" pouring "wicked martinis" and "classic Napa Cabernets", "why clog the arteries anywhere else?"

Cucina Paradiso   ▽ 22 | 15 | 23 | $30 |
Golden Eagle Shopping Ctr., 56 E. Washington St. (Petaluma Blvd.), Petaluma, 707-782-1130
■ Don't let the "strip-mall storefront" fool you – this "marvelous little Southern Italian" is "one of the better spots in Petaluma" with "consistently excellent" *cucina,* "accommodating service" and such niceties as "white tablecloths, napkins and fresh flowers"; there's even a seasonal patio ("next to the parking lot", granted), which "allows you to bring your dog", if you're so inclined.

Cucina Restaurant & Wine Bar   22 | 13 | 17 | $33 |
510 San Anselmo Ave. (Tunstead Ave.), San Anselmo, 415-454-2942
■ Jack Krietzman's recently rechristened and relocated San Anselmo trattoria is "just as good, if not better than its city sister" (Jackson Fillmore); expect the same "wonderful" Italian pastas, pizzas and wines "at affordable prices", in a "Pottery Barn" atmosphere; the staff seems more "helpful" since they moved to this "smaller, more intimate" spot, though that translates to "lines for a table" on weekends.

Della Santina's   23 | 19 | 21 | $34 |
133 E. Napa St. (1st St. E.), Sonoma, 707-935-0576; www.dellasantinas.com
■ "For a *bella notte*", locals head to this "old-world" "family-owned" trattoria just "off Sonoma Square", where the real-deal Tuscan fare, including "great items from the rotisserie", and a "charming" Decor score–boosting garden patio transport you to "Italy without the eight-hour flight"; "service can be slow" but it's nothing the ever-present "endearing owner" can't fix.

Deuce   ▽ 20 | 20 | 22 | $36 |
691 Broadway (Andrieux St.), Sonoma, 707-933-3823; www.dine-at-deuce.com
◪ Surveyors have dueling views about this Sonoma New American, set in a converted Victorian farmhouse; fanciers feel the "new chef is hitting his stride" and appreciate the "truly great" locally leaning wine list, "lovely leafy patio" and "friendly staff"; foes fret "for the price, we expected a little better" than food, decor and service "without much flair."

Dipsea Cafe, The   18 | 15 | 17 | $18 |
200 Shoreline Hwy./Hwy. 1 (Tennessee Valley Rd.), Mill Valley, 415-381-0298
2200 Fourth St. (W. Crescent Dr.), San Rafael, 415-459-0700
◪ You can't beat the location – "overlooking wetlands" and Mt. Tam – but it's the "good ol' USA-style" "hearty"

breakfasts and lunches for which "everyone still lines up" at these "bustling" Marin County cafes; the interiors have all "the charm of a local diner" and the service treats you "like rawhide – moves 'em in, cuts 'em out with great rapidity", but they remain the go-to places before or after a day outdoorsing.

Domaine Chandon
24 | 25 | 24 | $61

1 California Dr. (Hwy. 29), Yountville, 707-944-2892; www.chandon.com

■ If "sparkling wine with each course" is your "idea of heaven", then "finish off a tour of the champagne facility" with a tasting menu at this "beautiful indoor/outdoor" winery restaurant set on "romantic" "sylvan" grounds; gourmets grin that new chef Ron Boyd's "exquisite" Californian menu has "put this back on the Yountville food map", the service remains "elegance defined" and a recent remodel should bring some extra fizz to the 25-year-old dining room; it's "expensive", but an "epicurean delight."

Downtown Bakery & Creamery ∅
24 | 11 | 15 | $11

308A Center St. (Matheson St.), Healdsburg, 707-431-2719; www.downtownbakery.net

☑ "Ok, so it's not a restaurant per se" but this "fantastic" Healdsburg bakery does serve "spectacular" sandwiches and "pastry, ice cream and coffee – what more do you need?"; "service can be almost rude, but then you don't have to stay long", just seize your share of the "irresistible" treats and join the "locals and their dogs" who "hang out on two benches outside" or in the square.

Dry Creek Kitchen
23 | 23 | 19 | $54

Hotel Healdsburg, 317 Healdsburg Ave. (Matheson St.), Healdsburg, 707-431-0330; www.hotelhealdsburg.com

☑ There's "big-city dining" in them Maycamas hills – specifically, at Charlie Palmer's "ultramodern" venture "adjacent to the Euro-chic Healdsburg Hotel" that's "raised the bar" for the region with its "aesthetically prepared" New American cuisine complemented by an "all-Sonoma (and all good) wine list" (and "no corkage fee" if you bring your own); however, compliments dry up when it comes to the service, which many moan is quite "inconsistent" – and "at NYC prices", it shouldn't be.

Duck Club, The
20 | 21 | 20 | $42

Bodega Bay Lodge & Spa, 103 Coast Hwy. 1 (Doran Park Rd.), Bodega, 707-875-3525; www.bodegabaylodge.com

See review in South of San Francisco Directory.

EL PASEO
24 | 27 | 23 | $51

17 Throckmorton Ave. (bet. Blithedale & Sunnyside Aves.), Mill Valley, 415-388-0741

■ A "brick walkway leads to another place and era" at this Mill Valley "classic French" (yeah, "the name belies the menu") with a "retro romantic" ambiance that bears "an abundance of charm", "attentive-but-not-snooty" staffers and a kitchen "that takes the time to make it right"; despite all this, oenophiles insist "the wine is why you dine here", citing the "sensational" 1,400-label list.

Emporio Rulli 23 | 23 | 16 | $16 |

464 Magnolia Ave. (bet. Cane & Ward Sts.), Larkspur, 415-924-7478; www.rulli.com

■ In Larkspur, this "caffeine and sugar" emporium makes you feel "like you've walked right off the streets of California" and into "a bit of Rome"; perhaps it's *un poco* pricey, but these "ethereal goodies, from panini to pastries to gelati" and coffee, savored in a "gorgeous" Euro cafe atmosphere (complete with sidewalk seating), "put Starbucks to shame"; P.S. there are "civilized" siblings in SF now too.

FARMHOUSE INN & RESTAURANT, THE ▽ 27 | 26 | 26 | $53 |

Farmhouse Inn, 7871 River Rd. (Wohler Rd.), Forestville, 707-887-3300; www.farmhouseinn.com

■ "One of the best-kept secrets in the wine country... until now", this "splurge-worthy" "brother-and-sister–run" Forestville getaway embodies "what Sonoma is all about"; guests swoon over a "daily changing" Cal menu based on "whatever is fresh and in season" and the "impeccable" locally leaning wine list, "not to mention the cheese cart and the gracious service"; the overall effect is "like dining in someone's fancy dining room", which, in a way, it is.

fig cafe & winebar ▽ 22 | 19 | 23 | $38 |

(fka the girl & the gaucho)

13690 Arnold Dr. (Warm Springs Rd.), Glen Ellen, 707-938-2130; www.thefigcafe.com

■ Owner Sondra Bernstein has transformed her Latin-leaning Glen Ellen eatery into a "more casual" "country cousin" of her the girl & the fig and the result is a place now "packed on weekends"; fans will recognize the same "laid-back, friendly" staff serving "reasonably priced" Provençal-inspired comfort dishes, but it's the wine that's "the real standout here."

First Crush 17 | 15 | 17 | $37 |

24 Sunnyside Ave. (E. Blithedale Ave.), Mill Valley, 415-381-7500; www.firstcrush.com

See review in City of San Francisco Directory.

Fish ⊟ – | – | – | M |

350 Harbor Dr. (foot of Clipper Yacht Harbor), Sausalito, 415-331-3474; www.331fish.com

Chef-owner Chad Callahan hopes to make a big splash at this cafe perched at the foot of Clipper Yacht Harbor; a former big fish himself at Masa's, his concept is as simple as the name suggests: grilled sandwiches and other straightforward preparations of sustainably caught or responsibly farmed seafood in a funky, restored 1950s boat shop; chalkboards list the day's catch, wines come in mason jars, customers order at the counter and the entire seating area is comprised of unadorned redwood picnic tables.

Foothill Cafe
24 | 14 | 21 | $35

J&P Shopping Ctr., 2766 Old Sonoma Rd. (Foothill Blvd.), Napa, 707-252-6178

☑ A "crummy strip-mall setting" hides one of "Napa's best-kept secrets" – this "reasonably priced" "source for ribs" and other "well-prepared" all-American barbecue-type eats that's "made a name for itself in the Valley"; those who "schlep" out of their way to find it are sometimes disappointed by "overcrowded" conditions and "significant waits", but others affirm it's "a must every summer."

FORK ☒
27 | 20 | 23 | $47

198 Sir Francis Drake Blvd. (bet. Bank St. & Tunstead Ave.), San Anselmo, 415-453-9898; www.marinfork.com

☑ "Big city dining comes to the country" at this Californian–New French in San Anselmo that offers a "spectacular selection of little plates", "perfect for diners who have culinary attention deficiency disorder and want to try everything"; the vibe is "relaxed", the servers seem "knowledgeable" and the "prix fixe is a very good value", but to some, it seems like "the only thing smaller than the plates is the cramped space itself."

Frantoio
21 | 20 | 18 | $40

152 Shoreline Hwy./Hwy. 1 (west of Hwy. 101), Mill Valley, 415-289-5777; www.frantoio.com

☑ "Forget that this place is adjacent to a Holiday Inn" in Mill Valley insist fans, for the Northern Italian fare's "shockingly good" and there are "many options" from which to choose; service can be "condescending" and the "noise level too high", but "during the harvest season" diners are happily distracted by the on-site "authentic" "*frantoio* [olive press] in action."

FRENCH LAUNDRY
28 | 26 | 27 | $135

6640 Washington St. (Creek St.), Yountville, 707-944-2380; www.frenchlaundry.com

■ Enthusiasts are "excited about returning" to Thomas Keller's reopened Yountville institution; the "Herculean effort" "to get a reservation could lead to disappointment" but they "wow you", from the "impeccably served" French–New American menus, "a whirlwind" of tiny tastes and big sensations, to the "gorgeous gardens" or "understated" interior; a few snap it's "stuffy", literally and figuratively, but to most, "no prose can do justice" to this "once-in-a-lifetime experience (twice on someone else's dime)."

Fumé Bistro & Bar
▽ 21 | 18 | 21 | $33

4050 Byway St. E. (Wine Country Ave.), Napa, 707-257-1999;
www.fumebistro.com

■ Although "it almost fades into the background with all the famous restaurants around", this Napa New American bistro is too "good to be forgotten" says a "mostly local" clientele that includes "winemakers sneaking a quick lunch away from the crowds" and others who likewise appreciate the "friendly" service, "comfortable, casual" atmosphere and outdoor seating.

Gary Chu's
21 | 18 | 20 | $30

611 Fifth St. (bet. D & Mendocino Sts.), Santa Rosa,
707-526-5840; www.garychus.com

■ "The Chu empire seems to be expanding" in other Asian territories, but "what brings back the crowds" to his eponymous flagship in Downtown Santa Rosa are his "upscale", and some would say "Westernized", renditions of Chinese staples served in a "classier" atmosphere than others of its ilk ("you won't see ducks in the window" here); N.B. a work-in-progress remodel may outdate the Decor score.

General's Daughter, The
19 | 23 | 21 | $39

400 W. Spain St. (bet. 4th & 5th Sts.), Sonoma, 707-938-4004;
www.thegeneralsdaughter.com

☑ You can't touch the "attractive setting" and sense of history of this "country cute" Californian set in an 1864 house "built by General Vallejo for his daughter" and boasting "lovely" gardens and a patio that's "perfect" for "drinking in the beauty of Sonoma"; while it's a hit "with the tourists", the food quality is "uneven" and the room "noisy", leading some to demote it to "The Sergeant's Daughter."

Geyser Smokehouse
▽ 15 | 14 | 16 | $22

21021 Geyserville Ave. (Hwy. 128), Geyserville, 707-857-4600;
www.geysersmokehouse.com

☑ "When you've had too much" of the "froufrou" dining scene and "want a beer in wine country", come on down and belly up to the bar of this "funky", "kick-back joint" in "tiny" Geyserville where "Sonoma County locals" queue up for 'cue even though it's "nothing amazing."

Gira Polli
20 | 13 | 17 | $22

590 E. Blithedale Ave. (Camino Alto), Mill Valley,
415-383-6040

See review in City of San Francisco Directory.

girl & the fig, the
22 | 20 | 20 | $38

110 W. Spain St. (1st St.), Sonoma, 707-938-3634;
www.thegirlandthefig.com

☑ A "must-hit" for many at the "end of a day of wine tasting", Sondra Bernstein's "quaint" Sonoma bistro offers "something for everyone" off its "inspired" French menu ("if you like figs – wow") and wine list sampled via "creative flights"; the room itself is "inviting", but fair weather permits seating outside on the "delightful" patio; N.B. the short-lived Petaluma branch is no longer.

Glen Ellen Inn Restaurant   ▽ 20 | 20 | 20 | $39 |
13670 Arnold Dr. (Warm Springs Rd.), Glen Ellen, 707-996-6409; www.glenelleninn.com

☑ Owned by a husband-and-wife team, this "cozy country place" in Glen Ellen serves "innovative" and "eye-pleasing" Cal-Fusion fare that can be sampled à la carte or on the "amazing" Saturday night tasting menu; although some folks' meals have been of "variable" success, optimists claim it's presently "working its way up"; N.B. creek-side cottages house guests who can't bear to leave.

Gordon's   24 | 17 | 17 | $27 |
6770 Washington St. (Madison St.), Yountville, 707-944-8246

■ In what's perhaps Yountville's most "poorly kept secret", this "funky, rustic-casual" American cafe harbors a "world-class" chef who creates "out-of-sight" breakfast pastries and desserts; insiders acclaim the "hard-to-get-into" Friday-only dinners but warn "if you're in the wine biz, don't come here on a bad hair day because you're guaranteed to see someone you know" among the "non-touristy" crowd.

Green Valley Cafe 🚫   ▽ 18 | 13 | 18 | $28 |
1310 Main St. (Hunt Ave.), St. Helena, 707-963-7088; www.greenvalleycafe.com

■ "Hearty, classic Northern Italian cuisine" is on hand at this "intimate little bistro in St. Helena"; "friendly service and friendly prices" make it "favored by locals" (you might "meet your favorite winemaker" here), and though it's not fancy – the "small, tight space" has a "jeans-and-boots atmosphere" – it "hits the spot after a day of tiring wine-country touring."

Guaymas   17 | 20 | 15 | $31 |
5 Main St. (Tiburon Blvd.), Tiburon, 415-435-6300

☑ The Tiburon "to-die-for view of SF" makes this "a no-brainer place to take the out-of-towners", especially if they crave "fresh seafood that's a refreshing change from the usual Tex-Mex" meals; there are those who "can't handle the crowds" or "questionable service" for fare that "isn't exactly extraordinary"; still, you can always "forget the food" and just enjoy "the dynamite margaritas" and "unbeatable" setting.

Guernica   ▽ 17 | 15 | 21 | $33 |
2009 Bridgeway (Spring St.), Sausalito, 415-332-1512

☑ Seems like this "charming little" "Sausalito institution" "hasn't changed in ambiance or menu much since the

'70s" when it opened; all agree the super-"friendly owner/host" and "enthusiastic waiters" "make dining here like going to a friend's house"; but aside from the signature paella, "not much stands out" on the Basque bill of fare, while the decor could "stand a serious rehab."

Hana Japanese Restaurant   25 | 15 | 19 | $38 |
Doubletree Plaza, 101 Golf Course Dr. (Roberts Lake Rd.), Rohnert Park, 707-586-0270; www.hanajapanese.com
☑ His shopping-mall "surroundings are uninspired" but his cuisine is anything but, rave Rohnert Park rangers about chef-owner Ken Tominaga, aka "the master Japanese chef of Northern California", who "masterfully prepares" some of "the freshest sushi in Sonoma" and cooked "European-influenced dishes" too; for maximum impact, sit at the "black-lacquered" "bar and have him prepare something for you."

Harmony Club   ▽ 21 | 24 | 19 | $42 |
Ledson Hotel, 480 First St. E. (Napa St.), Sonoma, 707-996-9779; www.ledsonhotel.com
■ The joint is jumpin' at this "handsomely built" new eatery/club overlooking the Sonoma Plaza; the kitchen prepares an Eclectic selection of "small plates that sparkle" – served on equally dazzling "fancy, exquisite china with grand silver utensils" – while the bar (doing double duty as a tasting room) pours predominantly Ledson wines ("since they own the place"); be prepared for "pricey" tabs and some noise from the "live music" that rollicks the room nightly.

Hurley's Restaurant & Bar   ▽ 18 | 19 | 18 | $35 |
6518 Washington St. (Yount St.), Yountville, 707-944-2345; www.hurleysrestaurant.com
☑ You can dine "without breaking the bank" at this "locals' hangout" in Yountville, where the "well-chosen, limited" Cal-Med menu includes "interesting wild game dishes"; alas, the "gorgeous high ceilings and tile flooring" create a din at dinner, and given the "so-so service" and oft-"inconsistent" eats, the hostile huff it's "not worth the trouble with so many wonderful places in Napa Valley."

Il Davide   21 | 17 | 19 | $34 |
901 A St. (bet. 3rd & 4th Sts.), San Rafael, 415-454-8080
☑ With "wonderful frescoed walls" within and "sidewalk seating" for lazy lunches alfresco, this send-up of a Florentine trattoria is about the "closest you get to Tuscany" in San Rafael; it's "always crowded and always good", with "tasty, unfussy" fare and a staff that stays "pleasant" despite the demanding Marin clientele.

IL FORNAIO   19 | 20 | 18 | $34 |
223 Corte Madera Town Ctr. (Madera Blvd.), Corte Madera, 415-927-4400; www.ilfornaio.com
See review in City of San Francisco Directory.

Insalata's   23 | 21 | 20 | $39

120 Sir Francis Drake Blvd. (Barber Ave.), San Anselmo,
415-457-7700; www.insalatas.com

☑ "Do yourself a huge favor" and come to this "San Anselmo
spot" for Mediterranean meals that mix "comfort and
sophistication" in a "bright" interior; chef-owner Heidi
Krahling charms many with her "warmth and charisma",
though a few complain that the "servers can be indifferent";
still, most San Franciscans agree it's "worth a journey and
a bridge toll."

Izzy's Steak & Chop House   19 | 16 | 18 | $36

55 Tamal Vista Blvd. (Madera Blvd.), Corte Madera,
415-924-3366; www.izzyssteaksandchops.com
See review in City of San Francisco Directory.

Jimtown Store   21 | 19 | 18 | $15

6706 Hwy. 128 (1 mi. east of Russian River), Healdsburg,
707-433-1212; www.jimtown.com

■ When near Healdsburg, "Harley riders, cyclists and
locals" alike stop for the "not-your-ordinary deli" delights
served at this shop (no indoor tables, but there is a "tree-
lined patio"); crammed with "novelty items", its "funky
country-store atmosphere" – the building dates from 1893 –
attracts as much attention as its "inventive" sandwiches,
"delicious" tapenades and the "cheerful crew."

Joe's Taco Lounge & Salsaria   19 | 17 | 16 | $16

382 Miller Ave. (Montford Ave.), Mill Valley, 415-383-8164

☑ Mill Valley's "no-frills" fish shack is the "quintessential
Marin hangout" for families, "bikers, hikers and their dogs
outside waiting for leftovers" of "tasty" "down-home
Mexican" meals, including "mouthwatering fish tacos" at
"correspondingly tasty prices"; just "don't let the religious
icons [everywhere] scare you" and "don't go too hungry",
'cuz it's dogged by "substantial waits" and "slow service."

John Ash & Co.   24 | 25 | 23 | $53

Vintners Inn, 4330 Barnes Rd. (River Rd.), Santa Rosa,
707-527-7687; www.johnashrestaurant.com

■ "Quietly romantic", this "spacious" "Santa Rosa
standard" "may be the most beautiful place in Sonoma
County" ("get a table overlooking the vineyards" for
maximum impact); though lacking a little "variety", the Cal
cuisine is "impeccable", the "wine list impressive" and the
service is "polished without ever feeling stuffy"; no wonder
some sigh "I'm just sorry that I never made it sooner."

Julia's Kitchen   23 | 18 | 19 | $44

COPIA, 500 First St. (bet. Silverado Trail & Soscol Ave.),
Napa, 707-265-5700; www.copia.org

☑ "How can any place live up to being named after Julia
Child?" – well, it can start by taking "hand-picked, fresher-

than-fresh vegetables from the COPIA gardens" and using them in "inventive", "beautifully presented" Cal-French dishes to be delivered by "surprisingly pleasant staffers"; dissenters profess "disappointment", especially in the "industrial atmosphere", but if this "Napa secret" "doesn't knock your socks off, it will at least loosen your shoes."

K&L Bistro
▽ | 25 | 19 | 21 | $41 |

119 S. Main St. (Bodega Hwy./Hwy. 12), Sebastopol, 707-823-6614
■ For some "French fare with flair" in Sebastopol, surveyors stop by this *petit* place proffering "honest" "bistro classics" and a "very sharp wine list"; its combination of "big-town food and neighborhood feel" is "worth the drive", even if the digs are a bit "nondescript."

Kenwood
| 23 | 20 | 21 | $41 |

9900 Sonoma Hwy./Hwy. 12 (Warm Springs Rd.), Kenwood, 707-833-6326; www.kenwoodrestaurant.com
◪ "The noise level's deafening, but the food's delightful" at this Kenwood veteran surrounded by "vineyards and killer views"; "local winemakers are regulars", commandeering a "table on the terrace" that's "meant for lingering over just one more glass of wine" after consuming a "satisfying" French–New American meal that hops "hodgepodge"like from roast duck to tapioca pudding.

La Ginestra
| 18 | 13 | 19 | $28 |

127 Throckmorton Ave. (Miller Ave.), Mill Valley, 415-388-0224
■ This "family-owned red-sauce Italian "has been a Mill Valley landmark for 40 years" by delivering "nothing fancy" – just "good old-fashioned" "homemade pizzas and pastas" in an "informal" "family-oriented atmosphere"; "it can get a little loud and crowded sometimes" (reservations aren't accepted) but insiders just wink "talk to mama – she'll treat you right."

LARK CREEK INN, THE
| 26 | 25 | 24 | $52 |

234 Magnolia Ave. (Madrone Ave.), Larkspur, 415-924-7766; www.larkcreek.com
■ Bradley Ogden's Larkspur "flagship" "temple to farm-fresh fare" is "something of an icon", proffering "polished", "plentiful" and "perfected" portions of "grandma's cooking", a "strictly American wine list" and a staff that "knows how to make guests feel at home"; the "picturesque" "100-year-old Victorian house's" "out-of-the-way location" discourages eating here on a lark, but a meal "on the sublime patio" "surrounded by redwood groves" is "worthy of a long drive" from anywhere.

LaSalette
| 24 | – | 24 | $41 |

Sonoma Plaza, 452 First St. E. (bet. Napa & Spain Sts.), Sonoma, 707-938-1927; www.lasalette-restaurant.com
■ Recently relocated to Sonoma Plaza, this family-run favorite furnishes loyal locals with a "down-to-earth" taste

of the Lisbon table "without the travel"; the "welcoming" staff makes "spot-on recommendations" off the "intriguing" menu and the "superb", "almost all Portuguese" wine list (with a "dizzying selection of ports"); N.B. Friday Fado Nights feature a fixed menu and *fadista* musicians.

Las Camelias   21 | 16 | 19 | $24 |
912 Lincoln Ave. (bet. 3rd & 4th Sts.), San Rafael, 415-453-5850
☑ This "real find" in San Rafael goes way "beyond tacos" to serve Mexican cuisine that "seems like the kind of thing a grandmother somewhere would cook"; the "owner-created ceramic sculptures" are "fabulous" to some and "off-putting" to others, but they create "a more upscale environment than most"; P.S. meat-abstainers, take note: the vegetarian options are "tasty, tasty, tasty."

LA TOQUE   27 | 24 | 27 | $93 |
1140 Rutherford Rd. (Hwy. 29), Rutherford, 707-963-9770; www.latoque.com
■ From the "exquisite" "menus du jour" to the suggested "dress code" to the "serene" room, this Rutherford refuge "is French in every classic sense of the word, and yet it's definitely Napa Valley" with "minimal pretension"; "great" as the Gallic gastronomy is, "what really shines is the service", from the sommelier who "recommends wineries to visit" to chef-owner "Ken Frank himself" who "comes out to shave the truffles" on your dinner, if you're lucky enough to be there "in January, when they're featured."

Ledford House   23 | 23 | 23 | $45 |
3000 N. Hwy. 1 (Spring Grove Rd.), Albion, 707-937-0282; www.ledfordhouse.com
■ Day-trippers find "heaven on Hwy. 1" at this "favorite" "Mendocino coast establishment"; angelic "husband-and-wife team" Tony and Lisa Greer "do a wonderful job of making everyone feel as if they're guests in their home", one where she prepares "creative" Cal-Med menus enlivened by "live jazz each evening"; surveyors also shout hosannas for the unrivalled "ocean-sunset views from the bar" ("if there's no fog"; otherwise, snuggling up to the "welcome fireplace" will have to do.)

LEFT BANK   20 | 21 | 18 | $36 |
Blue Rock Inn, 507 Magnolia Ave. (Ward St.), Larkspur, 415-927-3331; www.leftbank.com
☑ "If only my *grand-mère* could cook like this" sigh Larkspurites who claim "nothing can quite compare" with this "bustling" French brasserie ("outside tables help avoid" the "brutal acoustics" within); still, the "service could use some spiffing up", and those who "want to love it" wish it were more consistent, saying "when it's good", it's "great", but "when it's not . . . well, you want to go somewhere else"; N.B. it has *copains* South and East of SF too.

Little River Inn　　23　23　24　$39

*Little River Inn, 7901 N. Hwy. 1 (Little River Airport Rd.),
Little River, 707-937-5942; www.littleriverinn.com*

■ "There's nothing little about this gem" in Little River,
where there's "actually two eating facilities", both with
"exceptional service"; the Garden Dining Room, with "fine"
Cal food, a "lovely lit garden view and outrageous flower
arrangements", caters to tourists celebrating "special
occasions"; the "casual, lively" Ole's Whale Watching Bar,
sporting "killer ocean" vistas and pub grub, is the locals'
preferred perch to "see whales and drink like a fish."

Lotus Cuisine of India　　22　18　20　$25

*704 Fourth St. (bet. Lincoln & Tamalpais Aves.), San Rafael,
415-456-5808; www.lotusrestaurant.com*

■ Enlightened suburbanites achieve "nirvana in San
Rafael" simply by supping at "the best Indian in Marin", with
"tremendous" food and "attentive service"; the interior
is "that stereotypical pink and glittery mishmash", with
"statues of gods adorning the walls", but "it's impossible
to argue with a retractable roof", which "they pull all the
way back" so "you eat under the stars"; P.S. while it's
"reasonably priced", the real "bargain is the lunch buffet."

Lucy's　　▽　18　16　14　$32

*6948 Sebastopol Ave. (bet. Main St. & Petaluma Ave.),
Sebastopol, 707-829-9713*

◪ This "wholesome, eco-friendly alternative cafe" is
"enormously popular" with the Sebastopol set for "a simple
meal"; despite a full Cal-Med menu, pizza "out of the brick
ovens" "is the best thing here"; "service is chaotic", but
it's about "the only non-dive bar in town where you can get
a decent drink with decent food", "so it all evens out."

MacCallum House　　23　20　21　$43

*MacCallum House Inn, 45020 Albion St. (bet. Kasten &
Lansing Sts.), Mendocino, 707-937-5763;
www.maccallumhouse.com*

◪ A grand ol' historic inn in Mendocino Village that exudes
"late-19th-century charm", with a warren of "quaint",
"intimate" "odd-shaped rooms" in which to enjoy longtime
chef Alan Kantor's "intelligently prepared, perfectly
seasoned" Cal cuisine; the presence of "new owners"
hasn't manifested itself in the dining room – guests joke
"you need the olive oil tasting appetizer to slide into the
small tables" – but "hopefully they'll perk up the service."

MADRONA MANOR　　25　27　24　$61

*Madrona Manor Inn, 1001 Westside Rd. (W. Dry Creek Rd.),
Healdsburg, 707-433-4231; www.madronamanor.com*

■ "Take your date" to this historic Healdsburg landmark
(built 1881), the "perfect place to be with someone you love
who loves fine food"; "service is professional, yet warm"

whether you're enjoying the "sophisticated, well-prepared" New American–French bistro cuisine on the "lovely" terrace or in the "elegant dining room"; those carried away by romance suggest "renting one of their lovely suites."

Manka's Inverness Lodge   25 | 24 | 21 | $66
30 Callendar Way (Argyle St.), Inverness, 415-669-1034; www.mankas.com

☑ "Walk all day then eat all night" at this Inverness "hunting lodge" serving "sophisticated" yet "rustic" Cal meals of "über-local food" (i.e. it's all raised, foraged or fished in the Point Reyes region), which is "expertly prepared" in the fireplace warming the "snug room" "while a dog scratches itself on the floor"; cynics say the scene is "terminally precious" and the "staff can be a bit prickly", but to most, it's a "magical" experience.

Manzanita   22 | 18 | 20 | $44
336 Healdsburg Ave. (North St.), Healdsburg, 707-433-8111

☑ A "menu highlighting seasonal ingredients" (plus "great wood-burning-oven pizza"), a "bartender who knows his wines" and servers who are "really good folks" make this Med "probably Healdsburg's most underrated restaurant" to fans; "not bad, but there are better in town" retort foes, who cite a "cold atmosphere" and "uncreative" vittles.

Marché aux Fleurs ⑧   ▽ 24 | 21 | 24 | $44
23 Ross Common (off Lagunitas Rd.), Ross, 415-925-9200; www.marcheauxfleursrestaurant.com

■ "In sleepy Ross", this "pretty little" New French owned by a "lovely couple" blossoms with his "exquisite", "expertly prepared" "seasonal menus", her "amazing", "affordable" wine list and "wonderful personal service" from both of them.

Marin Joe's ◐   17 | 11 | 16 | $29
1585 Casa Buena Dr. (south of Tamalpais Dr.), Corte Madera, 415-924-2081

☑ "One of the last" of the "old-school" Italian eateries (does that make it "retro cool or just weird"?), this "circa 1954"–decorated "throwback" is "a Marin County standby" for pastas, steaks and Caesar salad "prepared tableside" by "black tie–clad" waiters; a no-reservations policy, plus being "about the only post-10 PM game in town", means you should "be prepared to wait" with the "blue hairs" drinking in the piano bar – the only thing, moan modernists, that "makes the food halfway palatable."

Market   21 | 20 | 21 | $33
1347 Main St. (bet. Adam & Spring Sts.), St. Helena, 707-963-3799; www.marketsthelena.com

☑ The "professional staff, warm decor", plus one of the "most reasonably priced wine lists" around ensure a "perfect balance of price, place and people" at this "wine-country winner"; its Traditional American eats make a "nice break from all the haute cuisine" in Napa Valley – though since it's "comfort food as executed by a world-class chef" (Douglas Keane, ex Jardinière, to be precise), clearly "this is not your mother's mac 'n' cheese."

MARTINI HOUSE   25 26 23 $53
1245 Spring St. (bet. Main & Oak Sts.), St. Helena, 707-963-2233; www.martinihouse.com

■ "I wanted to move in but was only able to stay for lunch" sums up the sentiment inspired by St. Helena's "extremely romantic" ("complete with blazing fireplace"), "converted Craftsman house"; "always creative", Todd Humphries' "terrific" New American cuisine "perfectly complements the incredible wine list" and "superb" namesake cocktails brought by an "enthusiastic staff"; in short, "sorta spendy, but worth it" for an "over-the-top" experience.

Max's   16 13 16 $22
60 Madera Blvd. (Hwy. 101), Corte Madera, 415-924-6297; www.maxsworld.com

See review in City of San Francisco Directory.

Meadowood Grill   22 22 24 $48
Meadowood Resort, 900 Meadowood Ln. (Howell Mountain Rd., off Silverado Trail), St. Helena, 707-963-3646; www.meadowood.com

■ Whether "you're staying at the hotel" or just "stargazing" at the A-list regulars, this St. Helena Cal with a country-lodge setting ("feels like a mountain resort rather than the wine country") can be ideal "for a romantic and relaxed" meal, thanks to the exhaustive all-Napa wine list, "first-rate service" and "lovely patio" "overlooking the golf course" and croquet lawns; P.S. the post-*Survey* arrival of chef Vincent Nattress, who has revamped the "typical grill-oriented menu", may outdate the Food score.

Mendo Bistro   ▽ 23 16 19 $32
The Company Store, 301 N. Main St., 2nd fl. (Redwood Ave.), Fort Bragg, 707-964-4974; www.mendobistro.com

☑ Chef-owner Nicholas Petti's "goofy hat makes the papers" and his "crab cakes win the awards", but his "cavernous" Fort Bragg bistro has "developed a loyal following" as a "neighborhood restaurant that overachieves"; accompanied by an all-Mendo wine list, the New American–Med menu lets "you choose how you want your meat cooked and sauced"; the "iffy service" is nothing to bragg about, though.

Mirepoix ☒   ▽ 26 18 25 $46
275 Windsor River Rd. (Bell Rd.), Windsor, 707-838-0162

■ "Some of the best food" in Sonoma County can be had – as long as you "make reservations" – at this "homey" New American–New French in Windsor that's "worth the detour" off Hwy. 101; it's "small enough" that "you might get to meet the chef" and be treated to "excellent, attentive service" (that happily replenishes the "platters of heavenly flatbread" accompanying the meal); they'll also waive the corkage fee on any Sonoma wine not offered from their tiny cellar.

Mixx Restaurant ⊠   21 | 19 | 19 | $39 |

135 Fourth St. (Davis St.), Santa Rosa, 707-573-1344; www.mixxrestaurant.com

☑ "Great food" and even "better desserts" (courtesy of co-owner/pastry chef Kathleen Berman) make this "somewhat funky" Californian that "fits the mood" of "quirky Railroad Square" "worth visiting regularly"; adventurous eaters, however, wish they would mixx it up a bit, muttering that the menu has "no imagination."

Model Bakery   ∇ 22 | 11 | 13 | $12 |

1357 Main St. (bet. Adams & Spring Sts.), St. Helena, 707-963-8192; www.themodelbakery.com

■ "Who needs Starbucks when you have" this retro-looking "St. Helena institution" servicing "the elite of Napa Valley"; granted, it's just a "walk-in, order your stuff, walk-out bakery", but that stuff ("killer cookies", brick-oven "pizza to die for" and "fabulous grilled panini") provides a delectable "high-carb start" or "stop in-between winery tastings."

Monti's Rotisserie & Bar   – | – | – | M |

Montgomery Village Shopping Center, 714 Village Ct. (Parker Hill Rd.), Santa Rosa, 707-568-4404

Restaurateurs Mark and Terri Stark, the duo behind Willi's Wine Bar, offer *petit* plates as well as family-style platters at their newest venture at the Montgomery Village Shopping Center; the homey farmhouse-inspired decor is matched by an equally rustic Med menu, while their signature eclectic wine program features pours in many sizes.

Moosse Cafe   20 | 16 | 17 | $34 |

Blue Heron Inn, 390 Kasten St. (Albion St.), Mendocino, 707-937-4323; www.theblueheron.com

☑ Situated in the Blue Heron Inn, this casual Cal cafe gets "Mendocino insiders'" vote as a "must-stop for lunch", thanks to "imaginative, delicious salads and sandwiches" and an "enchanted garden with a glimpse of the sea" visible from the "quirky", "intimate" interior; "very slow" staffers, however, have caused the Service score to sink.

Mustards Grill   24 | 18 | 21 | $39 |

7399 St. Helena Hwy./Hwy. 29 (Washington St.), Yountville, 707-944-2424; www.mustardsgrill.com

■ "There is a reason that this place is still so hard to get into": celebrity chef/co-owner Cindy Pawlcyn is "at her best" at this "country roadhouse–like" Napa New American that's perfect "when you've had fusion up to here" and just want "down-home cooking with a gourmet touch"; it's a bit loud, but the signature "Mongolian pork chop is worth sitting next to a jet engine for", and the servers are "jolly people."

Napa General Store　　▽ 18 | 14 | 14 | $21 |

500 Main St. (5th St.), Napa, 707-259-0762;
www.napageneralstore.com

☑ "Unpretentious yet delicious (a difficult combo in Napa)", this family-friendly, "informal" "self service" cafe within a gourmet food shop is "good for the odd" midday hour when you want to grab a "quick bite" of glorified deli and "watch the river roll by" from the deck; N.B. at press time, new chef Nam Phan (ex Slanted Door) had begun offering an eclectic Pacific Rim small-plate menu weekend evenings.

Napa Valley Grille　　20 | 19 | 19 | $39 |

Washington Sq., 6795 Washington St. (Madison St.),
Yountville, 707-944-8686; www.napavalleygrille.com

☑ Surveyors are split on this old "reliable" "right in Downtown Yountville": certainly, the "nice patio" is a "great place for an outdoor" meal, and you can feast on the "fine" Cal cuisine (including "desserts that could replace antidepressants") "and still come home with your wallet intact"; but critics decry a "corporate food and service" mentality (it's "part of a chain"), shrugging it's "too standard to be worth a stop in Napa."

Napa Valley Wine Train　　17 | 24 | 20 | $64 |

1275 McKinstry St. (bet. 1st St. & Soscol Ave.), Napa,
800-427-4124; www.winetrain.com

☑ "Go during the daytime" "so you really get to see the beauty of the Napa Valley" while riding a "restored" train, urge those who are on board with this meals-on-wheels adventure; the Cal cuisine is "surprisingly palatable", though "of course not gourmet level", and the service "professional"; "certainly, it's a tourist trap", but a nice "onetime experience" as well.

955 Ukiah　　▽ 21 | 19 | 21 | $41 |

955 Ukiah St. (School St.), Mendocino, 707-937-1955;
www.955restaurant.com

■ Yes, the "funky" '70s decor of this "tucked-away-off-the-beaten-path Mendocino Village secret" "takes you back" – but what brings you back is the "delicious seasonal" New American–New French fare fashioned "from local farms' and fishermen's" wares that's "cooked with love" and served "with panache" by "gracious, informative servers" who "even have suggestions about events going on" around the county.

Olema Inn　　▽ 22 | 22 | 19 | $35 |

Olema Inn, 10000 Sir Francis Drake Blvd. (Hwy. 1), Olema,
415-663-9559; www.theolemainn.com

■ "What a treat!" exclaim those who, after "an exhausting day hiking", stumble on this "spare and elegant option in the wild country of Point Reyes National Seashore"; the Cal-Med cuisine stars "local, organically grown produce and bounty" "simply but well prepared" ("the Tomales Bay oysters reign"); the 1876 inn setting is "long on charm" too.

Osake ☒
▽ 22 | 18 | 18 | $35

2446 Patio Ct. (Farmer's Ln.), Santa Rosa, 707-542-8282; www.garychus.com

■ There's just "no stopping Gary Chu" who, when not running his eponymous Chinese, is "often here behind the sushi counter with fast hands and a hearty laugh", preparing "outrageous" "fusion rolls" and other "eclectic" Cal-Japanese dishes; his "pleasing personality" pervades the "friendly", "well-designed" space that includes a 250-gallon decorative "fish tank in the entrance bar area."

Pangaea
▽ 22 | 18 | 19 | $40

39165 Shoreline Hwy./S. Hwy. 1 (eastern side of the Hwy.), Gualala, 707-884-9669

■ Having moved from Pt. Arena to Downtown Gualala, this Mendocino coast sleeper is "better than ever" swear supporters of its self-billed "zaftig" Cal cuisine – "eclectic, robust" offerings like a "bittersweet chocolate cake", washed down with organic and biodynamic bottlings; the owners have made the new surroundings "in the middle of nowhere" more inviting, with "a bright mix of Provençal charm and urbane funk."

Pasta Pomodoro
15 | 13 | 16 | $18

Montecito Plaza, 421 Third St. (Irving St.), San Rafael, 415-256-2401

See review in City of San Francisco Directory.

Pearl ☒
▽ 22 | 17 | 22 | $29

1339 Pearl St. (bet. Franklin & Polk Sts.), Napa, 707-224-9161; www.therestaurantpearl.com

■ This "quaint" Downtown Napa joint is "the place locals hope you don't find out about" – "where winemakers go" when they want "terrific food but with none of the fanfare of the up-valley dining temples"; the "friendly" husband-and-wife owners "do a bang-up job" "in the kitchen and on the floor", serving Cal comfort food "like mom used to make if she were a heckuva good cook"; P.S. the "delicious oyster" selection is considered the pearl of the menu.

Père Jeanty
21 | 21 | 19 | $43

6725 Washington St. (Madison St.), Yountville, 707-945-1000; www.perejeanty.com

☑ Francophiles who travel for a taste of chef-entrepreneur Philippe Jeanty's French food now have this "fun new option", complete with a communal table and antique Gallic bric-a-brac; *la différence* here is that this large Yountville outpost's "interesting" Provençal menu features "lighter fare" – seafood, pizzas, "even a great hamburger";

comparison shoppers say it's not up to "sibling Bistro Jeanty" (particularly the "unpolished staff") but concede "it's a good second choice."

Piatti   18 19 18 $34

625 Redwood Hwy. (Hwy. 101), Mill Valley, 415-380-2525
El Dorado Hotel, 405 First St. W. (Spain St.), Sonoma, 707-996-2351
6480 Washington St. (Oak Circle), Yountville, 707-944-2070
www.piatti.com

☑ With branches throughout the Bay, this "kid-friendly" "cheerful chain" is "not like mama's, but good"; a "cozy atmosphere" and "solid Italian food" win over many, especially since you can "enjoy your meal without breaking the bank"; but service that "can be, at times, indifferent" and "cookie-cutter" choices leave some saying "ho-hum."

Piazza D'Angelo   17 18 17 $34

22 Miller Ave. (bet. Sunnyside & Throckmorton Aves.),
Mill Valley, 415-388-2000; www.piazzadangelo.com

☑ "A Mill Valley institution where people go to see and be seen", as the line of "expensive celebrity cars parked in front" attests, this "bustling" trattoria is "more than the sum of its parts", "conjuring up warm feelings" despite its "erratic" fare; maybe it's the all-day dining, "the efficient staff" or those "heated outdoor patios" or perhaps it's simply the "we-think-we're-in-LA bar scene."

Pilar ☒   – – – M

807 Main St. (3rd St.), Napa, 707-252-4474

Named for the Food Network personality Pilar Sanchez, working with co-chef/husband Didier Lenders, this new eatery near the Napa River is all about the wine country, from the local, seasonally driven Cal menu to the dining room's focal visual, a woodblock triptych ('The Farmer', 'The Winemaker', 'The Cook'); however, the actual vino list, which is categorized by varietal, carries both U.S. producers (listed on one side) and their foreign counterparts (on the other).

Pinot Blanc   20 23 21 $47

641 Main St. (Grayson Ave.), St. Helena, 707-963-6191;
www.patinagroup.com

☑ Set in the heart of St. Helena, this send-up of a Provençal country inn with a "posh" interior and "great alfresco dining" is a "gorgeous setting" for a "relaxing" "sit-down lunch while on the prowl for wine", enhanced by "service at your choice of pace" and a "broad by-the-glass" list; however, considering that this pricey Cal–New French is "part of the Splichal empire in LA", "it should be great, but it just misses."

Pizza Azzurro ☒   ▽ 21 12 17 $20

1400 Second St. (Franklin St.), Napa, 707-255-5552

☑ "For a quick meal in Downtown Napa", this pie shop offers something more than your "ordinary pepperoni pizza stop"; though the setting may be "rather utilitarian" and the servers "pretty amateur", the "terrific thin-crust" pies crowned with "unique gourmet toppings" and the wines from "local boutique wineries" "overshadow any complaint one might have with the decor or service."

Pizzeria Tra Vigne
20 | 18 | 17 | $23

(fka Vitte)

Inn at Southbridge, 1016 Main St. (Pope St.), St. Helena, 707-967-9999; www.pizzeriatravigne.com

■ After years of being known as 'that pizza joint run by Tra Vigne', this Italian now officially bears the mother ship's name; the menu offers "fab pizzas", pasta and piadine – "salad wrapped in flatbread" – as well as a "great wine list (for a pizzeria)" or "free corkage" if you bring your own; TVs and a pool table lend a casual feel, making it "a favorite to take children to."

Poggio Ristorante
21 | 25 | 18 | $41

777 Bridgeway (Bay St.), Sausalito, 415-332-7771

◪ Larry Mindel (founder of Il Fornaio) "has done it again" with this "delightful addition to the Sausalito waterfront"; the trattoria's "fabulous finished" Florentine interior "with doors opening" onto the sidewalk is a fitting backdrop for Chris Fernandez's (ex Oliveto's) "honestly prepared, rustic" Tuscan fare, complemented by a "great value" wine list; it's "one of the few places in town where the food matches the beautiful" views of SF Bay, but a weak spot is the staff, which is "nice, when it finally gets around to your table."

Ravenous
23 | 18 | 20 | $38

420 Center St. (North St.), Healdsburg, 707-431-1770

◪ This "quintessential neighborhood cafe", set in a "charming" "little white" cottage near "the Plaza stores", has "become a destination in its own right"; "lunch is for sure a hit", to the extent "they run out of half" of the Cal menu "by the end of the day", but dinner "in the garden" or in the dim, "intimate" interior is rather "romantic"; however, "the name describes the condition" many get into, due to "quirky service"; P.S. heartsick Healdsburgers "miss [late sibling] Ravenette next to the Raven Theater."

Rendezvous Inn & Restaurant
∇ 25 | 19 | 21 | $43

647 N. Main St. (Bush St.), Fort Bragg, 707-964-8142; www.rendezvousinn.com

◪ "An auberge in Fort Bragg? – well, not really", but that's what "passionate" chef-owner Kim Badenhop's "outstanding" New French aspires to be; his "creative" dishes, each "complemented by an amazing wine" suggestion, are "absolutely impeccable", and they're served by an "eloquent staff"; some new gardens may mollify those who say the 1897 B&B "needs help in the looks department"; otherwise, a visit "makes a Mendocino weekend perfect."

RESTAURANT AT STEVENSWOOD, THE
26 | 24 | 26 | $53

*Stevenswood Lodge, 8211 Shoreline Hwy./Hwy. 1
(2 mi. south of Mendocino), Little River, 707-937-2810;
www.stevenswood.com*

■ "Chef Marc Dym deserves to swim in a much bigger pond", so Little River "couldn't be luckier to have him" cooking up "beautifully presented" Mediterranean cuisine that's "always a half-step ahead of others"; "everything [else] is superlative" at this "stunner", too, from the "elegant", "intimate setting" to the highly "helpful waiters."

Restaurant 301
▽ 22 | 22 | 24 | $44

*Carter House Inn, 301 L St. (3rd St.), Eureka, 707-444-8062;
www.carterhouse.com*

■ Explorers who make "the detour off 101" shout Eureka – what a "surprisingly" "high-class" establishment "so far up the North Coast"; the high-ceilinged Victorian room provides ambiance for the garden-fresh (from the inn's own garden) New American–New French fare that occasionally "overreaches" but often is "outstanding"; the "educated staff has helpful ideas on wine pairings" from the 3,800-label cellar, but also "knows how to point you to a bargain."

Ristorante Allegria
▽ 20 | 23 | 21 | $36

*1026 First St. (Main St.), Napa, 707-254-8006;
www.ristoranteallegria.com*

☑ Endowed with a "killer location" – a Downtown Napa "beautiful, restored old bank building" – this Italian "fittingly pays a dividend" in the shape of sake cocktails, "attentive service" and quite "good food"; however, the sound "echoes insanely on busy nights", and skeptics sigh that while the sophomore "started off with a well-deserved bang", it's "sort of settled down into a less-spectacular version"; P.S. high rollers should "ask for the vault room for special occasions."

Ristorante Fabrizio ☒
20 | 16 | 21 | $31

455 Magnolia Ave. (Cane St.), Larkspur, 415-924-3332

■ It's "a li'l bit old-fashioned, but the regulars love it" at this Larkspur "reliable", serving "Northern Italian food at a reasonable price"; locals testify they've "never had a bad meal – though never had a great one, either"; however, "under the watchful eye of its namesake" chef-owner, the service is now quite "efficient", as a rise in the score attests.

Robata Grill & Sushi
20 | 16 | 16 | $33

*591 Redwood Hwy./Hwy. 101 (Seminary Dr. exit), Mill Valley,
415-381-8400; www.robatagrill.com*

☑ When folks crave raw fish "with no fancy overlay" – or a wait to get in – they head to this Mill Valley standby; the "paddle presentation [of the food] at the sushi bar is certainly unique", as are the "interesting vegetarian items" cooked on the namesake grill; but while it may offer the county's "best variety" of Japanese eats, sophisticates shrug that in the grand scheme of sashimi things, it's "standard."

Royal Thai 24 │ 17 │ 19 │ $23 │

610 Third St. (Irwin St.), San Rafael, 415-485-1074;
www.royalthaisanrafael.com

■ This "cute" "old Victorian home" is San Rafaelites' "favorite place to Thai one on", with a menu of "fresh, spicy-where-appropriate" fare that "goes beyond the typical"; throw in the "warm service" and you've got "one of the best" Bangkoks for your buck.

Rutherford Grill 21 │ 19 │ 20 │ $34 │

1180 Rutherford Rd. (Hwy. 29), Rutherford, 707-963-1792;
www.houstons.com

☑ "The scene is a who's-who of the Napa Valley wine industry" (maybe because they can bring their own with "no corkage fee") at Rutherford's "down-homey grill house" where "unhurried servers" deliver American eats that range from "knife-and-fork ribs" to "spectacular teriyaki ostrich"; and if it "seems like a Houston's", well, that's because they own it; P.S. reservations are now accepted, which may ease the "long waits."

Sam's Anchor Cafe 14 │ 19 │ 15 │ $26 │

27 Main St. (Tiburon Blvd.), Tiburon, 415-435-4527;
www.samscafe.com

☑ "Spandex-clad yuppies" stir up quite a singles scene as they swizzle a Bloody Mary or three at this Tiburon hangout that hoists "a breathtaking view" of the Bay; the cognoscenti confide "you don't go here for the food" or service, but there's "deck dining" on "average" American eats; just "watch the seagulls, or they'll take your fries."

Santé ▽ 20 │ 21 │ 22 │ $48 │

Sonoma Mission Inn & Spa, 100 Boyes Blvd. (Sonoma Hwy.), Sonoma, 707-939-2415; www.fairmont.com

☑ "To see the impressive Sonoma Mission Inn" is reason alone for a visit, but those who've "been pampered all day at the spa" also laud the Cal fare ("this is the way all health food should taste") offered by "attentive, yet discreet service" in this "posh", "peaceful" place; the recent arrival of chef Bruno Tison (ex NYC's The Plaza Hotel) may smooth out the "uneven" edges some cite.

Santi 24 │ 20 │ 22 │ $41 │

21047 Geyserville Ave. (Hwy. 128), Geyserville, 707-857-1790;
www.tavernasanti.com

■ When "everything in Healdsburg is booked up", take your wine-country visitors to this Geyserville "sleeper" – or better yet, "send them here first", as it's "one of the few out there" "that really tastes like Italy", with "lovingly prepared" and "graciously served" "soul food" from the northern regions that can be enjoyed in the "cozy inside" or on "a lovely garden out back"; the wine list features the "familiar" along with "new things to try."

Sassafras Restaurant &   ∇ 20 | 17 | 21 | $33 |
Wine Bar
Santa Rosa Business Park, 1229 N. Dutton Ave. (College Ave.), Santa Rosa, 707-578-7600
◪While the Santa Rosa "business park setting is a bit off-putting, once inside" customers "run to the wine bar" for "fun and educational flights" from the born-in-the-USA cellar at this vino and food "pairing paradise"; "new chef-owner Jack Mitchell has improved the quality" of the New American eats, but "that ratty decor has got to go."

Scoma's   21 | 17 | 19 | $39 |
588 Bridgeway (Princess St.), Sausalito, 415-332-9551; www.scomassausalito.com
See review in City of San Francisco Directory.

Sea Ranch Lodge Restaurant   ∇ 18 | 19 | 17 | $43 |
Sea Ranch Lodge, 60 Sea Walk Dr. (Hwy. 1), Sea Ranch, 707-785-2371; www.searanchlodge.com
■ Perched on the northern Sonoma coastline, this "remote, romantic" resort restaurant is a "welcome refuge off Highway 1"; "killer views of the ocean" lend themselves to "leisurely dinners" of locally caught seafood and "monthly winemaker dinners that are a treat"; however, old ranch hands prefer watching the sunset and "having a drink" "in the glassed-in sun room", which offers a "good bar menu."

Seaweed Café   – | – | – | M |
(fka Seaweed House)
1580 Eastshore Rd. (Hwy. 1), Bodega Bay, 707-875-2700; www.seaweedcafe.com
"Surely one of the best in Bodega Bay" say the few who know this mustard-colored cafe where French-born chef/co-owner Jackie Martine relies predominantly on local Sonoma larders to create an "eclectic", all-organic Cal version of 'coastal cuisine', which is paired with an exclusive Sonoma wine list (anything grown west of Highway 101); N.B. the prix fixe dinner is served Friday–Monday only.

Sharon's By the Sea   ∇ 20 | 13 | 18 | $31 |
Noyo Harbor, 32096 N. Harbor Dr. (Hwy. 1), Fort Bragg, 707-962-0680
Hill House Inn, 10701 Palette Dr. (Lansing St.), Mendocino, 707-937-3200
www.sharonsbythesea.com
■ This "hidden" "harborside hangout" perched on the pier in Fort Bragg offers "the best bang for the buck on the North Coast" – "and such a tasty bang" it is, with its "always good" Italianate seafood; the interior has been expanded, but "outside on the deck" under the bridge is preferred to "just watch the seagulls", "seals at play" and

fishermen reeling in what's likely to be on your plate;
P.S. "Sharon's just started cooking at the Hill House Inn
in Mendocino Village."

Sonoma Meritage & Oyster Bar
∇ 22 18 20 $38

*522 Broadway (bet. E. Napa & Patten Sts.), Sonoma,
707-938-9430; www.sonomameritage.com*
◪ Though the bivalves are "as fresh as can be", "don't be
fooled – this oyster bar serves one heck of an osso buco"
or whatever French–Northern Italian dishes the chef is
making that day; "generous portions" and an "excellent
wine list" featuring local and imported selections make it
ideal for "lunch just off the Sonoma Square"; doubters
who say "a new location might help" the dark digs will
delight in a move, scheduled in September at press time,
to 165 Napa Street.

Sonoma Saveurs
∇ 26 20 20 $32

*487 First St. W. (bet. Napa & Spain Sts.), Sonoma,
707-996-7007; www.sonomasaveurs.com*
■ "Get ready to say ooh-la-la" at this "brilliant new"
bistro/wine bar/retail store just off Sonoma Square;
although it serves "lovingly prepared classic French
fare" along with locally made "picnic food", it's already
known as "the home of the perfect foie gras", served in
an adobe-walled room that's "cozy or cramped, depending
on your viewpoint."

Station House Café
18 15 16 $27

*11180 State Rte. 1 (Sir Francis Drake Blvd.), Point Reyes
Station, 415-663-1515*
◪ "After a day of hiking at nearby Point Reyes National
Seashore", hungry diners stop at this station "straddling
the line between white tablecloth and greasy spoon" for
refueling on "solid" "down-home" Cal "grub" – particularly
"anything taken from the sea"; a "classy bar" and "live
music on weekend evenings" make it a "regular haunt for
locals", but killjoys claim the "long lines on the weekends"
reflect the fact "there's not much to choose from in
this remote locale."

St. Orres
∇ 24 24 23 $54

*36601 Shoreline Hwy./Hwy. 1 (2 mi. north of Gualala),
Gualala, 707-884-3303; www.saintorres.com*
◪ Chef Rosemary Campiformio puts her "little candied"
"heart in the salads" and everything else she prepares on
her "whimsical" prix fixe dinners in a Gualala B&B "way out-
of-the-way up the coast"; saints say "it's a sin not to go when
she's cooking" just to sample the Cal "menu of all things
hunted – shark, boar, venison and more [served] under the
onion-domed dining room hanging gardens"; but devils
declare the "contrived cuisine" "could use updating."

SUSHI RAN   27 | 20 | 21 | $44

107 Caledonia St. (bet. Pine & Turney Sts.), Sausalito,
415-332-3620; www.sushiran.com

■ "In a town that knows good, fresh fish", this "Tokyo-class"
Japanese stalwart in Sausalito has achieved "near-cult
status" for its "artistically presented" "Ameri-makis" and
sashimi, as well as "innovative Cal-Japanese" cooked
offerings "for those who stay away from the raw stuff"; it
also "scores high on the trend-o-meter" with "chichi
crowds" peopling the "lovely Zen-like room" or cooling
their jets on the patio of the stellar sake bar as they wait
for a table (which "can take forever" some grouse).

Syrah ☒   24 | 18 | 22 | $44

205 Fifth St. (Davis St.), Santa Rosa, 707-568-4002;
www.syrahbistro.com

◪ Centrally located in "historic Railroad Square", this Cal-
French bistro "is becoming the place to go in Santa Rosa"
for an "intimate dinner" at "reasonable prices", featuring
a "constantly changing menu", "fantastic wine list" and
"friendly service"; chef-owner Josh Silvers' passion is
evident whether he's in the "open kitchen that's fun to
watch" or "chatting with customers", and enables many to
overlook the "industrial feeling" of the dining room and the
outdoor seating in an "office-building atrium."

Tapeo   – | – | – | M

916 B St. (bet. 3rd & 4th Sts.), San Rafael, 415-453-2849

Tapas mania has reached the suburbs at this San Rafael
outpost, which doles out hot and cold Spanish-Med small
plates as well as a classic paella; the cosmopolitan dining
room is lavished with earth tones and Venetian plastered
columns, while the granite bar lounge serves a selection of
international beers, sangrias and *agave* wine cocktails.

Taylor's Automatic Refresher   22 | 14 | 16 | $15

933 Main St. (bet. Charter Oak Ave. & Pope St.), St. Helena,
707-963-3486; www.taylorsrefresher.com

■ "Not your father's roadside hamburger stand" – more
like "a D.Q. that died and went to heaven", this "iconic" St.
Helena "'50s" "walk-up" diner is "a junk-food lover's
dream", flipping classics like "blue-cheese burgers so
messy they drip down your arm" along with "seared ahi" and
killer vinos; "it's always jammed" and "a little overpriced"
but still "one of the cheaper places" in the area; N.B. the
new SF Ferry Building outpost's sit-down dining and Bay
views have elevated the Decor score.

TERRA   26 | 24 | 25 | $60

1345 Railroad Ave. (bet. Adams & Hunt Sts.), St. Helena,
707-963-8931; www.terrarestaurant.com

■ "Trust your culinary fortunes to Hiro Sone and his wife,
Lissa Doumani", who deliver "all the bang-for-big-bucks"

with an "exquisite", "flawlessly executed" New American (with Southern French and Northern Italian influences) menu at their Napa Valley "destination" housed in a "beautiful old" fieldstone building; the "wine list is more like a dictionary" and the "gracious" staff so "knowledgeable it was as if they were in the kitchen preparing the food."

TRA VIGNE   24 ⎟ 25 ⎟ 22 ⎟ $48 ⎟

1050 Charter Oak Ave. (Hwy. 29), St. Helena, 707-963-4444;
www.travignerestaurant.com

■ A stop at St. Helena's "quintessential Napa Valley restaurant" is like being "wined and dined at a private Tuscan villa" by "attentive" hosts who "know every wine and every vineyard"; dazzled devotees are undecided whether the "excellent" Italian fare "enhances the sun-dappled courtyard setting, or the other way around", but it's moot for most who can't think of a better way "to spend a romantic afternoon before hitting the wineries"; P.S. the "bar is a great place" to "drop in without a reservation" and "meet local vintners."

Tuscany   17 ⎟ 21 ⎟ 17 ⎟ $35 ⎟

1005 First St. (Main St.), Napa, 707-258-1000

☑ For Northern Italian "country-style cuisine" "with a wine-country accent", *amici* aver this Napa spot "can deliver" "really good food" and "fine service", but locals lament that "it's devolved into a tourist mill" with "unpredictable" fare that's "not worth the wait" or the "noise during the summer"; still, many are drawn by the "regional decor" – think "weathered wood beams", "flower boxes" and "French doors that open up to the warm weather."

Underwood Bar & Bistro   ▽ 21 ⎟ 22 ⎟ 18 ⎟ $39 ⎟

9113 Graton Rd. (Edison St.), Graton, 707-823-7023

■ "You'd swear you were in a great NY bistro", not "the middle of rural Sonoma", at this bustling "cosmopolitan" Graton spot fans consider to be one "of the best in the area"; the Southern Med fare is "well prepared" and the "portions are generous, even on the tapas plates", but the "lively" "bar's the thing here", and has become a late-night "social spot" for locals.

Uva Trattoria & Bar   ▽ 21 ⎟ 18 ⎟ 20 ⎟ $31 ⎟

1040 Clinton St. (Main St.), Napa, 707-255-6646;
www.uvatrattoria.com

■ Though it's centrally located near the opera house and shopping, this "pleasant and hip" Southern Italian "date place" is something of a "secret of Downtown dining" in Napa; "finding it can be a challenge", but locals laud its "nice, fresh" fare and wines at "reasonable prices" and staff that treats you "like a royal subject" in a "charming" setting; P.S. many "dishes are offered in both small and full-size portions."

Victorian Gardens   ▽ 24 | 26 | 27 | $75

The Inn at Victorian Gardens, 14409 Shoreline Hwy./Hwy. 1 (south of Elk, 8 mi. north of Pt. Arena), Manchester, 707-882-3606

■ "Dining with the Zambonis" at their exclusive B&B in Mendocino's Manchester is "like dining in with your best friends" (who happen to live in a "storybook" Victorian house on a 92-acre farm); "you may meet Luciano in the hen house with an axe or in the garden" as he "lovingly prepares" the nightly prix fixe of "homey Italian cuisine", while Pauline can be found in the 16-seat dining room doling out "old world hospitality."

Villa Corona   23 | 11 | 16 | $14

3614 Bel Aire Plaza (Trancas St.), Napa, 707-257-8685
1138 Main St. (bet. Pope & Spring Sts.), St. Helena, 707-963-7812

◪ "Once you get over the plastic lawn chairs" at these "small and basic" Napa and St. Helena spots, you'll appreciate the "delicious", "hearty" and "affordable" Mexican fare that amigos attest is some of "the best in the Valley"; the staff is "accommodating" and "takeout is fast when you call ahead", all of which makes it a "favorite among locals."

Wappo Bar Bistro   23 | 19 | 18 | $36

1226 Washington St. (Lincoln Ave.), Calistoga, 707-942-4712; www.wappobar.com

■ "It's simply divine" to "eat outdoors under the vine-covered arbor" at this "old reliable" in Calistoga offering a "wonderful, inventive" Eclectic menu and "fair-priced" wines, and while "some of the dishes are a bit of a stretch, nothing is poorly done"; the service can be "slow", but the staff is a "hoot", "gladly sharing interesting life stories if your dinner companions get boring."

Wappo Taco   ▽ 22 | 15 | 16 | $22

1458 Lincoln Ave. (Fair Way), Calistoga, 707-942-8165

■ The folks behind the globally inspired Wappo Bar Bistro have narrowed their focus with this "inviting" sit-down Mexican in the historic Calistoga Depot serving "flavorful", "ultra-fresh" south-of-the-border *cocina* in a brightly painted tropical interior (hanging chiles, potted palms and a salsa bar) or on an outdoor patio; cervezas, sangria and agua frescas are the beverages of choice.

Water Street Bistro ⊄   ▽ 23 | 14 | 17 | $19

100 Petaluma Blvd. N. (Western Ave.), Petaluma, 707-763-9563

■ "Everything is made from scratch" by chef-owner Stephanie Rastetter at her "cute little cafe" overlooking the Petaluma River, from "creative breakfasts" to "consistently satisfying" French bistro fare; "excellent prices" also make it a sweet spot for your morning meal or "lunch on the way to the wine country", but "alas, she's only open one night

a month" for eight-course theme dinners, Friday and
Saturday nights in the summer.

Willi's Seafood & Raw Bar 25 22 22 $41
403 Healdsburg Ave. (North St.), Healdsburg, 707-433-9191
◪ "A happening place to see and be seen" in Healdsburg,
where you can "sit out on the patio, drink a mojito and
relax", this "fab" seafood-tapas restaurant dishes out
"fresh, fresh" fin fare and "masterfully prepared" small
plates (including "imaginative" seviches and some of
"the best oysters in town"); "pairing wines is easy and
affordable", as they're "all available by the half-bottle" or
glass, but frugal finatics fume over the "little dishes" with
"big-plate prices."

Willi's Wine Bar 24 19 21 $41
*Orchard Inn, 4404 Old Redwood Hwy. (River Rd.), Santa Rosa,
707-526-3096; www.williswinebar.net*
◼ "Creative" international tapas "done to perfection" is the
draw of "one of the hottest restaurants" in Santa Rosa,
where a "friendly and knowledgeable" staff and "lovely
patio" also contribute to an "extraordinary experience";
oenophiles appreciate that all the wines on the global list are
available by the taste, glass, half-bottle or bottle, while
wallet- watchers warn that the "grazing menu encourages
ordering lots" of "small plates that can add up to big dollars."

Willow Wood Market Cafe ▽ 23 14 15 $27
9020 Graton Rd. (Edison St.), Graton, 707-522-8372
◪ "Russian River wine folks know" this "complete country
charmer" in the "one-horse town" of Graton, an Eclectic
"hippie-inspired market/restaurant" that is the "antithesis"
of many chichi wine-country competitors; everything is
so "fresh" coming out of the "tiny kitchen" ("awesome
breakfasts", "excellent soups", "homemade bakery items
galore"), and the "casual, whimsical atmosphere" has "lots
of soul", excusing the sometimes "apathetic" service.

Wine Spectator Greystone 23 23 21 $47
*Culinary Institute of America, 2555 Main St. (Deer Park Rd.),
St. Helena, 707-967-1010; www.ciachef.edu*
◼ In the Culinary Institute of America complex, this Cal is
"a fun place for foodies" where you can enjoy not only
"creative, cutting-edge" cuisine and "superb service", but
also "free entertainment as you watch your meal prepared"
by professional chefs in the open exhibition kitchen; the
"cavernous" dining room "can get very loud", but the "patio
is one of the most beautiful spots for lunch in the Valley."

Yankee Pier 18 15 16 $31
*286 Magnolia Ave. (bet. King St. & William Ave.), Larkspur,
415-924-7676; www.yankeepier.com*
◪ Nautical noshers note the "bare-bones surroundings"
at this transplanted "New England clam shack" in Larkspur

"are entirely obscured by fantastic fish 'n' chips, marvelous mussels and crusty cornbread"; while parents praise the "super kid-friendly" atmosphere, foes fume that it "misses the boat" due to "out-of-line" prices and a "cantankerous crew"; N.B. there's a sibling in San Jose.

zazu 24 | 18 | 22 | $43 |
3535 Guerneville Rd. (Willowside Rd.), Santa Rosa, 707-523-4814; www.zazurestaurant.com

☑ In Santa Rosa, chef-owners Duskie Estes and John Stewart "run a classic mom-and-pop restaurant" serving "sophisticated yet homey", "consistently excellent" New American–Northern Italian cuisine from an "ever-changing" menu; a "very accommodating staff" works hard to make you "comfortable" in the "roadhouse" setting, even if the noise level "makes it an excellent place to practice lip reading on busy nights."

Zin 21 | 19 | 20 | $37 |
344 Center St. (North St.), Healdsburg, 707-473-0946; www.zinrestaurant.com

☑ This "informal" "blue-plate" paradise "one street off the town square" is "probably the best dining value in Healdsburg", thanks to "generous portions" of "great American comfort food" and a "super selection of namesake wines"; it's popular with "grape growers" as well as tourists eager to "wind down after a day visiting wineries", and while the service can be "uneven" and the decor is a bit "stark", the "reliable fare" makes up for any number of zins.

Zinsvalley ⊠ ▽ 22 | 19 | 21 | $31 |
Browns Valley Shopping Ctr., 3253 Browns Valley Rd. (bet. Austin & Larkin Sts.), Napa, 707-224-0695; www.zinsvalley.com

■ "Do your zinning here" insist imbibing locals of this "local hangout" "tucked away in Browns Valley" that "deserves to be known by a wider crowd"; not only is "the wine list of Zinfandels hard-to-beat", but it "matches well" with the "wonderful", affordable New American fare, and the "owners greet you warmly"; all's best savored on the "gorgeous back patio", and "cellar rats" revel in the fact there's "no corkage fee."

Zuzu 23 | 17 | 20 | $33 |
829 Main St. (bet. 2nd & 3rd Sts.), Napa, 707-224-8555; www.zuzunapa.com

■ "Tapas are the topic" at this stylish, snug Spaniard just "along the Napa River", where guests "make a fun evening of tasting" "inventive small plates", "mighty fine sangria" and "bottles of little-known gems from Spain that won't break the bank"; but since this "naturally noisy" "social scene" is strictly first-come, first-served, "prepare to wait if you show up" at prime time.

South of San Francisco

Top Ratings

Except where indicated by a ∇, top lists exclude places with low voting.

Top Food

27 Le Papillon	Chez TJ
Marché	Cafe Gibraltar
Marinus	Evvia
26 John Bentley's	Emile's
Sierra Mar	La Forêt
Café Marcella	Passionfish*
Manresa	Amber India
Omei	Flying Fish Grill
25 Pacific's Edge	Koi Palace
Tamarine	Mei Long

By Cuisine

American
26 John Bentley's
25 Pacific's Edge
Chez TJ
231 Ellsworth
24 Parcel 104

Asian (misc.)
25 Tamarine
Amber India
24 Roy's/Pebble Bch.
22 Three Seasons
Straits Cafe

Californian
27 Marinus
Bouchée∇
26 Sierra Mar
Manresa
25 Passionfish

Chinese
26 Omei
25 Koi Palace
Mei Long
24 Fook Yuen
21 Hunan Home's Rest.

Continental
25 Emile's
Fresh Cream
23 Anton & Michel
20 Dal Baffo
19 Shadowbrook

French
27 Le Papillon
Marché
26 Sierra Mar
Manresa
25 Chez TJ

Italian
26 Café Marcella
23 Casanova
Osteria
Bella Vista
22 Mezza Luna

Japanese
25 Flying Fish Grill
23 Fuki Sushi
22 Higashi West
Blowfish Sushi
20 Juban

Mediterranean
25 Cafe Gibraltar
Evvia
Viognier
22 71 Saint Peter
Cetrella Bistro

Seafood
25 Passionfish
Flying Fish Grill
Koi Palace
24 Navio
Fook Yuen

---

* Indicates a tie with restaurant above

By Special Feature

Breakfast/Brunch
25 Pacific's Edge
　　La Forêt
　　Koi Palace
　　Viognier
24 Gayle's Bakery

Outdoor Seating
27 Marinus
26 Sierra Mar
24 Roy's/Pebble Bch.
　　Flea St. Café
23 Casanova

People-Watching
25 Tamarine
　　Evvia
　　Viognier
24 Village Pub
22 Spago Palo Alto

Romance
27 Le Papillon
　　Marinus
26 John Bentley's
　　Sierra Mar
25 La Forêt

Singles Scenes
22 Higashi West
　　Seven Rest.▽
19 Zibibbo
　　E&O Trading Co.
　　Kingfish

Small Plates
25 Tamarine
22 Three Seasons
　　Straits Cafe
19 Zucca Ristorante
　　Zibibbo

Tasting Menus
27 Le Papillon
　　Marché
　　Marinus
26 Manresa
25 Pacific's Edge

Winning Wine Lists
27 Marché
　　Marinus
　　Boucheé▽
25 Pacific's Edge
19 Zibibbo

By Location

Carmel/Monterey
27 Marinus
　　Boucheé▽
26 Sierra Mar
25 Pacific's Edge
　　Passionfish

Half Moon Bay/Coast
25 Cafe Gibraltar
24 Navio
22 Mezza Luna
　　Cetrella Bistro
　　Pasta Moon

Palo Alto/Menlo Park
27 Marché
25 Tamarine
　　Evvia
24 Bistro Elan
　　Flea St. Café

Peninsula
25 Koi Palace
　　Viognier
　　231 Ellsworth
24 Fook Yuen
23 Pisces

Santa Cruz/Capitola
26 Omei
　　Oswald's▽
24 Gayle's Bakery
21 Gabriella Café▽
19 Shadowbrook

Silicon Valley
27 Le Papillon
26 John Bentley's
　　Café Marcella
　　Manresa
25 Chez TJ

Top Decor

28	Sierra Mar		Anton & Michel
	Pacific's Edge		Le Papillon
	Navio		Village Pub
26	Shadowbrook		Tamarine
	Marinus		A.P. Stump's
	Cetrella Bistro		Evvia
25	Nepenthe		Bella Vista
	Roy's/Pebble Bch.		Chez TJ
24	Marché		La Forêt*
23	Casanova	22	Arcadia

Top Service

27	Le Papillon		Bella Vista
25	Chez TJ		La Forêt
	John Bentley's		Navio
	Emile's		Café Marcella
	Sierra Mar	23	Plumed Horse
	Marinus		231 Ellsworth
	Marché		Passionfish
	Pacific's Edge		Flying Fish Grill
24	Fresh Cream		Anton & Michel
	Manresa		Viognier

Top Bangs for the Buck

1. Pancho Villa
2. La Taqueria
3. La Cumbre Taq.
4. Burger Joint
5. Gayle's Bakery
6. Palo Alto Creamery
7. Amici East Coast
8. Tomatina
9. Zao Noodle
10. Pasta Pomodoro
11. Hunan Home's Rest.
12. ¡ZCool
13. North Bch. Pizza
14. Pizza Antica
15. Amber India
16. Chef Chu's
17. Omei
18. Barbara Fishtrap
19. Mei Long
20. Duarte's Tavern

subscribe to zagat.com

South of San Francisco

F D S C

Amber India   25 | 19 | 20 | $28
*Olive Tree Shopping Ctr., 2290 W. El Camino Real
(Rengstorff Ave.), Mountain View, 650-968-7511
Santana Row, 1140 Olsen Dr. (bet. Santana Row &
Winchester Blvd.), San Jose, 408-248-5400
www.amber-india.com*
■ Ask the "programming teams" and "Indian expats where
to find great food, and the answer is always" this Moghlai
Mountain Viewer (and its new "sharp-looking" Santana
Row sibling), which sets the amber, er, "gold standard" for
subcontinental eats ("the butter chicken alone leaves you
with an overwhelming desire to lick your plate"); fine china
and "professional service" create a "refined atmosphere",
all of which explains "why there's such a huge line" at the
bountiful lunch and weekend buffets.

Amici's East Coast Pizzeria   21 | 12 | 16 | $18
*790 Castro St. (Church St.), Mountain View, 650-961-6666
226 Redwood Shores Pkwy. (Twin Dolphin Dr.),
Redwood Shores, 650-654-3333
69 Third Ave. (San Mateo Dr.), San Mateo, 650-342-9392
www.amicis.com*
See review in City of San Francisco Directory.

Anton & Michel Restaurant   23 | 23 | 23 | $48
Mission St. (bet. Ocean & 7th Aves.), Carmel, 831-624-2406
■ Though it is "not cutting-edge", this "sedate" "old-
timer's place", celebrating its own silver anniversary this
year, offers "the most elegant" dining experience "in Carmel
proper", thanks to a "well-prepared" "classic Continental
menu" complemented by an "excellent wine list", "great
service" and a "gorgeous European-style decor" replete
with fireplaces within and bubbling fountains in the "nice
courtyard"; however, expect to pay a pretty price for
the "pretty setting."

A.P. Stump's   22 | 23 | 20 | $44
*163 W. Santa Clara St. (bet. Almaden Blvd. & San Pedro St.),
San Jose, 408-292-9928; www.apstumps.com*
☑ Chef/co-owner Jim Stump's "class act" destination, a
"beautiful", gorgeously transformed historic pueblo, is
where "South Bay power brokers" and "special-occasion"
celebrants "go to impress", thanks to Cal–New American
cuisine "that entices the mind and taste buds" and an

"amazing" 500-bottle wine list, at newly "reasonable prices (compared to the competition)"; cynics shrug off the "extremely small portions" but scold the staff for being "a bit snooty, considering it's only San Jose."

Arcadia
22 | 22 | 22 | $52

San Jose Marriott, 100 W. San Carlos St. (Market St.), San Jose, 408-278-4555

☑ Michael Mina (ex Aqua) has imported his city savoir faire to San Jose at this "beautiful" "Manhattan-esque dining room" catering to conventioneers with a "whimsical menu" that takes a New American "twist on old favorites" (i.e. duck fat–fried chicken); "you could easily forget you are in a hotel" except for the wails that it's "waaaaaay overpriced."

A Tavola
21 | 21 | 19 | $33

716 Laurel St. (bet. Cherry & Olive Sts.), San Carlos, 650-595-3003; www.atavoladining.com

☑ "Although you can tell it's run by a restaurant group" (the one behind Mistral and Kingfish), this "hopping" "hangout" "in Downtown San Carlos" manages to "cater to the cocktail crowd without alienating the family clientele" thanks to "excellent renditions of Italian–New American dishes", a "slightly swanky" decor and waiters who go "out of their way" for you; however, with an open kitchen and "upbeat bar scene", it can "get unbearably loud", so "consider eating at the sidewalk tables."

Barbara's Fishtrap ⊄
19 | 12 | 17 | $22

281 Capistrano Rd. (Hwy. 1), Princeton by the Sea, 650-728-7049

☑ If you don't mind standing in "absurdly long lines" for "greasy" ("in a good way") fish 'n' chips and "fresh – just look outside the window" – fin fare, then you'll love this "dive" "on the harbor in Princeton by the Sea"; true, there's "no ambiance [sitting] under nets", "service is sluggish" and you have to "watch for pelicans diving for [scraps] from your table", but then "what do you expect from a fish trap?"

Basin, The
∇ 19 | 20 | 23 | $40

14572 Big Basin Way (5th St.), Saratoga, 408-867-1906; www.thebasin.com

☑ While it may not be known far and wide, they seem to "care about you" at this Saratogan boasting a "nice small town feel", "innovative wine list" and organically driven New American–Med menu; if critics cry there are "better choices in the area" for the money, even they "must admit the [20 different] martini offerings are excellent."

Basque Cultural Center
∇ 19 | 13 | 19 | $26

599 Railroad Ave. (bet. Orange & Spruce Aves.), South San Francisco, 650-583-8091; www.basqueculturalcenter.com

■ Though it may "feel like a foreign country", full of "grandmas and grandpas from the old country drinking and eating" "well-prepared country Basque favorites", this quirky "sleeper" is only as distant as South SF; it's "worth the drive" if you "don't expect gourmet food", just "cheap" "homey" fare served "family-style" in a "large institutional setting", complete with handball courts and lecture halls.

Bella Vista ⊠   23 | 23 | 24 | $48
13451 Skyline Blvd. (5 mi. south of Rte. 92), Woodside, 650-851-1229; www.bvrestaurant.com
◪ Despite "giving every appearance of being a cowboy bar" from the outside, this "classic" "in the Redwoods" is one of the most "elegant" places for miles, with "wonderfully formal" service from "jacketed waiters" and "breathtaking" views "overlooking the South Bay" ("if you can't get romantic in this place, join a monastery"); modernists may mutter the "excellent" but "aging French-Italian menu" and interior "could use updating", but solid scores attest it's "worth the long drive from wherever."

Bistro Elan ⊠   24 | 19 | 21 | $41
448 California Ave. (El Camino Real), Palo Alto, 650-327-0284
■ "Hidden behind ferns" on "California Avenue's Restaurant Row", this "bustling little bistro" is ground zero for "Sand Hill–set power-lunchers" and well-heeled romancers who enjoy the "exquisite" Cal–French countryside" fare ("famous for foie gras" and artisanal breads to *mourir* for), an "eclectic wine list" and service with élan; the dining room "gets really loud", but "the tiny garden" out back offers a "heavenly" option in nice weather.

Bistro Vida   20 | 20 | 19 | $33
641 Santa Cruz Ave. (El Camino Real), Menlo Park, 650-462-1686
■ "You could swear that you were in Paris" at this "cozy" "low-key" Menlo Park bistro, due to its *très* "cosmopolitan atmosphere" "right down to the copies of *Le Figaro* to read while you wait for your table"; and while it may "not be as chic as its expensive French neighbors", the "classic, simple and well-executed" menu is "every bit as good" and the "friendly owners" dish out far "less attitude"; P.S. the weekend *petit déjeuner* alone is "worth a visit."

Blowfish, Sushi to Die For   22 | 21 | 17 | $37
335 Santana Row (bet. Stevens Creek & Winchester Blvds.), San Jose, 408-345-3848; www.blowfishsushi.com
See review in City of San Francisco Directory.

Bouchée   ▽ 27 | 22 | 21 | $56
Mission St. (bet. Ocean & 7th Aves.), Carmel, 831-626-7880; www.boucheecarmel.com
◪ This "innovative" sophomore, with a small "adjoining wine shop", may just be the "best thing to happen to Carmel since Clint"; expect Cal fare that's "different without being

contrived" and served in "beautiful" copper-accented digs; "yes, the food arrives so very slow", but an order of the "homemade breadsticks with butter and artisanal olive oils will keep you munching away until dinner arrives"; N.B. at press time, an offshoot in the new Auberge Carmel was due to open nearby.

Buca di Beppo   14   16   16 $24

Pruneyard, 1875 S. Bascom Ave. (Campbell Ave.), Campbell, 408-377-7722
643 Emerson St. (bet. Forest & Hamilton Aves.), Palo Alto, 650-329-0665
www.bucadibeppo.com

■ "Serious garlic and gaudy decor" sums up the scene at these Silicon Valley sites that are "good for gorging in groups" ("don't go alone") on "mountains of mediocre Southern Italian food" "served family-style" beneath a "kitschy" display of "attic art"; gourmets growl it's a "dumbed-down" eating experience, but the "raucous atmosphere" "makes up for a lot", particularly if you reserve the "Vatican-themed" Pope's Table; N.B. there's a branch in the City of SF.

Burger Joint   20   12   15 $11

San Francisco Int'l Airport, Int'l Terminal, Boarding Area A, South San Francisco, 650-583-5863;
www.burgerjointsf.com
See review in City of San Francisco Directory.

Cafe Gibraltar   25   20   22 $37

425 Ave. Alahambra (Palma St.), El Granada, 650-728-9030;
www.cafegibraltar.com

■ Unsuspecting day, trippers think they've "found the pearl in the oyster" upon encountering this North African–inspired Med in El Granada that has a rotating menu of "excellent", "unusual" dishes enlivened with "interesting spices and ingredients"; additional assets include a staff that's "happy to answer your questions" and a room that's "spartan" yet "comfortable."

CAFÉ MARCELLA   26   18   24 $41

368 Village Ln. (bet. Hwy. 9 & Santa Cruz Ave.), Los Gatos, 408-354-8006

■ Los Gatos denizens looking for a "special-occasion" site or a little "romance" head to this "very happening" spot known for "fabulous" French-Italian offerings; the staff "hovers like bees on a flower, providing exactly what you need when you need" it, and if the room's "cramped" and "noisy", sensible folk ask "what good bistro isn't?"

Café Niebaum-Coppola   16   20   15 $31

473 University Ave. (bet. Cowper & Kipling Sts.), Palo Alto, 650-752-0350; www.cafecoppola.com
See review in City of San Francisco Directory.

Cafe Pro Bono 18 13 19 $32
2437 Birch St. (S. California Ave.), Palo Alto, 650-326-1626;
www.cafeprobonorestaurant.com
☑ "You're likely to spot bigwigs lingering over linguine"
and other "old-school Italian" options at this "reliable"
Palo Alto cafe blessed with a "relaxing" atmosphere and
"amicable owner"; but while everyone raves about "their
signature dish", Susan's Downfall (herb ravioli blanketed
in an "artery-clogging" cheese sauce), some feel the rest
of the menu and the decor could use "updating."

Casanova 23 23 22 $46
Fifth Ave. (bet. Mission & San Carlos Sts.), Carmel, 831-625-0501;
www.casanovarestaurant.com
☑ For a "respite from shopping" or for a "romantic"
interlude, Carmelites consider this "old-world" French–
Northern Italian that serves "very good" food accompanied
by a "wonderful wine list", either in the "warm" interior or
out on the "charming patio"; a few hint that it's "lost some
of its sparkle over the years", but if "overpriced at dinner",
it's a "better value at lunch" or breakfast.

Central Park Bistro 19 21 18 $34
181 E. Fourth Ave. (San Mateo Dr.), San Mateo, 650-558-8401;
www.centralparkbistro.com
☑ A "find in Downtown San Mateo", this "classy" boîte
presents an "adventurous" New American menu, featuring
"especially delicious" "small dishes for sharing", and has
"inviting decor" and "outdoor tables that are a plus"; if
critics contend it's "not quite up to its ambitions foodwise",
they concede that it's still "pleasant" for a "drinks-and-
live-music" combo on weekends.

Cetrella Bistro & Café 22 26 21 $44
845 Main St. (Monte Vista Ln.), Half Moon Bay, 650-726-4090;
www.cetrella.com
☑ "Tuscan charm" abounds at this hangout in "sleepy" Half
Moon Bay, in both the "blend of Med cuisines" and the
"warm" room whose "huge fireplaces" are draws on "cool
coastal nights"; optimists underscore "markedly improved"
service, although some still think it's "up and down"; live jazz
on weekends "keeps you coming back" for Sunday brunch.

Chantilly ☒ ▽ 23 23 24 $52
3001 El Camino Real (Selby Ln.), Redwood City, 650-321-4080;
www.chantillyrestaurant.com
☑ Those looking for a place to mark a "special occasion"
or host a "corporate function" in Redwood City applaud
this Continental now in its third decade; a crowd composed
of "local senior execs" enthuses over the "superb service"
in "quiet", "elegant surroundings" (brocade-covered walls,
marble fireplaces), but modernists bemoan what they opine
is "overpriced" food and the "sleepy" pulse.

Cheesecake Factory, The ●   16   16   15 $25
*Westfield Shoppingtown Valley Fair, 3041 Stevens Creek Rd.
(bet. S. Redwood Ave. & Winchester Blvd.), San Jose,
408-246-0092; www.thecheesecakefactory.com*
See review in City of San Francisco Directory.

Chef Chu's   21   15   19 $25
*1067 N. San Antonio Rd. (El Camino Real), Los Altos,
650-948-2696; www.chefchu.com*
☑ "You can always count on" a "solid" and "flavorful", if
"Americanized", Chinese meal at chef-owner Lawrence
Chu's "busy" Los Altos "institution" where locals "have
been eating for years"; while the "decor isn't fantastic",
service is "lightning-quick" and an open kitchen provides
a modicum of drama, as do the "photos of the chef with
famous folks" who've partaken here.

Chez TJ ⌧   25   23   25 $67
*938 Villa St. (bet. Castro St. & Shoreline Blvd.), Mountain View,
650-964-7466; www.cheztj.com*
■ After more than 20 years, this "charming Victorian
cottage" is arguably "the View's best" when you want to
"splurge with your sweetie to spark some romance"; it's
your classic "special-occasion" site with "doting service", a
"quiet", "elegant" environment and a strictly prix fixe menu
featuring "artfully crafted" New French–New American
food at "really expensive prices"; P.S. the recent arrival of
a "new executive chef may change things, however."

Club XIX   ▽ 23   24   23 $62
*The Lodge at Pebble Beach, 17 Mile Dr. (Hwy. 1), Pebble Beach,
831-625-8519; www.pebblebeach.com*
☑ "Gorgeous views to the 18th hole" and of "stunning
sunsets" drive this "clubby" Cal–New American in The
Lodge at Pebble Beach; the "rich food for the rich",
"outstanding wine list" ("priced so high you will think
you've ordered a case instead of a bottle") and premium
service put it on par with "the Monterey Peninsula's best"
for fans; the post-*Survey* arrival of a "new chef" may mollify
the minority that sinks the cuisine as "not as impressive
as the surroundings."

Cool Café   ▽ 20   20   11 $19
*Stanford University Cantor Arts Ctr., 328 Lomita Dr.
(Museum Way), Palo Alto, 650-725-4758;
www.cooleatz.com*
☑ "The magic of eating" in the Cantor Arts Center's sculpture
garden "overlooking some of Rodin's finest creations" is too
Cool for words marvel fans of the "proprietor of Flea Street
Café's" all-organic venue (from the "potato chips, salt, sugar,
etc." to the "disposable utensils made from wheat"); true,
the Cal cuisine "can be a bit costly" for "salads and
sandwiches", but it's a "nice indulgence" – especially at

the unadvertised "stealth dinners" served Thursday nights.

Dal Baffo ⊠   20 | 18 | 20 | $61
878 Santa Cruz Ave. (University Dr.), Menlo Park, 650-325-1588;
www.dalbaffo.com
☑ Menlo Park's "special-occasion" site since the '70s
stands apart from its trendy neighbors with its "handsome",
"staid", hushed surroundings, "old-school Northern
Italian"–Continental "classics", "courteous" staff and
"amazing wines, including a few you'd have to sell your
car to order"; however, Decor and Service score drops
suggest it's "too dang expensive" for the "under-50" set,
who sneer "if your country club is closed for the evening,
this is the place to go."

Duarte's Tavern   20 | 12 | 18 | $24
202 Stage Rd. (Pescadero Rd.), Pescadero, 650-879-0464;
www.duartestavern.com
■ "After a foggy day at the beach", there's no better "stop-
off" than this "run-down" "old roadhouse" in the Pescadero
boondocks filled with a "mix of locals and tourists" who
fill up on the "deservedly legendary" soups and "housemade
pies" (particularly the "fabulous olallieberry" version in
season); though "out-of-the-way", it's "worth the drive",
"which along the coast is pretty in any case."

Duck Club, The   20 | 21 | 20 | $42
Stanford Park Hotel, 100 El Camino Real (Sand Hill Rd.),
Menlo Park, 650-330-2790; www.stanfordparkhotel.com
Monterey Plaza Hotel & Spa, 400 Cannery Row
(Wave St.), Monterey, 831-646-1700;
www.woodsidehotels.com
■ A "quiet, clubby atmosphere" prevails at this Menlo Park
and Monterey pair of "special-occasion" spots, catering
to a mix of "venture capitalists", "blue hairs" and students
with "parents in town"; both are "as good as it gets" for
suburban hotel dining, with "well-done", "if not spectacular"
New American dinners (though the signature dish "puts all
other ducks to shame") and "pleasant" service; P.S. there's
also a branch with a "beautiful view of Bodega Bay" and
an "East Bay edition" as well.

E&O Trading Company   19 | 20 | 17 | $33
96 S. First St. (San Fernando St.), San Jose, 408-938-4100;
www.eotrading.com
See review in City of San Francisco Directory.

Ecco Restaurant ⊠   ▽ 24 | 17 | 22 | $45
322 Lorton Ave. (Burlingame Ave.), Burlingame, 650-342-7355;
www.eccorestaurant.com
■ If you're looking for San Francisco "city quality" food and
service without leaving "the burbs", *ecco* – this 18-year-
old "Burlingame classic" "is the place"; although it is still
largely "undiscovered" by outsiders, locals go "to be seen"

in a setting that's as "stylish" as the "nicely presented", "creative" Continental concoctions.

El Palomar   ▽ 18 17 17 $22

Palomar Hotel, 1336 Pacific Ave. (Soquel Ave.), Santa Cruz, 831-425-7575

■ "Get there early if you want to eat and then stay for the party" at this Downtown Santa Cruz "hot spot", known as much for its "consistently good" seafood-oriented Mexican menu as for its "sure-to-please tropical margaritas" (the reason for the "noisy" "lively" scene at the bar); "the wait is always long" but the setting – a "wonderful old hotel lobby" with an atrium ceiling – "is so cool" you won't mind "hanging out."

Emile's ⌧   25 19 25 $57

545 S. Second St. (bet. Reed & William Sts.), San Jose, 408-289-1960; www.emiles.com

◪ Seems like this "out-of-the-way" "San Jose tradition" has "been around forever" – and "rightfully so" say surveyors who swoon over the soufflés, "wonderful Franco-Swiss entrees" and service (owner and former chef Emile Mooser is often spotted "stopping by each table"); perhaps the "unimpressive" "interior should be updated", but the "consistent quality" of the fine food remains the focal point.

Eulipia Restaurant and Bar   ▽ 21 17 21 $37

374 S. First St. (bet. San Carlos & San Salvador Sts.), San Jose, 408-280-6161; www.eulipia.com

■ This 26-year-old beacon of creative New American cuisine in Downtown San Jose has had "its ups and downs" over the years, but it remains the place to "see local politicians at play" and playgoers dining "before a show"; although the "reliable" eats don't earn a standing ovation, the "cool atmosphere", "good, informal service" and lively (read: "noisy") bar make this long-running production "worth a return visit."

EVVIA   25 23 22 $43

420 Emerson St. (bet. Lytton & University Aves.), Palo Alto, 650-326-0983; www.evvia.net

■ One of Palo Alto's finest, this Hellenistic hot spot has got the Grecian formula down, serving "utterly awesome lamb dishes" along with other "lusty" classics "as good as any on the real Evvia" in a "gorgeous, rustic taverna setting" with a "huge fireplace" that "warms your soul" (or is that the ouzo?); although it's "packed as tight as one of those dolmas" and noisy as a gladiator game, the "professional" staff knows how to attend to the "venture capital crowd" who feast like gods and aren't fazed by the Olympic-size bill.

Fandango   21 | 20 | 21 | $38
223 17th St. (Lighthouse Ave.), Pacific Grove, 831-372-3456;
www.fandangorestaurant.com
■ Like its namesake dance, this "long-established" haunt "in
an old home" exudes a "cheerful" aura that's "a welcome
relief" from its tony Monterey Peninsula brethren; though
"somewhat traditional", the menu offers almost everything
under the Mediterranean sun, plus "outstanding wine
selections"; however, the "charming French country
ambience" and "warm service is what makes it a favorite."

Faz   17 | 18 | 17 | $33
Sunnyvale Sheraton, 1108 N. Mathilda Ave. (Moffett Park Dr.),
Sunnyvale, 408-752-8000; www.fazrestaurants.com
See review in City of San Francisco Directory.

Fish Market, The   17 | 13 | 16 | $28
3150 El Camino Real (Page Mill Rd.), Palo Alto, 650-493-9188
1007 Blossom Hill Rd. (Winfield Blvd.), San Jose, 408-269-3474
1855 S. Norfolk (Fashion Island Blvd.), San Mateo, 650-349-3474
3775 El Camino Real (Halford Ave.), Santa Clara, 408-246-3474
www.thefishmarket.com
◪ "The West Coast's answer to Legal Sea Foods" can be
found at this "always packed" chain where the fin-fervent
go for "fresh, simple" specimens prepared "without any
big fuss" and paired with "sides that always satisfy"; but
critics claim the food's "nothing to write home about" and
the "overworked" staff "couldn't have been slower than if
you went fishing for your meal yourself."

Flea St. Café   24 | 17 | 22 | $41
3607 Alameda de las Pulgas (Avy Ave.), Menlo Park,
650-854-1226; www.cooleatz.com
■ In Menlo Park, the flagship of chef-owner Jesse Cool's
archipelago of organic eateries still pleases with "carefully
thought-out", "lovingly prepared" Cal–New American
dishes fashioned from "environmentally responsible"
foodstuffs; Ms. C. "often comes out to chat with patrons"
in the dining room, which is "more inviting" since a recent
redo (that perhaps outdates the Decor score); it's always
been a go-to spot for "special-occasion" dinners, but "their
best-kept secret is Sunday brunch."

Flying Fish Grill   25 | 19 | 23 | $36
Carmel Plaza, Mission St. (bet. Ocean & 7th Aves.), Carmel,
831-625-1962
■ "One of the best places" in Clint country ("if you can find
it" hidden in Carmel Plaza), this "homey" underwater-
themed "underground restaurant" reels in locals with its
"inventive" Japanese-influenced Californian menu that,
no surprise, "has an emphasis on fish"; but above all, it's
the welcoming "owners Tina and Kenny" Fukumoto that
"are the reason behind its success."

Fook Yuen Seafood
24 | 12 | 15 | $27

195 El Camino Real (Victoria Ave.), Millbrae, 650-692-8600
✉ Many rave about this "excellent" Millbrae dim sum and seafood house, claiming it's "as close to Hong Kong as you can get" in the South Bay; but lift your eyes from your steaming morsels and "chaos reigns" as "gruff" servers traverse a room that's crying out for "an extreme makeover."

Fresh Cream
25 | 22 | 24 | $62

Heritage Harbor, 99 Pacific St. (bet. Artillery & Scott Sts.), Monterey, 831-375-9798; www.freshcream.com
✉ While it's "an old-timer by Monterey standards", this Continental-French "holds up well" thanks to "wonderful" Bay views and food that's "conservative" and "rich" ("a reflection of the clientele"); if spoilers snap it's "overpriced and overrated for what it is", Romeos see it as a "romantic" rendezvous (so "don't go with your golf buddies").

Fuki Sushi
23 | 18 | 18 | $35

4119 El Camino Real (bet. Arastradero & Page Mill Rds.), Palo Alto, 650-494-9383; www.fukisushi.com
✉ "Stanford students" and business-folk gunning for "top-of-the-line sushi" and "other Japanese delicacies" head to this Palo Alto perennial; it's "spacious" enough to accommodate "spontaneous visits or larger parties" in the private "tatami rooms", but service is "slow" and some counsel that you're in for an "expensive" meal.

Gabriella Café
▽ 21 | 16 | 17 | $36

910 Cedar St. (bet. Church & Locust Sts.), Santa Cruz, 831-457-1677; www.gabriellacafe.com
✉ Short on space but long on "charm", this "romantic" Downtown Santa Cruz Cal–Northern Italian offers a menu "created around ingredients from local organic farms" (try any of the "slow-cooked dishes") in a "quaint atmosphere"; service is similarly of the "slower" nature, and "tight quarters require you" to "get cozy with your fellow diners."

Gayle's Bakery & Rosticceria
24 | 12 | 17 | $17

504 Bay Ave. (Capitola Ave.), Capitola, 831-462-1200; www.gaylesbakery.com
☐ Locals report having a "mystical experience" when "staring into the pastry case" at this Capitola site, whose sandwiches (made on some of "the best artisan breads") are "perfect for a picnic or quick lunch" and whose "upscale blue plates" are "recommended" for early suppers; there are always "long lines of hungry souls" on the same quest, but the counter staff "moves people through quickly."

Gaylord India
19 | 16 | 18 | $31

1706 El Camino Real (Encinal Ave.), Menlo Park, 650-326-8761; www.gaylords.com
See review in City of San Francisco Directory.

Gervais, Restaurant　　　▽ 20 | 19 | 19 | $53

14560 Big Basin Way (bet. 4th & 5th Sts.), Saratoga, 408-867-7017; www.gervaisrestaurant.com

◪ Certain Saratogans "like what the young new couple is doing" at this Silicon Valley French cuisine stalwart that they took over in summer 2003; citing a "reasonable wine list" and updated menu as auspicious signs, the more cautious suggest they "have the potential to be good" once they get over the initial "growing pains" manifested by "service that sometimes forgets about you."

Gordon Biersch　　　14 | 15 | 15 | $24

640 Emerson St. (bet. Forest & Hamilton Sts.), Palo Alto, 650-323-7723
33 E. San Fernando St. (bet. S. 1st & 2nd Sts.), San Jose, 408-294-6785
www.gordonbiersch.com

◪ During the day, these Palo Alto and San Jose outposts of a microbrewery chain are merely "mediocre business lunch places" serving "typical", "overly salty" American "pub grub"; but come quittin' time, they morph into veritable "yuppie body shops" as "screaming" singles have yet another round of the house's "decent beer" and "great garlic fries" "while waiting for some action"; P.S. a city cousin in South Beach boasts a "view of the Bay Bridge."

Grasing's Coastal Cuisine　　　22 | 17 | 20 | $46

Mission St. (6th Ave.), Carmel, 831-624-6562; www.grasings.com

◪ Chef Kurt Grasing and his co-owner, radio host Narsai David, "have a good thing going" at their cozy Carmel Downtowner showcasing amazing grazes of "farm-fresh" Cal fare and "an unusual list of old and current" Golden State wines; but grousers growl this "cutie" is coasting a little on its reputation, finding the food and service "disappointing."

Happy Cafe Restaurant ∉　　　▽ 19 | 3 | 10 | $14

250 S. B St. (bet. 2nd & 3rd Aves.), San Mateo, 650-340-7138

◪ To supporters, some of "the best Shanghai street stall–style food" (say that three times fast) can be found at this San Mateo "hole-in-the-wall" that's a "favorite among foodies" and "the Taiwan/Hong Kong set"; the less-happy, however, hiss it's little more than "a basic place to catch a cheap meal."

Higashi West ⬛　　　22 | 20 | 18 | $39

632-636 Emerson St. (bet. Forest & Hamilton Aves.), Palo Alto, 650-323-9378

◪ "The place to go in Palo Alto" when you want to eat 'em raw, this "Rico Suave" spot satisfies sushi seekers who are "ready to pay for" "the largest pieces west of the Pecos", "imaginative" rolls and "even better sake flights"; a "cool vibe" predominates, but "purists may be revolted" by the European-Japanese "fusion dishes" and "arrogant service."

Hong Kong Flower Lounge   21 | 14 | 14 | $28 |
51 Millbrae Ave. (El Camino Real), Millbrae, 650-692-6666
◪ "There's good reason for the huge crowds" at this "enormous" Millbrae mainstay: it's a "delicious" bit of "dim sum heaven" by day (until 2:30 PM) and by night, of dinners comprised of the "best ingredients available", including some still swimming in the "fish tank in front"; alas, while the fare's "fresh", the interior isn't (decor "needs updating"), and "if you aren't a regular, you don't rate" with the staff.

Hunan Home's Restaurant   21 | 10 | 17 | $20 |
4880 El Camino Real (Showers Dr.), Los Altos, 650-965-8888
See review in City of San Francisco Directory.

Iberia   21 | 22 | 17 | $44 |
1026 Alma St. (bet. Oak Grove & Ravenswood Aves.), Menlo P⌐rk, 650-325-8981; www.iberiarestaurant.com
◪ "They have a touch" with tapas at this Menlo Park "crowd-pleaser" that's "worth every penny" if you "long for a trip back to Spain"; the setting is "lovely and romantic", be it the "tree-shaded garden in summer" or "cozy fireplace" in winter; but while the Service score has risen, several still scold the staffers for being "slow"; P.S. there's now an adjacent "retail store with Spanish groceries."

IL FORNAIO   19 | 20 | 18 | $34 |
327 Lorton Ave. (bet. Burlingame Ave. & California Dr.), Burlingame, 650-375-8000
The Pine Inn, Ocean Ave. (Monte Verde St.), Carmel, 831-622-5100
Garden Court Hotel, 520 Cowper St. (bet. Hamilton & University Aves.), Palo Alto, 650-853-3888
Hyatt Sainte Claire, 302 S. Market St. (San Carlos St.), San Jose, 408-271-3366
www.ilfornaio.com
See review in City of San Francisco Directory.

Izzy's Steak & Chop House   19 | 16 | 18 | $36 |
525 Skyway Rd., San Carlos, 415-924-3366; www.izzyssteaksandchops.com
See review in City of San Francisco Directory.

JoAnn's Café ⊟   ▽ 23 | 9 | 17 | $15 |
1131 El Camino Real (Westborough Blvd.), South San Francisco, 650-872-2810
■ "Even with JoAnn gone", her fan base still lines up for some of "the best breakfast in the greater Bay Area", served ("if you can find it") in a small, '50s-style South San Francisco "strip-mall coffee shop"; "arrive hungry", since the morning meals and "Latin-influenced lunches" just "like the ranch hands used to make" come in "large portions"; as for service, it depends on whether you "love being called 'hon.'"

JOHN BENTLEY'S 🚫 26 21 25 $50
2915 El Camino Real (bet. Berkshire & Columbia Aves.),
Redwood City, 650-365-7777
2991 Woodside Rd. (bet. Cañada & Whiskey Hill Rds.),
Woodside, 650-851-4988
www.johnbentleys.com
■ "It takes guts to put your name on a restaurant" and
chef-owner John Bentley has the gall to do it twice; his
"intimate" converted Woodside firehouse remains an
"institution" for its "satisfying" New American food and
"unbelievable" "nurturing" service; but the man is now
mostly manning his new, larger (and unrated) Redwood
City outpost, which features a more casual menu and a full
bar; all of this means he no longer runs "one of the best
places on the Peninsula" – he runs two of them.

Juban 20 18 17 $32
1204 Broadway (bet. California Dr. & El Camino Real),
Burlingame, 650-347-2300
712 Santa Cruz Ave. (El Camino Real), Menlo Park,
650-473-6458
www.jubanrestaurant.com
☑ "Enjoyable" "Japanese-style BBQ", "courteous" service
and a "quiet atmosphere" (that's boosted the Decor score)
make Asian visitors "very nostalgic" at this *yakiniku* duo in
Burlingame and Menlo Park; but while do-it-yourselfers
declare it's "great fun" playing chef at "your on-table
grill", dissenters wonder "why should I pay to do my own
cooking?", especially when it's "too many dollars for too
little food"; P.S. there's "one in SF's Japantown" too.

jZCool 🚫 19 10 13 $17
827 Santa Cruz Ave. (bet. Crane St. & University Dr.),
Menlo Park, 650-325-3665; www.cooleatz.com
☑ "Flea St. Café's proprietor" Jesse Cool "has created a
stripped-down" offshoot at this "casual" "organic lunch
haven" cranking out a "satisfying" "selection of Cal comfort
food"; however, while well-heeled Menlo Parkers don't
mind "paying for quality ingredients", a drop in the Decor
score suggests they're more apt to take it out than to dine
in the "no-atmosphere" room with "deli-style service."

Kingfish 19 22 16 $36
201 S. B St. (2nd Ave.), San Mateo, 650-343-1226;
www.kingfishblues.com
☑ An ersatz "Mardis Gras atmosphere" reigns at this
ragin' Cajun in Downtown San Mateo; three "festive"
floors, enlivened by Southern folk art, "live music"
and "imaginative" cocktails, make it a popular "drinks
hangout", and while mavens "wouldn't describe the food
as authentic", the Eclectic offerings are "respectable"
enough; however, the "amateur" service "really misses
the [fishing] boat."

Koi Palace
25 | 15 | 13 | $31

Serramonte Plaza, 365 Gellert Blvd. (bet. Hickey & Serramonte Blvds.), Daly City, 650-992-9000; www.koipalace.com
☑ "The king of the dim sum" castles reigns at this palace-size Chinese in Daly City, whose little treasures "rival the great houses of Hong Kong" (as do the prices); true to its name, it also offers "spectacular", "fresh seafood – still swimming in the tank until you order it"; but weekenders can't afford to be koi about landing a table – "go early" and "be prepared to wrestle with the [others] waiting in line" because, despite "poor service", it's "always packed."

Kuleto's
20 | 19 | 18 | $38

1095 Rollins Rd. (Broadway), Burlingame, 650-342-4922; www.kuletos.com
See review in City of San Francisco Directory.

La Cumbre Taqueria
21 | 8 | 14 | $10

28 N. B St. (bet. 1st & Tilton Aves.), San Mateo, 650-344-8989
See review in City of San Francisco Directory.

La Forêt
25 | 23 | 24 | $58

21747 Bertram Rd. (Almaden Rd.), San Jose, 408-997-3458; www.laforetrestaurant.com
■ "Worth the drive out into the wilderness" – it's "tucked away" in an "old house by a creek" in the woods near San Jose – this "incredibly romantic" "getaway" charms with "exotic wild game" and other "excellent", if "a bit high-priced", French favorites; most find the waiters "wonderful."

La Taqueria ☒⌿
24 | 7 | 13 | $10

15 S. First St. (Santa Clara Ave.), San Jose, 408-287-1542
See review in City of San Francisco Directory.

LEFT BANK
20 | 21 | 18 | $36

635 Santa Cruz Ave. (Doyle St.), Menlo Park, 650-473-6543
377 Santana Row (S. Winchester Blvd.), San Jose, 408-984-3500
Bay Meadows, 100 Park Pl. (Saratoga Dr.), San Mateo, 650-345-2250
www.leftbank.com
See review in North of San Francisco Directory.

LE PAPILLON
27 | 23 | 27 | $62

410 Saratoga Ave. (Kiely Blvd.), San Jose, 408-296-3730; www.lepapillon.com
■ Although "nondescript on the outside", this "classy French" is "excellent in all respects inside" offering "the real deal" fine-dining experience – the kind with "old-fashioned fussing over the customers" and "beautifully presented" tasting menus that culminate with soufflés slashed open tableside; no wonder that for nearly 30 years it's been seen as "San Jose's finest" for "a special-

occasion meal for that special someone" (with "top-tier" prices to match).

Lion & Compass ☒   22 | 18 | 20 | $39 |
1023 N. Fair Oaks Ave. (Weddell Dr.), Sunnyvale, 408-745-1260; www.lionandcompass.com
☑ "Silicon Valley's ultimate power-broker deal-making locale" is still buzzing with "BMWs, Porsches, Hummers, Ferraris" and the "venture capitalists" who drive them; while this Sunnyvale "hot spot's" decor comes off as "somewhat cold", the nicely presented New American meals "remain good" and bonuses like valet parking are well appreciated.

MacArthur Park   16 | 18 | 16 | $36 |
27 University Ave. (El Camino Real), Palo Alto, 650-321-9990
See review in City of San Francisco Directory.

Maddalena's & Café Fino ☒   ▽ 19 | 19 | 21 | $36 |
544 Emerson St. (bet. Hamilton & University Aves.), Palo Alto, 650-326-6082; www.maddalenasrestaurant.com
☑ "Live jazz" and a "well-serviced bar" are the "best things" about this set of "old-school" dining venues in Palo Alto; maestro Fred Maddalena "hosts the nightly party" at Café Fino, a "moody nightclub" made for "music and martinis"; next door, "Maddalena's is more subdued", with "formal waiters" that score better than the French-Italian fare and a "vibe that screams senior-citizen crowd" or "for business meetings only."

Manresa   26 | 22 | 24 | $80 |
320 Village Ln. (N. Santa Cruz Ave.), Los Gatos, 408-354-4330; www.manresarestaurant.com
☑ "Run, run, run to eat" at this "South Bay standout" sing enthusiasts enchanted with chef David Kinch's Los Gatos endeavor that "pushes the envelope of bold culinary ideas"; "spoil yourself" on his flexible prix fixes featuring a string of "unusual pairings" of Cal–New French food that "delivers the thrills you should expect at these prices"; still, man-eaters moan the "small portions" and the "smiling" but sluggish service don't support the "stratospheric" tabs.

MARCHÉ ☒   27 | 24 | 25 | $61 |
898 Santa Cruz Ave. (University Dr.), Menlo Park, 650-324-9092
■ "It's just Menlo Park", but it "feels like you're in the big city" (with prices to match) at chef-owner Howard Bulka's "posh" "destination"; his daily changing New French à la carte and tasting menus – "based on the seasons and the market" ("as the name implies") – and "brilliant wine selections" are "serious business"; but what really shines is the service, from the "chef visits at each table" to the "friendly, professional" staff that "remembers diners."

MARINUS   27 | 26 | 25 | $72
Bernardus Lodge, 415 Carmel Valley Rd. (Laureles Grade Rd.), Carmel, 831-658-3500; www.bernardus.com
■ "The absolute star of the Carmel dining scene" resides at this "pastoral" "getaway"; first "wear a belt you can loosen a notch" and then "sit back and be pampered" by "perfectly professional servers" dishing up "insanely delicious" Cal–New French cooking and a "bank-breaking wine list" (weighted with Bernardus Winery bottlings) in "one of the all-time great dining rooms" – "elegant, yet rustic" when "next to the cozy fireplace"; P.S. true sports can "spend the weekend" at the lodge.

Max's   16 | 13 | 16 | $22
1250 Old Bayshore Hwy. (Broadway), Burlingame, 650-342-6297
711 Stanford Shopping Ctr. (Sand Hill Rd.), Palo Alto, 650-323-6297
1001 El Camino Real (James Ave.), Redwood City, 650-365-6297
www.maxsworld.com
See review in City of San Francisco Directory.

Mei Long   25 | 20 | 22 | $31
867 E. El Camino Real (east of Hwy. 85), Mountain View, 650-961-4030
■ Say so long to "the standards" and hello to the "inventive", "sublimely subtle Chinese cuisine" created at this "formal" Mountain Viewer where "linen-clad tables" and orchids "hide behind the suburban strip mall"; you're encouraged to "put yourself in the waiters' hands" for the tasting menus enhanced by "great wine pairings"; penny-pinchers point out "lunch is a real treat, since the menu is almost the same as dinner, while prices are very close to basic eateries'."

Mezza Luna   22 | 19 | 21 | $32
459 Prospect Way (Capistrano Rd.), Princeton by the Sea, 650-728-8108; www.mezzalunabythesea.com
☑ If 'authentic' means "everyone from the owners on down are from Italy, then this is the most authentic place you'll ever find" say the luna-struck about this "laid-back" trattoria in Princeton by the Sea; it's known for "Calabrian specials" and "fish so fresh you can still smell" the harbor nearby; though the decor has warmed up in the ratings, some still shrug it's "ho-hum."

Mistral ☒   21 | 19 | 19 | $35
370-6 Bridge Pkwy. (Marine World Pkwy.), Redwood Shores, 650-802-9222; www.mistraldining.com
☑ "A power-lunch place for Silicon Valley execs (lots of Oracle folks)", this "unexpected" site in a Redwood Shores office park serves "quite good", "if not gourmet" French-Italian fare; though the interior can be "noisy as a rock

concert", outdoor tables take advantage of the "lovely location overlooking the lagoon"; N.B. recent renovations may outdate the Decor score.

Montrio Bistro ▽ 23 | 20 | 21 | $42 |
414 Calle Principal (Franklin St.), Monterey, 831-648-8880;
www.montrio.com
☑ "One of the few options for a good meal" (plus a stiff drink) in touristy Downtown Monterey, this "lively", "wildly decorated" "firehouse-turned-bistro" offers "innovative" Cal-Italian entrees, many of 'em prepared on a wood-burning rotisserie, plus "little $5 plates that are great" bar snacks; too bad the "terrible acoustics" cause some to scream the "food is second to the noise."

NAVIO 24 | 28 | 24 | $66 |
Ritz-Carlton Hotel, 1 Miramonte Point Rd. (Hwy. 1),
Half Moon Bay, 650-712-7000; www.ritzcarlton.com
■ "Breathtaking views of the beach" from every table in the "beautiful dining room" are the reason many navigate their way to Half Moon Bay, especially for splashy Sunday brunch buffets deemed "the best on the Peninsula"; however, chef Peter Rudolf's "healthy", "stylish" seafood creations and the "intelligent", "polite service" are worth a visit anytime, particularly if you "splurge" on the tasting menu; of course, "like all Ritz-Carltons, it's expensive."

Nepenthe 14 | 25 | 16 | $33 |
Hwy. 1 (¼ mi. south of Ventana Inn & Spa), Big Sur,
831-667-2345; www.nepenthebigsur.com
☑ "Spectacular views of the coastline and ghostly memories of Orson Welles and Rita Hayworth" (who briefly owned the place) make this "laid-back hippie throwback" a "must-stop on your way up" Hwy. 1; "they could serve leftovers and one would still enjoy" "sitting on the deck to watch the sunset over the Pacific", even if the "perch over Big Sur isn't as high" as the prices; and if the service is "notoriously bad", at least it "leaves plenty of time to take in the romantic ambiance."

Nola 17 | 21 | 17 | $28 |
535 Ramona St. (bet. Hamilton & University Aves.), Palo Alto,
650-328-2722; www.nolas.com
☑ "Every day is Mardi Gras" at this "festive", "funky" Palo Alto place that's "always packed" with "the young and restless"; spoilsports snap the "ultra-spicy" Cajun-Southwestern cuisine makes a "sorry substitute" for a "meal in the Big Easy", but still, it'll serve for sobering up after the "killer drinks."

North Beach Pizza ● 17 | 8 | 13 | $16 |
240 E. Third Ave. (B St.), San Mateo, 650-344-5000;
www.northbeachpizza.com
See review in City of San Francisco Directory.

Oak City Bar & Grill
20 | 20 | 19 | $40 |

1029 El Camino Real (Ravenswood Ave.), Menlo Park, 650-321-6882; www.oakcitybarandgrill.com

☒ "Located in the site" of "the late, lamented Wild Hare", this "bright", "trendy" New American newcomer is a "worthy successor", "a good place to take the men in your life who prefer food that's not weird"; and though a few fret "the service still has some kinks to work out", most agree it's "a welcome addition to the improving Menlo Park restaurant scene."

Omei
26 | 14 | 17 | $27 |

2316 Mission St. (King St.), Santa Cruz, 831-425-8458

☒ "Omei! O'my!" gush fans of "spicy to the point of perfection" Chinese fare with "lots of vegetarian options" ("of course, it's Santa Cruz") and "mysteriously thick sauces"; service "can be slow", but mainly it's the "minimalist, blasé decor" that "could stand to be spruced up so that it would fit the wonderful food."

Original Joe's ●
17 | 12 | 17 | $27 |

(aka Joe's, OJ's)

301 S. First St. (San Carlos St.), San Jose, 408-292-7030; www.originaljoes.com

See review in City of San Francisco Directory.

Osteria ⊠
23 | 16 | 19 | $31 |

247 Hamilton Ave. (Ramona St.), Palo Alto, 650-328-5700

☒ "You're treated like family" at "one of the best Northern Italian places in Palo Alto", where your "well-priced", "consistently good" food stays "steaming hot from the minute they set it down to when your're sopping up the sauce with bread"; though the "loud", close quarters may work for a "cozy dinner for two", claustrophobes find it "terribly cramped"; P.S. "everyone waits, reservations or not."

Oswald's
▽ 26 | 19 | 24 | $45 |

1547 Pacific Ave. (Cedar St.), Santa Cruz, 831-423-7427

■ For a "piece of the city down by the surf", "the snooty crowd" heads to Santa Cruz's "most sophisticated" site ("not a skateboard in sight"); "great organic products" are the foundation of the "excellent" "innovative" Cal cuisine (explaining why "you might even see Paul Newman dining with daughter Nell when he's in town") culminating in the chocolate soufflé; however, the art-filled, "quaint" quarters have "no waiting area, so make reservations."

PACIFIC'S EDGE
25 | 28 | 25 | $65 |

Highlands Inn, 120 Highlands Dr. (Hwy. 1), Carmel, 831-620-1234; www.highlandsinn.hyatt.com

■ "The name says it all": "perched on the edge of a cliff over the Pacific", this Carmel getaway affords unrivaled "sunset views" that will "make you want to linger"; despite fears it would "lose its edge" when it lost its old chef, the New American–French "food doesn't disappoint" – especially if you sample the "superb tasting menus" ("the choice of foodies"), offered by "impeccable service"; pricewise, it's "no bargain", but "propose to her here and she can't say no."

Palo Alto Creamery   17 | 15 | 17 | $17 |

566 Emerson St. (Hamilton Ave.), Palo Alto, 650-323-3131
Stanford Shopping Ctr., 180 El Camino Real (University Ave.),
Palo Alto, 650-327-3141

☑ Take the kids on "a field trip to another era" at this duo of Palo Alto diners with "'50s style and '90s buzz"; with its "eat-with-a-spoon milkshakes" and "enormous breakfasts for cholesterol freaks", it "would be the perfect place on earth, but for the high prices", for coffee-shop cuisine; P.S. the Downtown original, a "beloved neighborhood institution", is preferred to the Stanford Shopping Center's "carbon-copy clone."

Pancho Villa Taqueria   23 | 9 | 15 | $10 |

365 S. B St. (bet. 3rd & 4th Aves.), San Mateo, 650-343-4123
See review in City of San Francisco Directory.

Parcel 104   24 | 22 | 22 | $48 |

Santa Clara Marriott, 2700 Mission College Blvd.
(Great America Pkwy.), Santa Clara, 408-970-6104;
www.parcel104.com

☑ Co-owned by Bradley Ogden of Lark Creek Inn fame, this "swank" New American "in a surprising location" (namely, a "suburban Marriott") dishes out "creative" food that has many "taste buds all aflutter"; some skeptics cite "hit-or-miss" experiences, especially with service ("without Bradley in the kitchen, it's just another hotel restaurant"), but most posit the "pricey" place is "well worth it."

Passage to India   ▽ 18 | 14 | 15 | $19 |

1991 W. El Camino Real (bet. Escuela & Rengstorff Aves.),
Mountain View, 650-969-9990; www.passagetoindia.net

☑ The "reasonably priced" buffet – "a completely satisfying meal" at lunch and weekend dinner – is the claim to fame of this Mountain View Indian; most happily hail the "huge variety" of dishes, "from Indian takes on Chinese" to the "great vegetarian selection"; naysayers note, however, that "few foods can survive the buffet treatment" – and the "inconsistent" fare here "is no exception."

Passionfish   25 | 17 | 23 | $39 |

701 Lighthouse Ave. (Congress Ave.), Pacific Grove,
831-655-3311; www.passionfish.net

■ Insiders insist this "little-known" Californian in Pacific Grove offers both the "best seafood on the Monterey Peninsula" and "deals on wine you'll find anywhere" thanks to near "at-cost" prices; the owners are "passionate

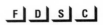
about food", "outstanding service" and protecting the environment; despite the "simple decor" and an "exterior that looks like a coffee shop", "reservations are a must, as locals can't stay away."

Pasta Moon 22 | 18 | 20 | $35
315 Main St. (Mills St.), Half Moon Bay, 650-726-5125; www.pastamoon.com

☑ "Fragrant smells waft out the door" of this "casual trattoria" on Half Moon Bay's main drag; all agree you can't find more "luscious homemade pastas" under the Tuscan sun or "warmer personal service"; but opinions on the digs are all over the moon – "casual" and "charming" to converts, "cramped" and "cluttered" to critics.

Pasta Pomodoro 15 | 13 | 16 | $18
Evergreen Mkt., 4898 San Felipe Rd. (Yerba Buena Blvd.), San Jose, 408-532-0271

See review in City of San Francisco Directory.

Pearl Alley Bistro ∇ 19 | 19 | 18 | $35
110 Pearl Alley (bet. Lincoln & Walnut Sts.), Santa Cruz, 831-429-8070; www.pearlalley.com

■ Tucked away "in the surfing capital of the world", Santa Cruz, this little pearl spans the globe with a "constantly updated menu" that mines a different land each month (with cooked-tableside Mongolian BBQ on permanent offering); but two constants – the "comfy" wine bar downstairs and 11 PM closing time – make it ideal for "after-movie dining and wine"-ing; P.S. Barossa Grill, an "Aussie-style" sibling, opened post-*Survey* at 515 Cedar Street.

P.F. Chang's China Bistro 18 | 19 | 17 | $27
900 Stanford Shopping Ctr. (El Camino Real), Palo Alto, 650-330-1782
Cherry Orchard Ctr., 390 W. El Camino Real (S. Mathilda Ave.), Sunnyvale, 408-991-9078
www.pfchangs.com

☑ Connoisseurs may cavil about "cookie-cutter Chinese", but South Bayers say "forget authentic – I want it to taste good"; hence, the popularity of these "cavernous" shopping-mall "staples in suburbia" for "fresh", "franchise food that works" ("you gotta love the lettuce wraps") served in "madcap", "meat-market" settings by "cute", if "overly helpful" staffers; just "call ahead for reservations" – "they accept them now" – because "it's bustling to the point of chaos"; N.B. there's a branch East of SF.

Piatti 18 | 19 | 18 | $34
Sixth Ave. (Junipero Ave.), Carmel, 831-625-1766
2 Stanford Shopping Ctr. (El Camino Real), Palo Alto, 650-324-9733
www.piatti.com

See review in North of San Francisco Directory.

Pisces 🅥   23   20   21 $50
1190 California Dr. (Broadway), Burlingame, 650-401-7500;
www.piscesrestaurant.com
☑ "All train stations should have food like this" signal
surveyors about this converted "old depot" in Burlingame,
a "more relaxed" "little sister to Aqua" whose atmosphere
"seems quaint until the Cal Train thunders by"; however,
while many still call the "seafood creative", a drop in the
Food score suggests that not everyone is all aboard with
the decisions to "redo the menu", axe the raw bar and
"lower the prices" – which remain startlingly "expensive"
for "scanty" portions.

Pizza Antica   22   15   17 $23
334 Santana Row (Stevens Creek Blvd.), San Jose, 408-557-8373
☑ "Unique, upscale pizza" "finally arrives in San Jose"
courtesy of chef/co-owner Gordon Drysdale's "deservedly
popular" pizzeria; "sidewalk tables for warm nights" and a
"cool, modern" interior make it a "great place to make
believe you're in Europe", but "if you want to talk to your
tablemates, come early, because the noise level is almost
painful" at prime time.

Plumed Horse 🅥   23   21   23 $57
14555 Big Basin Way (4th St.), Saratoga, 408-867-4711;
www.plumedhorse.com
☑ Since 1952, this Saratoga "special-occasion standard"
has taken the triple crown for "classic" Cal-French cuisine
featuring "aesthetically wondrous entrees" and desserts
(cherries jubilee, anyone?); some admire the "charming,
intimate environment", but high-stylers hint that "refreshing
the decor" could restore some faded plumage.

Rio Grill   21   18   19 $36
Crossroads Shopping Ctr., 101 Crossroads Blvd. (Rio Rd.),
Carmel, 831-625-5436; www.riogrill.com
☑ "Try anything from the oak smoker" at this Carmel Cal-
Southwestern and you'll see why "lots of locals eat here"
for "interesting takes on standard options"; some sigh
"the menu is getting a little long in the tooth" and its "tired"
decor and strip-mall "location don't do it justice"; but after
over 20 years, it's "still going strong."

Ristorante Capellini   19   20   18 $34
310 Baldwin Ave. (B St.), San Mateo, 650-348-2296;
www.capellinis.com
☑ "Expect to see lots of business transacted" at this "all-
around" San Matean that "holds up year after year", thanks
to "reliable Italian" fare, designer Pat Kuleto's "lovely
dark-wood room" and a "bustling" bar scene; however,
dissenters deem it "pricey, given the uneven service", and
the fact that it "hasn't changed since it opened" 15 years
ago disappoints others by more than a hair.

Robert's Whitehouse
∇ 24 | 21 | 21 | $46

*649 Lighthouse Ave. (bet. 18th & 19th Sts.), Pacific Grove,
831-375-9626; www.robertswhitehouse.com*

■ "Robert Kincaid's latest effort" in a charming vintage
venue in Pacific Grove is a bit of a "sleeper", but the "older
crowd" that flocks here appreciates the "great three-
course prix fixe French dinners", considered "the best
value in the Monterey Area" ("don't miss the signature
chocolate bag and milkshake dessert"); the "homey, yet
romantic setting" feels "like dining in someone's Victorian
dining room" (which we "guess it is, actually").

Roy's at Pebble Beach
24 | 25 | 22 | $51

*Inn at Spanish Bay, 2700 17 Mile Dr. (Congress Rd.),
Pebble Beach, 831-647-7423; www.roysrestaurant.com*

◪ Peripatetic chef Roy Yamaguchi "brings a little of his
famous" "Hawaii Regional treats" to the "après-golf crowd"
at Pebble Beach at "one of the best Roy's in the West";
settingwise, while "nothing compares to the beautiful
islands", "sweeping ocean views" and "the sound of
bagpipes" "on the tee" at sunset plays a darn good second
fiddle; though it's "unswervingly polite", "it's a shame the
service doesn't match the food or the environment."

Sardine Factory ⊠
21 | 21 | 22 | $47

*701 Wave St. (Prescott Ave.), Monterey, 831-373-3775;
www.sardinefactory.com*

◪ This "Cannery Row institution" is "a classy reminder of
Monterey in its heyday", where "career waiters reign, the
customer is queen" and prom-goers and the over-50 set
celebrate in sundry areas – "a studylike room by the
fireplace, another with a greenhouse feel" and a recently
remodeled piano bar; however, sharks snap the seafood
is "inconsistent", ranging from "as good as it gets" to
"not-so-good"; "it may be resting a bit on its laurels, but
they're impressive laurels."

Sent Sovi
∇ 26 | 20 | 25 | $56

*14583 Big Basin Way (5th St.), Saratoga, 408-867-3110;
www.sentsovi.com*

■ Saratoga's "only real entry" for fine dining may have
changed owners, but it remains a destination for "intimate
dinners" served by "intuitive staffers" within a copper-
and-wood "quaint atmosphere"; while the new "young
chef's" Cal-French bistro fare is "not as refined" as his
predecessor's, it's "beautifully presented" and "tastes
even better than it looks."

Seven Restaurant & Lounge ⊠
∇ 22 | 24 | 21 | $38

*754 The Alameda (Bush St.), San Jose, 408-280-1644;
www.7restaurant.us*

◪ "Feel like you're in the 'in' crowd" at this industrial-chic
new San Jose restaurant/"hip bar" that radiates "an electric

atmosphere"; despite being "too loud for aging eaters" (part of the "trendy setting"), surveyors are in seventh heaven about "twin chefs" Russell and Curtis Valdez for their "creative presentations and preparations" of the French–New American menu; however, many are at sixes and sevens over the "friendly, but not-too-competent service."

71 Saint Peter 🖼   22 | 18 | 21 | $35

71 N. San Pedro St. (bet. Santa Clara & St. John Sts.), San Jose, 408-971-8523; www.71saintpeter.com
■ There's a "definite European flavor" to this "jewel in the crown of Downtown San Jose", which "turns out some of the finest food, ambiance and service", from the "delicious" Med-French fare with "a fun wine list" down to its "comfortable, cozy" "rustic-looking" brick-walled interior and "charming" "tables on the street" and "prompt but not pushy" staff; while claustrophes "wish it were a little bigger", Romeos find it "great for romantic dates."

SHADOWBROOK   19 | 26 | 21 | $41

1750 Wharf Rd. (Capitola Rd.), Capitola, 831-475-1511; www.shadowbrook-capitola.com
■ "One can only wonder how many marriage proposals have occurred" in the "unique, terraced dining rooms" and "picturesque gardens" on a "lazy river" at this "unusual" Capitola "destination" "complete with cable-car approach"; "although the New American food is quite good, you end up paying some extreme prices for the atmosphere and service"; but it's still a choice "hideaway" to "celebrate a special occasion", so "reserve early."

SIERRA MAR   26 | 28 | 25 | $73

Post Ranch Inn, Hwy. 1 (30 mi. south of Carmel), Big Sur, 831-667-2800
■ "Suspended mid-air" "1,200 feet above the blue Pacific and nearly as far beyond your every expectation", this "absolutely phenomenal", "romantic" Big Sur site offers a "magnificent marriage" of "imaginative Cal–New French food", "fantastic wine", "wonderful service" and stunning setting; there's simply "no more spectacular view in the world" (or on the *Survey*'s Top Decor list), so even if you're "not staying at the exclusive retreat", it's "worthwhile just for drinks" at sunset to "watch the whales spout below."

Spago Palo Alto 🖼   22 | 22 | 20 | $52

265 Lytton Ave. (bet. Bryant & Ramona Sts.), Palo Alto, 650-833-1000; www.wolfgangpuck.com
☑ The South Bay's celebrity eatery (spottings include Joe Montana, Al Gore and even "Wolfgang Puck himself behind the stove") continues to offer "LA cool in Palo Alto" with a "light", "elegantly lively" decor and "serious" Cal-Med cuisine that's ideal for "impressing out-of-towners if you're on an expense account"; yeah, it's "pretty full of

itself", and the service and "food aren't consistent – but the experience is a delight."

St. Michael's Alley   22   18   21 $35
806 Emerson St. (Homer Ave.), Palo Alto, 650-326-2530; www.stmikes.com

■ Ok, so it's "not on an alley", but this "quaint little" Palo Alto "institution" is "far enough away from the University Avenue fray to keep the setting serene"; the Cal cuisine is "impeccable" for the price (particularly weekend brunches) and "endearing owners add a casual warmth" to the already "rather intimate" interior, making it a "cute" "date place."

Stokes Restaurant & Bar   ▽ 23   22   23 $44
500 Hartnell St. (bet. Madison & Polk Sts.), Monterey, 831-373-1110; www.stokesrestaurant.com

■ "There's no mud" at this "off-the-beaten path" "historic adobe" – just "marvelous presentations and great combinations" of Cal-Med flavors (in "tapas, small and large plates") and a "great wine list" delivered in a rambling of fireplace-lit "chic" dining rooms (think a 13th-century Italian villa gone to seed); "jaded diners" can't "believe the food, service and atmosphere that you get for the price", making it a "must-stop in Monterey."

STRAITS CAFE   22   20   18 $33
1100 Burlingame Ave. (Highland Ave.), Burlingame, 659-373-7883 ⊠
3295 El Camino Real (Lambert Ave.), Palo Alto, 650-494-7168
Santana Row, 333 Santana Row, Suite 1100 (bet. Olin Ave. & Tatum Ln.), San Jose, 408-246-6320
www.straitsrestaurants.com
See review in City of San Francisco Directory.

TAMARINE   25   23   22 $41
546 University Ave. (Tasso St.), Palo Alto, 650-325-8500; www.tamarinerestaurant.com

■ "Some of the most elegant Vietnamese south of SF and east of Ho Chi Minh City" awaits at this "smooth-as-silk" Palo Altan where "upscale" "tapas-style presentations" served on "arty tableware" "encourage group dining" in the "cool, subdued" space; it's the "'in' meeting place for venture capitalists and lawyers" at lunch, and the "lively bar scene" attracts "beautiful young professionals after work", but "expect long waits (even with reservations)" or try the "communal tables for walk-ins."

Tarpy's Roadhouse   23   21   21 $38
2999 Monterey-Salinas Hwy. (Canyon Del Rey Blvd.), Monterey, 831-647-1444; www.tarpys.com

■ "Don't let the name fool you": this "historic" stone manse "on the way into Monterey" serves "generous portions" of "solid, stick-to-your-ribs" American fare (including vegetarian offerings) that's way "better than

what you'd expect" from a roadhouse; a "friendly staff"
and a "great patio in warm weather" overlooking "planes
landing at the adjacent airport" all help make it worth the
"ride out into the country."

Taste Cafe & Bistro   ▽ 22 16 21 $37
1199 Forest Ave. (Prescott Ln.), Pacific Grove, 831-655-0324;
www.tastecafebistro.com
■ Though it's "way out of the way" and "in a strip mall"
to boot, loyalists "make the extra drive" to this "intimate"
bistro in Pacific Grove for "superb" Continental fare, a
"reasonably priced wine list" and "exceptional" service,
plus live jazz Thursdays–Saturdays; the "recently expanded"
Med-style space is more "comfortable" than ever.

Three Seasons   22 19 17 $31
518 Bryant St. (University Ave.), Palo Alto, 650-838-0353;
www.threeseasonsrestaurant.com
See review in City of San Francisco Directory.

Tomatina   18 14 16 $18
Mercado Ctr., 3127 Mission College Blvd.
(Great America Pkwy.), Santa Clara, 408-654-9000;
www.tomatina.com
☑ "Better-than-average pizzas made in squarer-than-
average shapes" and "yummy piadines" (flatbreads topped
with salads) win praise for this kid-friendly Italian-Med in
Santa Clara; the "noisy" scene and "spotty" service are
probably "not as much fun as" the eponymous "tomato-
throwing festival in Spain", but "if you're in a hurry", "it will
do the trick"; P.S. the East Bay has two branches, one of
which is the "best-kept secret" in Walnut Creek.

Trader Vic's   17 22 18 $41
Dina's Garden Hotel, 4269 El Camino Real (bet. Charleston &
San Antonio Rds.), Palo Alto, 650-849-9800;
www.tradervicspaloalto.com
See review in East of San Francisco Directory.

Turmerik   ▽ 21 18 19 $30
141 S. Murphy St. (bet. Evelyn & Washington Aves.),
Sunnyvale, 408-617-9100; www.turmerik.com
☑ "Be adventurous" and "you will be rewarded" at this
Sunnyvale spot serving "subtle, inventive" Indian-centric
Pan-Asian cuisine; critics complain that it's "overpriced
for its trendiness factor", but the dinner buffet is "an amazing
deal" and the lunch spread is "outstanding" say fans who
rate both "a cut above" the average.

231 Ellsworth ⌘   25 21 23 $54
231 S. Ellsworth Ave. (bet. 2nd & 3rd Aves.), San Mateo,
650-347-7231; www.231ellsworth.com
☑ "Whether you're dining *à deux*" "for a special occasion"
"or in a large group" "after your meeting", this "old-

school", "elegant" "San Mateo gem" is "an oasis in the [culinary] desert" "between SF and Palo Alto", plying Peninsula patrons with "fabulous service" and "over-the-top" New American tasting menus that include "unique pairings" from "the amazing wine list" that's "more like a book"; however, a money-conscious minority suggests the experience "costs more than it's [ells]worth."

Udupi Palace   ▽ 22 | 8 | 16 | $14 |
976 E. EL Camino Real (Poplar Ave.), Sunnyvale, 408-830-9600; www.udupipalaceca.com
See review in East of San Francisco Directory.

Village Pub, The   24 | 23 | 23 | $56 |
2967 Woodside Rd. (Whiskey Hill Rd.), Woodside, 650-851-9888; www.thevillagepub.net
■ This "Woodside wonder" "ain't no village pub" admirers attest, but rather a "pricey" "star restaurant on the Peninsula" with "sophisticated" New American cuisine and an "impressive wine list" served by a "pampering" staff in a "cozy" yet "posh" room; you can always opt for a burger in the "more casual bar area", but you're just as likely to "rub shoulders with the VCs in the Valley" there as well.

Viognier   25 | 22 | 23 | $49 |
Draeger's Mktpl., 222 E. Fourth Ave. (bet. B St. & Ellsworth Ave.), San Mateo, 650-685-3727; www.viognierrestaurant.com
■ "Whoever thought a restaurant on top of a supermarket could be so good?" ponder pros of this "lovely" Med in an "oddball location" over the gourmet Draeger's Marketplace in San Mateo; a "small but wonderful menu" (including an "outstanding" prix fixe), "superb wine choices", a "staff that gives you the feeling that they really enjoy their work" and a "beautiful setting" comprise a "recipe for a good evening."

Yankee Pier   18 | 15 | 16 | $31 |
378 Santana Row (S. Winchester Ave.), San Jose, 408-244-1244; www.yankeepier.com
See review in North of San Francisco Directory.

Zao Noodle Bar   15 | 12 | 14 | $16 |
261 University Ave. (bet. Bryant & Ramona Sts.), Palo Alto, 650-328-1988; www.zao.com
See review in City of San Francisco Directory.

Zibibbo   19 | 19 | 18 | $38 |
430 Kipling St. (bet. Lytton & University Aves.), Palo Alto, 650-328-6722; www.restaurantzibibbo.com
◪ A "high-class hot spot" in Palo Alto, this sibling of SF's Lulu offers an "eclectic Med menu" that "changes with the seasons", paired with an "interesting wine list", so "there's always something new to try"; a "professional, upbeat" staff keeps the atmosphere in the "cavernous

dining room" "relaxed and friendly", and while some feel it's "not as good as it was in the go-go '90s", at least it's "easier to get a seat these days."

Zucca Ristorante | 19 | 17 | 17 | $30 |

186 Castro St. (bet. Central & Villa Sts.), Mountain View, 650-864-9940; www.zuccaristorante.com

◪ At this "cute" Mountain View mainstay, "there's always something new" on the "middle-of-the-road Med" small-plates menu that mines the culinary traditions of Turkey, Greece, Italy, France, Spain and even India; "service is erratic", but you can always count on the "wonderful martinis", and "in warm weather, the front patio is the place to be" (if only to escape the "busy, loud" scene within).

Indexes

CUISINES
LOCATIONS
SPECIAL FEATURES

Places outside of San Francisco are marked as follows:
E=East of SF; N=North; and S=South.

CUISINES

Oswald's/S
Pacific
Palomino
Pangaea/N
Paragon
Paragon/E
Passionfish/S
Pearl/N
Pilar/N
Pinot Blanc/N
Pisces/S
Plumed Horse/S
PlumpJack
PlumpJack/E
Public, The
Ravenous/N
Rio Grill/S
Rivoli/E
Rubicon
Santé/N
Seasons
Seaweed Café/N
Sent Sovi/S
Sierra Mar/S
Silks
Soizic/E
Spago Palo Alto/S
Station House/N
Stinking Rose
St. Michael's/S
Stokes Rest./S
St. Orres/N
Syrah/N
Townhouse B&G/E
Venus/E
Waterfront Rest.
Wente Vineyards/E
Wine Spectator/N
Zax Tavern/E

Cambodian
Angkor Borei
Angkor Wat
Battambang/E

Caribbean
Cha Cha Cha
Charanga

Cheese Steaks
Jay's Cheese Steak

Chinese
(* dim sum specialist)
Alice's
Brandy Ho's
Chef Chu's/S
Eliza's
Eric's
Firecracker
Fook Yuen/S*
Fountain Court*
Gary Chu's/N
Great China/E
Great Eastern
Happy Cafe/S
Harbor Village*
Hong Kong Flower/S*
House of Nanking
Hunan
Hunan Home's Rest.
Hunan Home's Rest./S
Jade Villa/E*
Jai Yun*
Koi Palace/S*
Legendary Palace/E*
Little Shin Shin/E
Mandarin, The*
Mayflower
Mei Long/S
Omei/S
P.F. Chang's/E/S
R & G Lounge
Rest. Peony/E*
Shanghai 1930*
Shen Hua/E
Taiwan
Taiwan/E
Tommy Toy's
Ton Kiang*
Watercress
Yank Sing*
Yuet Lee

Coffee Shops/Diners
Bette's Oceanview/E
Bubba's Diner/N
FatApple's/E
It's Tops Coffee
Jimmy Bean's/E
JoAnn's Café/S
Mel's Drive-In

Palo Alto Creamery/S
Taylor's Automatic
Taylor's Automatic/N

Continental
Anton & Michel/S
Caprice, The/N
Chantilly/S
Dal Baffo/S
Ecco Rest./S
Fresh Cream/S
Maddalena's/S
Shadowbrook/S

Creole
PJ's Oyster

Cuban
Habana

Delis
Jimtown Store/N
Max's
Max's/E/N/S
Saul's Rest./E

Dessert
Boulange de Cole/Polk
Cafe Cacao/E
Cheesecake Factory/S
Citizen Cake
Downtown Bakery/N
Emporio Rulli
Emporio Rulli/N
Fenton's Creamery/E
Tartine Bakery

Eclectic
Albany Bistro/E
Andalu
Celadon/N
Delancey St.
Firefly
Harmony Club/N
Hayes & Vine
Kingfish/S
Nectar Wine
Pearl Alley Bistro/S
Pomelo
Samovar
Va de Vi/E
Wappo Bar/N

Willi's Wine Bar/N
Willow Wood Mkt./N

English
Liverpool Lil's
Lovejoy's Tea Rm.

Eritrean
Massawa

Ethiopian
Axum Cafe
Blue Nile/E
Massawa

French
Alamo Sq.
Alexander Valley/N
Angèle/N
Antidote/N
Aqua
Auberge du Soleil/N
Bambuddha Lnge.
Bella Vista/S
BIX
Bizou
Boulange de Cole/Polk
Boulevard
Cafe Beaujolais/N
Café Fanny/E
Cafe Jacqueline
Café Marcella/S
Campton Place
Casanova/S
Chaz Rest.
Chez Spencer
Christophe/N
Cinq/N
El Paseo/N
Emile's/S
fig cafe/N
First Crush
First Crush/N
French Laundry/N
Fresh Cream/S
Frisson
Gervais Rest./S
Grand Cafe
Isa
Jardinière
Julia's Kitchen/N

Cuisine Index

Caffe Macaroni (S)
Caffè Museo
Caffe Sport (S)
Caffé Verbena/E
Capp's Corner
Casanova/S (N)
Cena Luna/N
Cucina Paradiso/N (S)
Cucina Rest./N
Dal Baffo/S (N)
Delfina (N)
Della Santina's/N (N)
Dopo/E
E'Angelo (N)
Eccolo/E (N)
Emmy's Spaghetti
Emporio Rulli
Emporio Rulli/N
Faz
Faz/E/S
Florio
Frantoio/N (N)
Gabriella Café/S (N)
Gira Polli (S)
Gira Polli/N (S)
Globe
Green Valley Cafe/N (N)
Il Davide/N (N)
Il Fornaio
Il Fornaio/E/N/S
Incanto (N)
Jackson Fillmore
Julius' Castle
Kuleto's (N)
Kuleto's/S (N)
La Felce (N)
La Ginestra/N (S)
Last Supper Club
LoCoCo's Rest./E (S)
L'Osteria del Forno (N)
Marin Joe's/N (N)
Mario's Bohemian (N)
Merenda (N)
Mescolanza
Mezza Luna/S (S)
Michelangelo Rest.
Mistral/S
Montrio Bistro/S
Nizza La Bella/E
Nob Hill Café (N)

North Bch. Rest. (N)
Oliveto/E (N)
Original Joe's
Original Joe's/S
Osteria/S (N)
Palatino
Palio D'Asti (N)
Pane e Vino (N)
Parma
Pasta Moon/S
Pasta Pomodoro
Pasta Pomodoro/E/N/S
Pazzia (N)
Pesce (N)
Phoenix Next Door/E
Piatti/E/N/S
Piazza D'Angelo/N
Pizzeria Tra Vigne/N
Poggio Rist./N (N)
Postino/E
Prima/E
Quince
Rist. Allegria/N (N)
Rist. Bacco
Rist. Capellini/S (N)
Rist. Fabrizio/N (N)
Rist. Ideale
Rist. Milano (N)
Rist. Umbria (N)
Rose Pistola (N)
Rose's Cafe (N)
Santi/N (N)
Scala's Bistro (N)
Sharon's By Sea/N
Sociale
Sonoma Meritage/N (N)
Stinking Rose (N)
Tomatina/E/S
Tommaso's (S)
Tonno Rosso (N)
Tratt. Contadina
Tratt. La Siciliana/E (S)
Tra Vigne/N
Tre Fratelli
Tuscany/N (N)
Uva Tratt./N (S)
Valentina Rist. (N)
Venezia/E (N)
Venticello (N)
Victorian Garden/N

Izzy's Steak
Izzy's Steak/N/S
Morton's
Ruth's Chris
Vic Stewart's/E

Swiss
Emile's/S
Matterhorn Swiss

Tearooms
Lovejoy's Tea Rm.
Samovar

Tex-Mex
Guaymas/N

Thai
Basil Thai
Cha Am Thai
Cha Am Thai/E
Khan Toke
King of Thai
Koh Samui
Manora's Thai
Marnee Thai
Osha Thai
Plearn Thai/E
Royal Thai/N
Soi 4/E
Thai Hse.
Thep Phanom
Yukol Place

Tibetan
Lhasa Moon

Turkish
A La Turca

Vegan
Geranium
Herbivore
Millennium

Vegetarian
Fleur de Lys
French Laundry/N
Geranium
Greens
Herbivore
Millennium
Udupi Palace/E/S

Vietnamese
Ana Mandara
Crustacean
Golden Turtle
La Vie
Le Cheval/E
Le Colonial
Le Soleil
Slanted Door
Tamarine/S
Tao Cafe
Thanh Long
Three Seasons
Three Seasons/E/S
Tu Lan
Vi's/E

LOCATIONS

CITY OF SAN FRANCISCO

Location Index

Location Index

Santa Clara
Fish Market
Parcel 104
Tomatina

Santa Cruz/Aptos/Capitola
El Palomar
Gabriella Café
Gayle's Bakery
Omei
Oswald's
Pearl Alley Bistro
Shadowbrook

Saratoga
Basin, The
Gervais Rest.
Plumed Horse
Sent Sovi

South San Francisco/Daly City
Basque Cultural Ctr.
Burger Joint
JoAnn's Café
Koi Palace

Sunnyvale
Faz
Lion & Compass
P.F. Chang's
Turmerik
Udupi Palace

Woodside
Bella Vista
John Bentley's
Village Pub

SPECIAL FEATURES

(Indexes list the best in each category. Multi-location restaurants' features may vary by location.)

Business Dining

Special Feature Index

Catering

Special Feature Index

Celebrity Chefs

bacar, *Arnold Eric Wong*
Bistro Jeanty/N, *Philippe Jeanty*
Bocadillos, *Gerald Hirigoyen*
Boulevard, *Nancy Oakes*
Campton Place, *Daniel Humm*
Chef Chu's/S, *Lawrence Chu*
Chez Panisse/E, *Alice Waters*
Cindy's Backstreet/N, *Cindy Pawlcyn*
Citizen Cake, *Elizabeth Falkner*
Cool Café/S, *Jesse Cool*
Delfina, *Craig Stoll*
Dry Creek Kit./N, *Charles Palmer*
Eos Rest., *Arnold Eric Wong*
Farallon, *Mark Franz*
Fifth Floor, *Laurent Gras*
Flea St. Café/S, *Jesse Cool*
Fleur de Lys, *Hubert Keller*
French Laundry/N, *Thomas Keller*
Frisson, *Daniel Patterson*
Gary Danko, *Gary Danko*
Jardinière, *Traci Des Jardins*
Jeanty at Jack's, *Philippe Jeanty*
La Folie, *Roland Passot*
Lark Creek Inn/N, *Bradley Ogden*
La Toque/N, *Ken Frank*
Martini Hse./N, *Todd Humphries*
Masa's, *Richard Reddington & Gregory Short*
Michael Mina, *Michael Mina*
Mustards Grill/N, *Cindy Pawlcyn*
Oliveto/E, *Paul Bertolli*
Père Jeanty/N, *Philippe Jeanty*
Pilar/N, *Pilar Sanchez*
Pinot Blanc/N, *Joachim Splichal*
Piperade, *Gerald Hirigoyen*
Poggio Rist./N, *Chris Fernandez*
Ritz-Carlton D.R., *Ron Siegel*
Roy's/Pebble Bch./S, *Roy Yamaguchi*
Slanted Door, *Charles Phan*
Tartare, *George Morrone*
Terra/N, *Hiro Sone*
Town Hall, *Steven and Mitchell Rosenthal*
Zuni Cafe, *Judy Rodgers*

Child-Friendly
(Besides the usual fast-food places; * children's menu available)
Acme Chophse.
Ahwahnee/E*
Albona Rist.
Alexis Baking Co./N
Alioto's*
All Season's Cafe/N
Anzu*
Aperto*
Arcadia/S*
A. Sabella's*
Asqew Grill*
A Tavola/S*
Axum Cafe*
Balboa Cafe/E*
Barbara Fishtrap/S*
Barney Hamburger*
Barney Hamburger/E*
Basque Cultural Ctr./S*
Beach Chalet*
Bette's Oceanview/E
Blackberry Bistro/E
Bocadillos
Bo's Barbecue/E
Bubba's Diner/N*
Buca di Beppo*
Buca di Beppo/S
Bucci's/E
Buckeye Roadhse./N*
Burger Joint
Cactus Taqueria/E*
Cafe Citti/N
Cafe Marimba*
Cafe Riggio*
Caffè Museo
Calistoga Inn/N*
Campton Place*
Capp's Corner
Carneros/N*
Casanova/S*
Casa Orinda/E
Celadon/N*

Special Feature Index

Critic-Proof
(Get lots of business despite so-so food)

Dancing

Delivery

Fountain Court
Fuki Sushi/S
Gary Chu's/N
Gayle's Bakery/S
Geyser Smokehse./N
Hunan
Insalata's /N
King of Thai
La Méditerranée
La Méditerranée/E
Las Camelias/N
Mandalay
Max's
Max's/E/N/S
Mescolanza
Mistral/S
Montrio Bistro/S
Napa General/N
North Bch. Pizza
North Bch. Pizza/S
Original Joe's
Pasta Pomodoro/N
Piazza D'Angelo/N
Pizza Antica/S
Pizza Rustica/E
R & G Lounge
Ravenous/N
Rio Grill/S
Rist. Allegria/N
Shen Hua/E
Swan Oyster
Tapeo/N
Ton Kiang
Tratt. La Siciliana/E
Tra Vigne/N
Turmerik/S
Villa Corona/N
Village Pub/S
Vivande Porta Via
Wappo Bar/N
Yianni's
Yukol Place
Zante's Pizza

Dining Alone

(Other than hotels and places
with counter service)
Amber India/S
Ana Mandara
Blackhawk Grille/E

Boulevard
Buca di Beppo/S
Burger Joint/S
Cafe Cacao/E
Café Rouge/E
Caffè Museo
Caffé Verbena/E
Carnelian Room
Celadon/N
Cha Am Thai
Charles Nob Hill
Cheesecake Factory
Cheesecake Factory/S
Chow/Park Chow/E
Citizen Cake
Cool Café/S
Cosmopolitan
Cucina Paradiso/N
Desiree Café
Duck Club/N
Faz
Ferry Plaza Seafood
Flying Fish Grill/S
Foothill Cafe/N
Fresh Cream/S
Frjtz Fries
Gaylord India
Hard Rock Cafe
Hog Island Oyster
Il Fornaio
Juban
Julia's Kitchen/N
Koi Palace/S
LaSalette/N
Left Bank/S
Maki
Mandarin, The
MarketBar
Max's
Max's/E
Mendo Bistro/N
Mifune
Monti's Rotisserie/N
Mo's
Napa Valley Grille/N
Palo Alto Creamery/S
Pasta Pomodoro/N/S
P.F. Chang's/E/S
Piatti/S
Rest. Peony/E

Rio Grill/S
Rotunda
Sanraku
Sassafras/N
Scoma's
Sea Ranch Lodge/N
Sharon's By Sea/N
Slanted Door
Sonoma Saveurs/N
South Park
Straits Cafe/S
Taylor's Automatic
Tomatina/S
Town's End
Tre Fratelli
Viognier/S
Willi's Wine Bar/N
Wine Spectator/N
Yank Sing
Yoshi's/E
Zinsvalley/N

Entertainment

(Call for days and times of performances)
Ahwahnee/E (piano)
Albion River Inn/N (piano)
Alegrias (flamenco/guitar)
Ana Mandara (jazz)
Asia de Cuba (latin house)
AsiaSF (gender illusionists)
Axum Cafe (acoustic/jazz)
Aziza (belly dancer)
bacar (jazz)
Bambuddha Lnge. (DJ)
Beach Chalet (jazz)
Big 4 (piano)
BIX (jazz)
Blowfish Sushi/S (DJ)
butterfly embarc. (DJ/jazz)
Cafe Bastille (jazz)
Café Claude (jazz)
Calistoga Inn/N (open mike)
Carneros/N (local bands)
Catch (piano)
Central Park Bistro/S (jazz)
Cetrella Bistro/S (jazz)
Chaya Brasserie (jazz)
Chez Spencer (piano)
Circolo (DJ)

Cityscape (DJ)
Cosmopolitan (piano)
Deep Sushi (DJ)
Destino (varies)
downtown/E (jazz)
Duck Club/S (piano)
E&O Trading Co. (DJ/jazz)
Eastside West (bands/DJs)
El Palomar/S (mariachis)
Emmy's Spaghetti (DJ)
Enrico's Sidewalk (jazz)
Erna's Elderberry/E (jazz)
Everett & Jones/E (blues/jazz)
Faz/E/S (varies)
First Crush (jazz)
Foreign Cinema (films)
Frisson (DJ)
Frjtz Fries (DJ)
Garden Court (harpist/jazz)
Geyser Smokehse./N (karaoke)
Gordon Biersch/S (jazz)
Hard Rock Cafe (pop/rock)
Harmony Club/N (piano)
Harris' (jazz/piano)
Hurley's Rest./N (live music)
Jardinière (jazz duo)
Jitney's B&G (varies)
Jordan's/E (jazz)
Kan Zaman (belly dancer)
Katia's Tea Rm. (accordion)
Kingfish/S (r&b/rock)
La Luna (folk dance/tango)
La Note/E (accordion)
La Scene Café (piano)
Left Bank/N (jazz)
Lhasa Moon (Tibetan music)
Liberty Cafe (band/vocals)
Little River Inn/N (guitar)
Maddalena's/S (jazz trio)
Madrona Manor/N (jazz)
Marin Joe's/N (jazz/piano)
Marinus/S (jazz)
Max's/S (singing waiters)
Mecca (DJ)
Millennium (jazz)
Moose's (jazz)
Napa General/N (varies)
Napa Valley Train/N (piano)
Navio/S (jazz)

Olema Inn/N (live music)
Olive Bar (DJ)
Original Joe's (piano)
Pacific (piano)
Pacific's Edge/S (piano)
Paragon/E (jazz)
Pasta Moon/S (jazz)
Pearl/N (live music)
Pinot Blanc/N (jazz)
Plumed Horse/S (jazz/piano)
Ponzu (DJ)
Prima/E (jazz)
Public, The (DJ/jazz)
Puerto Alegre (mariachi trio)
Ramblas (Flamenco guitar)
Rist. Allegria/N (accordion)
Ritz-Carlton D.R. (harp)
Roe (DJ/jazz)
RoHan Lounge (DJ)
Rose Pistola (jazz)
Rose's Cafe (guitar)
Samovar (jazz)
Santé/N (piano)
Sardine Factory/S (piano)
Sassafras/N (jazz)
Seaweed Café/N (readings)
Shadowbrook/S (jazz)
Station House/N (jazz)
Straits Cafe/S (DJ/jazz)
Sushi Groove (DJ)
Tapeo/N (live music)
Taste Cafe/S (jazz)
Trader Vic's/S (varies)
Uva Tratt./N (piano)
Vic Stewart's/E (piano)
Washington Sq. (jazz)
XYZ (DJ)
Yoshi's/E (jazz)
Zuni Cafe (piano)

Fireplaces

Albion River Inn/N
Alexander Valley/N
Anton & Michel/S
Applewood Inn/N
A. Sabella's
Auberge du Soleil/N
Barney Hamburger/E
Bella Vista/S

Betelnut
Big 4
Bistro Don Giov./N
Bistro Jeanty/N
Boonville Hotel/N
Boulange de Cole/Polk
Brannan's Grill/N
Brix/N
Cafe Citti/N
Caprice, The/N
Casanova/S
Casa Orinda/E
Catch
Cetrella Bistro/S
Chantilly/S
Chez TJ/S
Chow/Park Chow
Chow/Park Chow/E
Dal Baffo/S
Della Santina's/N
Dipsea Cafe/N
Domaine Chandon/N
Duck Club/E/N/S
El Paseo/N
Erna's Elderberry/E
Evvia/S
Fandango/S
Farmhouse Inn/N
Faz/E
Fleur de Lys
Flying Fish Grill/S
Foreign Cinema
French Laundry/N
Fresh Cream/S
Gaylord India/S
Gervais Rest./S
Guaymas/N
Harmony Club/N
Harris'
Home
House of Prime Rib
Hurley's Rest./N
Iberia/S
Il Fornaio/E/N/S
John Ash & Co./N
Kenwood/N
Kokkari Estiatorio
Kuleto's
Lark Creek Inn/N

Historic Places
(Year opened; * building)

1909 Miss Millie's*
1910 Campton Place*
1910 Catch*
1912 Swan Oyster
1913 Zuni Cafe*
1914 Balboa Cafe
1915 Jordan's/E*
1915 Napa Valley Train/N*
1916 Pork Store Café*
1917 Pacific's Edge/S*
1920 A. Sabella's
1920 El Palomar/S*
1920 Kingfish/S*
1920 Rist. Capellini/S*
1920 Sam's Anchor/N
1922 Hawthorne Lane*
1922 Julius' Castle*
1923 Martini Hse./N*
1923 Palo Alto Creamery/S
1925 Alioto's
1925 John Bentley's/S*
1925 Palomino*
1927 Ahwahnee/E
1927 Townhouse B&G/E*
1928 Alfred's Steak
1930 Caprice, The/N*
1930 Foreign Cinema*
1930 Lalime's/E*
1932 Casa Orinda/E*
1934 Caspers Hot Dogs/E
1934 Trader Vic's/E
1935 It's Tops Coffee*
1935 Tommaso's
1937 Buckeye Roadhse./N
1937 Original Joe's
1940 Glen Ellen Inn/N*
1945 Tonga Room
1947 Shadowbrook/S
1949 House of Prime Rib
1949 Nepenthe/S
1949 Taylor's Automatic/N

Hotel Dining

Adagio Hotel
  Cortez
Ahwahnee Hotel
  Ahwahnee/E
Auberge du Soleil
  Auberge du Soleil/N

Bernardus Lodge
  Marinus/S
Blue Heron Inn
  Moosse Cafe/N
Blue Rock Inn
  Left Bank/N
Boonville Hotel
  Boonville Hotel/N
Calistoga Inn
  Calistoga Inn/N
Campton Place Hotel
  Campton Place
Carter House Inn
  Rest. 301/N
Claremont Resort & Spa
  Jordan's/E
  Paragon/E
Clift Hotel
  Asia de Cuba
Dina's Garden Hotel
  Trader Vic's/S
Doubletree Plaza
  Hana Japanese/N
El Dorado Hotel
  Piatti/N
Fairmont Hotel
  Tonga Room
Farmhouse Inn
  Farmhouse Inn/N
Four Point Sheraton Hotel
  Faz/E
Four Seasons Hotel
  Seasons
Garden Court Hotel
  Il Fornaio/S
Highlands Inn
  Pacific's Edge/S
Hill House Inn
  Sharon's By Sea/N
Hilton San Francisco
  Cityscape
Hotel Griffon
  Tonno Rosso
Hotel Healdsburg
  Dry Creek Kit./N
Hotel Monaco
  Grand Cafe
Hotel Nikko
  Anzu

Special Feature Index

Jacket Required

Special Feature Index

Grasshopper/E
Guaymas/N
Harmony Club/N
Hayes & Vine
Higashi West/S
Home
Hurley's Rest./N
Iberia/S
Incanto
Jardinière
Kan Zaman
Kingfish/S
Kokkari Estiatorio
Last Supper Club
Le Colonial
Left Bank/N/S
Le Petit Robert
Le Zinc
Liverpool Lil's
Luna Park
MacArthur Park/S
Maddalena's/S
Manzanita/N
MarketBar
Martini Hse./N
Mecca
Michael Mina
MoMo's
Montrio Bistro/S
Moose's
Mustards Grill/N
Nepenthe/S
Nizza La Bella/E
Nola/S
Olive Bar
Oliveto/E
One Market
Ozumo
Palio D'Asti
Pangaea/N
Paragon/E
Park Chalet
paul k
Pearl Alley Bistro/S
Père Jeanty/N
Picaro
Plouf
Plumed Horse/S
Ponzu
Public, The
Puerto Alegre

Ramblas
Rest. LuLu
Rica Rest.
Roe
RoHan Lounge
Rose Pistola
Rose's Cafe
Roy's
Samovar
Sam's Anchor/N
Sardine Factory/S
Shanghai 1930
Skates on Bay/E
Slow Club
Sonoma Meritage/N
Spago Palo Alto/S
Suppenküche
Sushi Groove
Tablespoon
Tallula
Tamarine/S
Tapeo/N
Tokyo Go Go
Tonga Room
Town Hall
Townhouse B&G/E
Trader Vic's/E
Tra Vigne/N
2223 Rest.
Underwood Bar/N
Va de Vi/E
Washington Sq.
Waterfront Rest.
Willi's Seafood/N
Wine Spectator/N
Zax Tavern/E
Zibibbo/S
Zin/N
Zuni Cafe
Zuzu/N

Microbreweries
Beach Chalet
Calistoga Inn/N
E&O Trading Co.
E&O Trading Co./S
Gordon Biersch
Gordon Biersch/S
Rose's Cafe

Venezia/E
Yoshi's/E
Zante's Pizza

Outdoor Dining

(G=garden; P=patio;
S=sidewalk; T=terrace;
W=waterside)
Absinthe (S)
À Côté/E (P)
Ahwahnee/E (P)
Alexander Valley/N (P)
Amici East Coast/S (S)
Angèle/N (P, W)
Anton & Michel/S (P)
Applewood Inn/N (G, T)
A.P. Stump's/S (P)
A 16 (P)
Asqew Grill/E (P)
A Tavola/S (S)
Auberge du Soleil/N (T)
Baker St. Bistro (S)
Balboa Cafe/E (T)
Barbara Fishtrap/S (P, S, W)
Barney Hamburger (P)
Barney Hamburger/E (P)
Basin, The/S (P)
Bay Wolf/E (T)
Beach Chalet (W)
Belle Arti/N (G, P)
Betelnut (S)
B44 (S)
Bistro Aix (P)
Bistro Don Giov./N (P, T)
Bistro Elan/S (P)
Bistro Jeanty/N (P)
Bistro Liaison/E (P)
Bistrot La Poste/N (P)
Blackberry Bistro/E (P)
Blackhawk Grille/E (P, T, W)
Blue Plate (G, P)
Boonville Hotel/N (G, P)
Bo's Barbecue/E (G)
Bouchon/N (P)
Boulange de Cole/Polk (S)
Brasserie/Mer/N (P)
Bridges Rest./E (P)
Brix/N (P)
Bucci's/E (P)
Buckeye Roadhse./N (P)

Cafe Bastille (S, T)
Cafe Citti/N (P)
Café Claude (S, T)
Café N.-Coppola (S)
Café N.-Coppola/S (P)
Café Tiramisu (S)
Caffe 817/E (S)
Caffè Museo (S)
Caffé Verbena/E (P)
Calistoga Inn/N (P)
Casanova/S (P)
Catch (P, S)
Celadon/N (P)
César/E (P)
Cha Am Thai/E (P)
Charanga (P)
Chaya Brasserie (P, S)
Cheesecake Factory (P, T)
Chez Felice/N (P)
Chez Spencer (G, P)
Chez TJ/S (T)
Chloe's Cafe (S)
Chow/Park Chow (P, T)
Chow/Park Chow/E (P)
Cindy's Backstreet/N (P)
Citron/E (P)
Club XIX/S (P, W)
Cole's Chop Hse./N (T, W)
Cool Café/S (P)
Cote Sud (P)
Cucina Paradiso/N (P, W)
Deep Sushi (P, S)
Delancey St. (P, S)
Della Santina's/N (G, P)
Deuce/N (G, P)
Dipsea Cafe/N (G)
Domaine Chandon/N (G, T, W)
Doña Tomás/E (G, P)
Duck Club/S (P)
Eccolo/E (P)
El Palomar/S (T)
El Paseo/N (P)
Enrico's Sidewalk (P)
Erna's Elderberry/E (T)
Farmhouse Inn/N (T)
Faz (G, T)
Faz/E/S (P, T, W)
Fenton's Creamery/E (P)
Ferry Plaza Seafood (P)
Fillmore Grill (P)

People-Watching

Christophe/N
Clémentine
Fifth Floor
Grand Cafe
Indigo
La Scene Café
Postrio

Private Rooms
(Call for capacity)
Absinthe
Acme Chophse.
Acquerello
Alfred's Steak
Alma
Ana Mandara
Andalu
Angèle/N
Antidote/N
Anton & Michel/S
A.P. Stump's/S
Arcadia/S
Auberge du Soleil/N
Aziza
bacar
Balboa Cafe/E
Baraka
Basin, The/S
Bay Wolf/E
Bella Vista/S
Betelnut
Big 4
Blue Plate
Boulevard
Bridges Rest./E
Brix/N
Brother's Korean
Buca di Beppo/S
Campton Place
Caprice, The/N
Carnelian Room
Carneros/N
Casanova/S
Central Park Bistro/S
Cetrella Bistro/S
Cha Cha Cha
Chantilly/S
Charles Nob Hill
Chez TJ/S
Cindy's Backstreet/N

Citron/E
Club XIX/S
Cortez
downtown/E
Dry Creek Kit./N
Duck Club/E/N/S
E&O Trading Co.
E&O Trading Co./S
El Paseo/N
Emile's/S
Farallon
Fifth Floor
500 Jackson
Flea St. Café/S
Fleur de Lys
Fonda Solana/E
Foreign Cinema
Fork/N
Fountain Court
Fournou's Ovens
Frantoio/N
Frascati
French Laundry/N
Fresh Cream/S
Frisson
Fuki Sushi/S
Garibaldis/E
Gary Danko
General's Daughter/N
Gervais Rest./S
Glen Ellen Inn/N
Globe
Grand Cafe
Grasing's Coastal/S
Guaymas/N
Guernica/N
Harbor Village
Hong Kong Flower/S
House of Prime Rib
Iberia/S
Il Fornaio
Il Fornaio/S
Indigo
Insalata's /N
Jardinière
Jeanty at Jack's
John Ash & Co./N
Julia's Kitchen/N
Julius' Castle
Kenwood/N

Prix Fixe Menus

(Call for prices and times)

Venezia/E
Victorian Garden/N
Viognier/S
Watercress
Watergate
Zaré
Zazie
Zucca Ristorante/S

Quiet Conversation
Acquerello
Applewood Inn/N
Auberge du Soleil/N
Bay Wolf/E
Bella Vista/S
Cafe Jacqueline
Campton Place
Casanova/S
Chantilly/S
Charles Nob Hill
Chaz Rest.
Chenery Park
Chez Panisse/E
Chez TJ/S
Duck Club/E/N/S
El Paseo/N
Fifth Floor
Fleur de Lys
Fournou's Ovens
Frisson
Gary Danko
Gervais Rest./S
Iberia/S
Julius' Castle
Lalime's/E
La Salamandre/E
La Toque/N
L'Olivier
Lovejoy's Tea Rm.
Madrona Manor/N
Manresa/S
Marché aux Fleurs/N
Masa's
Ma Tante Sumi
Michael Mina
O Chamé/E
Oswald's/S
Pacific's Edge/S
Park Grill
Postino/E

Quince
Seasons
Silks
St. Orres/N
Uzen/E
Watergate
XYZ
Zaré
Zax Tavern/E

Raw Bars
Absinthe
Acme Chophse.
bacar
Bistro Vida/S
Blowfish Sushi
Blowfish Sushi/S
Bouchon/N
Café Rouge/E
Cetrella Bistro/S
downtown/E
Eastside West
Elite Cafe
Farallon
Ferry Plaza Seafood
Fish Market/S
Foreign Cinema
Fresca
Godzila Sushi
Grandeho's
Hog Island Oyster
Kingfish/S
Kirala/E
Kyo-Ya
Left Bank/S
McCormick Kuleto
Merenda
Nectar Wine
Olema Inn/N
Osake/N
Ozumo
Parcel 104/S
Pearl Oyster Bar/E
Pesce
Postrio
Rest. LuLu
Sierra Mar/S
Sonoma Meritage/N
Spenger's/E
Sushi Groove

Swan Oyster
Ten-Ichi
Ti Couz
Uzen/E
Willi's Seafood/N
Yabbies Coastal
Yankee Pier/N/S
Zibibbo/S
Zucca Ristorante/S
Zuni Cafe

Romantic Places
Acquerello
Ahwahnee/E
Ajanta/E
Albion River Inn/N
Alexander Valley/N
Ana Mandara
Anton & Michel/S
Applewood Inn/N
Auberge du Soleil/N
Aziza
Bella Vista/S
Big 4
Bistro Clovis
Bistro Elan/S
Bistro Vida/S
Blue Nile/E
Bouchée/S
Boulevard
Cafe Beaujolais/N
Cafe Jacqueline
Caprice, The/N
Carnelian Room
Casanova/S
Chantilly/S
Chapeau!
Charles Nob Hill
Chez Panisse/E
Chez Spencer
Chez TJ/S
Christophe/N
Citron/E
Cityscape
Cool Café/S
Dal Baffo/S
Della Santina's/N
Domaine Chandon/N
Duck Club/E/N/S
El Paseo/N

Emile's/S
Erna's Elderberry/E
Evvia/S
Fandango/S
Farmhouse Inn/N
Fifth Floor
Flea St. Café/S
Fleur de Lys
Foreign Cinema
French Laundry/N
Fresh Cream/S
Frisson
Gabriella Café/S
Garden Court
Gary Danko
General's Daughter/N
Gervais Rest./S
Glen Ellen Inn/N
Greens
Guernica/N
Harmony Club/N
Hyde St. Bistro
Iberia/S
Il Davide/N
Incanto
Indigo
Jardinière
John Ash & Co./N
John Bentley's/S
Julius' Castle
Katia's Tea Rm.
Kenwood/N
Khan Toke
La Folie
La Forêt/S
Lalime's/E
La Note/E
Lark Creek Inn/N
La Salamandre/E
La Toque/N
Le Papillon/S
Little River Inn/N
L'Olivier
MacCallum Hse./N
Maddalena's/S
Madrona Manor/N
Manka's Inverness/N
Marché/S
Marché aux Fleurs/N
Marinus/S

Martini Hse./N
Masa's
Matterhorn Swiss
Michael Mina
Moosse Cafe/N
Napa Valley Train/N
O Chamé/E
Olema Inn/N
Oliveto/E
Pacific's Edge/S
Postino/E
Quince
Rest. at Stevenswood/N
Ritz-Carlton D.R.
Ritz-Carlton Terr.
Robert's Whitehse./S
Roy's/Pebble Bch./S
Sent Sovi/S
71 Saint Peter/S
Shadowbrook/S
Sierra Mar/S
Silks
Slow Club
Soizic/E
St. Michael's/S
Stokes Rest./S
St. Orres/N
Tallula
Terra/N
Venticello
Victorian Garden/N
Viognier/S
Watergate
Wente Vineyards/E
Woodward Garden
Zaré
Zarzuela
Zax Tavern/E

Senior Appeal

Acme Chophse.
Acquerello
Alfred's Steak
Alioto's
Anton & Michel/S
Bella Vista/S
Big 4
Cafe For Seasons
Caprice, The/N
Chantilly/S

Charles Nob Hill
Christophe/N
Cole's Chop Hse./N
Dal Baffo/S
Duck Club/E/N/S
Emile's/S
Eulipia Rest./S
FatApple's/E
Fleur de Lys
Fly Trap
Fournou's Ovens
Garden Court
Gervais Rest./S
Harris'
Hayes St. Grill
House of Prime Rib
Izzy's Steak
La Felce
La Ginestra/N
Lalime's/E
Le Central
L'Olivier
Marin Joe's/N
Masa's
Mixx Rest./N
Morton's
North Bch. Rest.
Plumed Horse/S
Robert's Whitehse./S
Rotunda
Sardine Factory/S
Scoma's
Tadich Grill
Vic Stewart's/E

Singles Scenes

Ace Wasabi's
Alma
Andalu
Asia de Cuba
Balboa Cafe
Bambuddha Lnge.
Beach Chalet
Betelnut
Bistro La Mooné
BIX
Blowfish Sushi
Blue Plate
butterfly embarc.
Cafe Bastille

Special Feature Index

Special Feature Index

subscribe to zagat.com

Sushi Ran/N
Syrah/N
Tartare
Terra/N
Town Hall
Tra Vigne/N
231 Ellsworth/S
Va de Vi/E
Vic Stewart's/E
Village Pub/S
Viognier/S
Wappo Bar/N
Waterfront Rest.
Wente Vineyards/E
Willi's Seafood/N
Wine Spectator/N
Yabbies Coastal
Zibibbo/S
Zin/N
Zinsvalley/N
Zuni Cafe

Worth a Trip

EAST
Albany
  Fonda Solana
Berkeley
  César
  Chez Panisse
  Chez Panisse Café
  Eccolo
  Kirala
  Lalime's
  O Chamé
  Rivoli
  Zachary's Pizza
  Zax Tavern
Danville
  La Salamandre
Livermore
  Wente Vineyards
Oakhurst
  Erna's Elderberry
Oakland
  À Côté
  Bay Wolf
  Oliveto
  Zachary's Pizza
San Ramon
  Cafe Esin

Yosemite Nat'l Park
  Ahwahnee
NORTH
Albion
  Albion River Inn
  Ledford Hse.
Boonville
  Boonville Hotel
Eureka
  Rest. 301
Forestville
  Farmhouse Inn
Fort Bragg
  Mendo Bistro
  Rendezvous Inn
Geyserville
  Alexander Valley
  Santi
Graton
  Underwood Bar
Gualala
  St. Orres
Healdsburg
  Dry Creek Kit.
  Madrona Manor
  Manzanita
  Willi's Seafood
Inverness
  Manka's Inverness
Kenwood
  Kenwood
Larkspur
  Emporio Rulli
  Lark Creek Inn
  Left Bank
Little River
  Little River Inn
Manchester
  Victorian Garden
Mendocino
  Cafe Beaujolais
  MacCallum Hse.
Mill Valley
  Buckeye Roadhse.
Napa
  Angèle
  Celadon
  Julia's Kitchen
  Mustards Grill
  Napa Valley Train

Special Feature Index

Alphabetical Page Index

Places outside of San Francisco are marked as follows:
E=East of SF; N=North; and S=South.

Alphabetical Page Index

subscribe to zagat.com

Alphabetical Page Index

Alphabetical Page Index

Alphabetical Page Index

Alphabetical Page Index

Wine Vintage Chart

This chart is designed to help you select wine to go with your meal. It is based on the same 0 to 30 scale used throughout this *Survey*. The ratings (prepared by our friend **Howard Stravitz,** a law professor at the University of South Carolina) reflect both the quality of the vintage and the wine's readiness for present consumption. Thus, if a wine is not fully mature or is over the hill, its rating has been reduced. We do not include 1987, 1991–1993 vintages because they are not especially recommended for most areas. A dash indicates that a wine is either past its peak or too young to rate.

	'85	'86	'88	'89	'90	'94	'95	'96	'97	'98	'99	'00	'01	'02
WHITES														
French:														
Alsace	24	18	22	28	28	26	25	24	24	26	24	26	27	–
Burgundy	26	25	–	24	22	–	29	28	24	23	25	24	21	–
Loire Valley	–	–	–	–	24	–	20	23	22	–	24	25	23	–
Champagne	28	25	24	26	29	–	26	27	24	24	25	25	26	–
Sauternes	21	28	29	25	27	–	21	23	26	24	24	24	28	–
California (Napa, Sonoma, Mendocino):														
Chardonnay	–	–	–	–	–	–	25	21	25	24	24	22	26	–
Sauvignon Blanc/Semillon	–	–	–	–	–	–	–	–	–	25	25	23	27	–
REDS														
French:														
Bordeaux	24	25	24	26	29	22	26	25	23	25	24	27	24	–
Burgundy	23	–	21	24	27	–	26	28	25	22	28	22	20	24
Rhône	25	19	27	29	29	24	25	23	24	28	27	26	25	–
Beaujolais	–	–	–	–	–	–	–	–	22	21	24	25	18	20
California (Napa, Sonoma, Mendocino):														
Cab./Merlot	26	26	–	21	28	29	27	25	28	23	26	23	26	–
Pinot Noir	–	–	–	–	–	26	23	23	25	24	26	25	27	–
Zinfandel	–	–	–	–	–	25	22	23	21	22	24	–	25	–
Italian:														
Tuscany	26	–	24	–	26	22	25	20	29	24	28	26	25	–
Piedmont	26	–	26	28	29	–	23	27	27	25	25	26	23	–